BLACK SABBATH
THE VINYL TESTAMENT

AN UNAUTHORIZED BIOGRAPHY

BLACK SABBATH THE VINYL TESTAMENT

A FAN'S JOURNEY, ALBUM BY ALBUM, SONG BY SONG
by Matt (Matman) Herring

Edited by Vincent Ferrante
Graphic Design and Editorial Production by N. Blake Seals
Cover Illustration by Andrew Edge
Frontspiece band & Dio Portrait Illustrations by Blake

Black Sabbath The Vinyl Testament. Published by Monarch Books, a division of Monarch Comics, LLC. ©2021 Happy Family Media / Monarch Books. All Rights Reserved. No part of this publication may be reproduced or transmitted in any form or by any means except short excerpts for review without the express written permission of the author or publisher. All photographs, including photos of album covers, books, posters, magazines, advertisements, video captures, etc., are from the way-too-big collection of the author unless otherwise noted. No ownership or copyright to the original material is implied

To contact the author - matmancomics@yahoo.com and Facebook at Matt (Matman) Herring
Matt is on the web at **www.originalmatman.weebly.com**
Authors podcasts - **www.powerchordspodcast.com** and **www.podomatic.com** (The Radio Eclectic)

To contact Monarch Books or Monarch Comics - contact@monarchcomics.com
Monarch Comics and Monarch Books are on the web at **www.monarchcomics.com**

TABLE OF CONTENTS

THANK-YOU'S & DEDICATION
INTRODUCTION 1
THE ORIGINAL BIG FOUR 3

THE OLD TESTAMENT
BIRTH - THE BOOK OF SABBATH – CHAPTER ONE 13
1970 - BLACK SABBATH featuring Ian Gillan, Glenn Hughes, and The Crazy World Of Arthur Brown 14
      PARANOID featuring Mick Box (Uriah Heep) 22
1971 - MASTER OF REALITY featuring Bev Bevan, Cozy Powell, and Steve Howe (YES/ASIA) 31
1972 - VOL4 featuring Ronnie James Dio, Tony Iommi vs. Jimmy Page, and Phil Mogg (UFO) 38
1973 - SABBATH BLOODY SABBATH featuring Vinny Appice and James Pulli (Impellitteri) 47

FALL - THE BOOK OF SABBATH – CHAPTER TWO 57
1975 - SABOTAGE featuring Rich Williams/Kansas 58
      WE SOLD OUR SOUL FOR ROCK 'N' ROLL featuring REFLECTIONS and Oz Fox/Stryper 65
1976 - TECHNICAL ECSTASY featuring BLACK SABBATH GREATEST HITS,
      Bob Daisley and Brian Howe/Bad Company 70
1978 - NEVER SAY DIE! featuring Geoff Nichols, Neil Murray, and Rob DeLuca (Spread Eagle/UFO) 79

THE NEW TESTAMENT
REBIRTH - THE BOOK OF SABBATH – CHAPTER THREE 89
1980 - HEAVEN AND HELL featuring BLIZZARD OF OZZ, LIVE AT LAST
      and Graham Bonnet/Rainbow/MSG/Alcatrazz/Impellitteri..... 90
1981 - MOB RULES featuring DIARY OF A MADMAN, Bobby Rondinelli,
      and Vinny Appice (Black Sabbath/DIO/Last In Line) 99
1982 - LIVE EVIL featuring SPEAK OF THE DEVIL and Neil Carter (UFO/Gary Moore) 107

CRAWL - THE BOOK OF SABBATH – CHAPTER FOUR 115
1983 – BORN AGAIN featuring BARK AT THE MOON, HOLY DIVER, and George Lynch
      (Dokken/Lynch Mob) 116
1985 – LIVE AID featuring LIVE AT THE MARQUEE CLUB and Darryl McDaniels (Run DMC) 125
1986 – SEVENTH STAR featuring THE ULTIMATE SIN, INTERMISSION, Laurence Cottle,
      and Glenn Hughes (Deep Purple) 131

REBUILD - THE BOOK OF SABBATH – CHAPTER FIVE 141
1987 – THE ETERNAL IDOL featuring DREAM EVIL and Phil Soussan
      (Wildlife/Ozzy Osbourne/Vince Neil/Last In Line) 142
1989 – HEADLESS CROSS featuring BADLANDS and Geoff Downes (Buggles/Yes/Asia) 150
1990 – TYR featuring ALONG THE WAY, JUST SAY OZZY, LOCK UP THE WOLVES,
      and John Payne (Asia) 158

TABLE OF CONTENTS

CONCEDE - THE BOOK OF SABBATH – CHAPTER SIX 167
1992 – DEHUMANIZER featuring BACK WHERE I BELONG, Brad Wilk, and Michael Sweet (Stryper) 168
1994 – CROSS PURPOSES featuring NATIVITY IN BLACK and Gene Simmons (KISS) 178
1995 – CROSS PURPOSES – LIVE featuring Tony MacAlpine (M.A.R.S.) 186
1995 – FORBIDDEN featuring OZZMOSIS, PLASTIC PLANET, and Robert Mason (Lynch Mob/Warrant) 190

RESURRECTION - THE BOOK OF SABBATH – CHAPTER SEVEN 199
1998 – REUNION featuring THE SABBATH STONES and Ron 'Bumblefoot' Thal
    (Guns N' Roses/Sons Of Apollo/ASIA) 200
2000 – 2010 featuring Rob Rock (M.A.R.S./Impellitteri) 206
2013 – 13 featuring Chris Broderick (Jag Panzer/Megadeth/Act Of Defiance) 226
2016-2017 – THE END featuring Andrew Freeman (Last In Line) 232

ENCORE – FOR WHOM THE BELL TOLLS featuring Jimi Bell 236

THANK YOU GOODNIGHT 241

Author Matt Herring talks about Black Sabbath and the book on YOU CAN'T HANDLE THE PLOOF, the show where conversation is 'king' and opinions are honored. Pictured (left to right) is Brett Dumis, Jeff Ploof, and Matman. The show is on YouTube!

THANK-YOU'S AND DEDICATION

THANK YOU to those who supported our very successful Indie Go-Go campaign for this project! Your friendship and faith in me means the world and universe!

Jimi Bell - Mark Allen Lanoue (and Farmer Bob) – Ron 'Bumblefoot' Thal – Scott Fish - Brian LeTendre - Thomas, Kerry and Fin Hourihan – Bryan Grenier – Keith Partridge – Jeff (You Can't Handle The Ploof) – Lisa Hagar – Lea Cafferty – Jay Santo – Dirk McClure – Brandon Smith – Antonio Gherardi – Christopher McGough – Phillipe Warda – Jan Zajic – Amy Griffin - Matias Nastolin – Elliot and Linda McGough with Mustard Seed Productions, Monarch Comics and those who helped spread the word!

Andrew Edge, Rusty Gilligan and Maria Barnes for the art and making this book look so good!

On Facebook - Black Sabbath's Worldwide Legion Of Fans, Complete Black Sabbath, Black Sabbath Family, The Tony Martin Archives, Blackest Sabbath, Black Sabbath Fans Worldwide, Ozzy Osbourne Connection, Dio Fans Forever, National Acrobats, Tony Iommi Great Lefty, Melodic Mafia, Power Chords Podcast, Rock Candy Magazine, Official Stryper Fanclub, You Can't Handle The Ploof. Thank you for all your help in putting this book together.

Thank you to Amy, Beky and Samantha (and Troy) for letting me indulge in my passions and at times pretending to care and listen. Thanks to Tiki, Eli, Sagwa for being my support by laying on desks, knocking stuff over and well... just being loving. Thank you, Vincent Ferrante and Blake, for all their hard work in making this the best it possibly could... and better!

Thank you to the entire Stryper Family, Rob DeLuca, Andrew Freeman, Mandy Reid, the Lake Crew, Rob Gaylard, Shauna O'Donell, Frontiers s.r.l., Jim Peterik, John Kivel, Kevin Chairamonte, Dustin Hardman, Shaun Gold, Jon Freeman, all my friends at Amazon in the Boston Region and BDL2, especially the WHS crews! Thank you to all the bands, reps, labels and promoters who support me, my writings and my podcasts by providing me music and concerts to help review. Without you, it's just me....

With any book of this magnitude there are so many sources I drew on for quotes, comments and to clear up any holes like HIT PARADER, KERRANG, CIRCUS, CREAM, FACES, ROLLING STONE, METAL EDGE and RIP magazine who provided me quotes and info in the real time they were released. Also, these books were invaluable references (listed in order of height); DIARY OF A MADMAN (Carol Clerk), DOOM LET LOOSE (Martin Popoff), SYMPTOM OF THE UNIVERSE (Mick Wall), I AM OZZY (Ozzy Osbourne), IRON MAN (Tony Iommi), GLENN HUGHES THE AUTOBIOGRAPHY (Glenn Hughes), DIO – LIGHT BEHIND THE DARK (Martin Popoff), OZZY KNOWS BEST (Chris Nickson), AN ORAL HISTORY (Mike Stark) and IAN GILLAN (Ian Gillan).

I dedicate this book to my best friend Tiki who gave me so much happiness. Miss you big boy!

– *Matman* 7/10/2021

INTRODUCTION

"I have seen Black Sabbath 83 times!" - Michael Suilleabhain

If I was looking for who is the biggest Black Sabbath fan on the planet, the above statement answers that with an extra-large exclamation point. I certainly consider myself a massive fan, but my friend Michael sets the bar pretty high. When I began to get a good handle on what I wanted this book to be like, I reached out to the Facebook community and the many groups like Melodic Mafia, Black Sabbath Family, The Tony Martin Archives, Worldwide Legion Of Fans, Blackest Sabbath, Ronnie James Dio, Legion Of Fans, Tony Iommi Great Lefty, Cozy Powell Appreciation Society, Heavy Metal Rock, Tony Iommi The Music Machine, and Black Sabbath Complete Black Sabbath Page. I know I may have missed a few, but one of the constants on all these pages was Michael and his pictures, stories, and memories.

"I first heard Black Sabbath in 1983 when a mate in Ireland lent me BLACK SABBATH (their first album)," remembers Michael with excitement. "As soon as I heard the bells and rain, I knew that moment would change my life forever." A few years later, Michael made his first Black Sabbath vinyl purchase, SEVENTH STAR, and, like me, Michael loved it. This amazing and highly underrated Black Sabbath album would begin a lifetime of collecting for him of not only the traditional releases but anything with the Black Sabbath logo, including picture discs, concert recordings, posters, tour shirts, ticket stubs, etc....and etc. The list goes on and on into a collection of music and memorabilia numbering in the thousands!

The first time Michael would see Black Sabbath on stage was at an incredibly rare and intimate event on May 29, 1988, when Tony Iommi (guitar), Tony Martin (vocals), Geoff Nicholls (bass), and Terry Chimes (drums) tore through three songs, Neon Knights, Heart Like A Wheel, and Paranoid. History would show this as the only UK concert Black Sabbath played in the UK on THE ETERNAL IDOL tour and the first show with Tony Martin on his native soil. But the biggest proof of fandom is the project that Mike put together...Emerald Sabbath!

While I celebrate my fandom by writing a book and doing a podcast, Michael took it to the next level in a very entertaining way by making an album. Called NINTH STAR, Michael assembled an incredible array of musicians who had history with Black Sabbath and a story to tell. In the case of Ron Keel and Dave Walker, it involved them taking care of some unfinished business. As you will find out in this book, both singers spent time at the mic with Black Sabbath but never recorded anything with them. Also joining Michael on this project were former Black Sabbath players Bev Bevan (drums), Lawrence Cottle (bass), Bobby Rondinelli (drums), Tony Martin (vocals), Vinny Appice (drums), Neil Murray (bass), Adam Wakeman (keyboards), and Terry Chimes (drums). Within these pages, you will read all about their parts in the history of Black Sabbath. But Michael didn't just get the players who made the music, he brought in producers, arrangers, and Skaila Kanga, who played harp on sessions with Black Sabbath in the 1970s. Michael also sang on the album, doing a moody and emotional rendition of Changes. Very nice, my friend.

"Do you need anything else, mate?" was the reply I got from Michael following every post about needing pictures or autographed items for the book. Every email he sent me was full of amazing pictures, some featuring rare items I had never seen before, and always a story or two that made the pictures really come to life.

It was funny asking Michael about his favorite Black Sabbath moments because there are so many, and each has a great memory attached. "I saw every UK show on the CROSS PURPOSES and FORBIDDEN tours..."I remember meeting Ozzy for the first time in 1992..."..."I remember being on the guest list on the HEADLESS CROSS tour and the guy selling T-shirts hired me to do security."

But one of his most cherished moments, and possibly the greatest moment in Black Sabbath history, was the band's final bow in Birmingham, England. "Of course, The End shows in Birmingham!" Michael has developed so many friendships within the band and the fan base that he is, to me, the biggest Black Sabbath fan in the world. If you think you are, let me ask you this? Did you put together a well-reviewed tribute album to Black Sabbath? Go to wherever you buy your music and get a copy of EMERALD SABBATH – NINTH STAR!

Sure, I'm a huge fan and wrote this book, but Michael recorded an album...so he wins!

Michael Suilleabhain in the studio recording Emerald Sabbath's NINTH STAR album with many of the musicians and producers who had worked with Black Sabbath. Pictured is Michael with keyboardist Adam Wakeman (son of Rick Wakeman of YES and Black Sabbath/Ozzy Osbourne), Bev Bevan (Electric Light Orchestra and BORN AGAIN tour & THE ETERNAL IDOL), bassist Laurence Cottle (HEADLESS CROSS), bassist Neil Murray (Whitesnake/Black Sabbath), and drummer Terry Chimes (The Clash/THE ETERNAL IDOL tour.) The group shot is Neil Murray, Mike Exeter (production), the Man himself, Bev Bevan and Kevin Pree (engineer.)

www.emeraldsabbath.com

THE ORIGINAL BIG FOUR

GODS AMONG MEN

"If you look at the music that came in the late '60s in the form of Led Zeppelin, Sabbath, Deep Purple, and Uriah Heep... somebody gave it the name Heavy Metal!" - Ken Hensley (Uriah Heep)

What is Heavy Metal? And more importantly, who created Heavy Metal?
Depending on who you ask... and when, this will always be a hot topic for debate. This question has sparked some great conversations and a drunken fight or two over the years, but who is the band that can lay claim to creating this exciting genre of music? Any band that you may name can trace their sound and basic roots to American Blues artists like Willie Dixon, Bessie Smith, Muddy Waters, Howlin' Wolf, and so many other great performers. During the British Invasion, The Who brought the power and unpredictability, but it was The Kinks and their hits, *You Really Got Me* and *All Day And All Of The Night* that proved the true power of the guitar riff! What about the Beatles and their thrashy classic *Helter Skelter*, a burner of a song about just losing control? How about Jimi Hendrix with his showmanship and his feedback-filled fury? Cream? Blue Cheer? The Stooges? All these choices, not to mention your thoughts of who may have created the thrashy guitar riff, are all great answers and a great idea for a book... just not *this* book. Here, we will be focusing on the point in time when music changed forever with one band... one amazing, historic, and completely misunderstood band... Black Sabbath.

SHADES OF A CONCRETE GOD

To tell this story and their impact on the music scene, we must travel back to July of 1968 and the release of Deep Purple's debut album, SHADES OF DEEP PURPLE. Formed in 1968 in Herford, Hertfordshire, England, Deep Purple was primarily a psychedelic band with a very American sound. Heavily influenced by the Hammond-driven sounds of Vanilla Fudge and Steppenwolf, Deep Purple's original line-up of Richie Blackmore (guitar), Jon Lord (keyboards), Ian Paice (drums), Rod Evans (vocals) and Nick Simpler (bass) was ignored in their native UK but oddly found massive success in the US with a hit single, Hush. The band made an appearance on the Playboy After Dark TV show to perform the single, bringing Deep Purple (and singer Rod Evan's bright yellow pants) into American homes, along with even more success.

To capitalize on their growing success in North America, the band's management and their American record label (Tetragrammaton) wanted Deep Purple back in the studio right away. Five months after the release of the first, album number two, THE BOOK OF TALIESIN, hit the stores, followed by more roadwork. On album number two, surrounded by more of the same easy-to-digest music, was an instrumental called Wring That Neck that was as heavy as anything the band ever recorded and was a harbinger of things to come... a few years later. Deep Purple was already beginning to see the disastrous results of constantly being on the road and then forced back into the studio on their creativity. Unity within the band began to fracture and a struggle for leadership of the band between Blackmore and Lord began. Although the band's first two albums weren't heavy at all or in any way a reflection of what the band would become, for me, Heavy Metal, or at least the movement I will call "The Original Big Four," starts right here!

"Zeppelin had just done their heavy rock stuff, so we were aware of that sound." - Ian Paice (Deep Purple)

FLIGHT OF THE LEAD BALLOON

Five months later in London, 1968, from the ashes of the Yardbirds, guitarist Jimmy Page looked to put a band together to fulfill commitments in Scandinavia left by the demise of the band. His goal was to put together a blues-based band like the Yardbirds, but much heavier, and louder. First to come on board were two unknown players from the Midlands, vocalist Robert Plant and drummer John Bonham. The bass guitar role would be filled by session player and bassist/keyboardist John Paul Jones, who Page worked with before, meeting on Donovan's Hurdy Gurdy Man session. Following a meeting a few rehearsals, Led Zeppelin was born!

"I knew this was going to be great." - John Paul Jones (Led Zeppelin)

The new band, now christened Led Zeppelin, a name given to them by The Who's John Entwistle and Keith Moon, was able to sign a very lucrative deal with Atlantic Records (with the help and support of manager Peter Grant). The advance was the biggest ever given to a new band, but also important was that the deal would give the fledgling band complete control over their music, from album covers to what singles, if any, would be released. The band also had the luxury of working on their own timetable, fueling their creativity and giving their music a chance to grow at its natural pace. In January of 1969, Led Zeppelin would release their now-classic debut album, LED ZEPPELIN, a heavy, blues-filled release that introduced the prototypical "Heavy Metal Singer" in Plant as he swaggered and moved from full-on whaling to heartfelt and emotional ballads. By year's end, Led Zeppelin would release another album, the even more classic and much heavier LED ZEPPELIN II, the album that was the blueprint for this new musical movement.

"I left home at 16 and started my real education musically." - Robert Plant (Led Zeppelin)

EARTH TO SABBATH

Aware of what was going on with both groups, a band of four unlikely young men from the Industrial city of Birmingham would join forces in 1968 in a band called Earth. In 1969, they would discover another UK band with the same name was touring on their circuit, causing a bit of confusion. In 1969, Earth would not only change their name to Black Sabbath but would also change its musical identity. Combining the heaviness of Led Zeppelin with the almost hippy vibe of Deep Purple (at this time in their career), Sabbath created a very dark and sinister sound. In February of 1970, Black Sabbath released their self-titled debut album, a collection of songs driven by bone-crushing riffs, dark lyrics, and a very unorthodox vocal style that would defy the odds. That sound reached an audience looking for something different.

"At the time I was really aware we were an oddball band." - Bill Ward

THE SPICE OF LIFE

Partly due to the unexpected success of Black Sabbath and their debut album, June of 1970 would see the release of Uriah Heep's debut album, ...VERY 'EAVY ...VERY 'UMBLE (Vertigo Records). Formed in 1967 by guitarist Mick Box and criminally underrated vocalist David Byron, the duo would create the band Spice, and, for the next few years, see a number of musicians file in and out of the line-up. Uriah Heep would not have much of a direction until a name change and key addition to the band in 1969. Taking their name from the character in David Copperfield by Charles Dickens, the band would soon find the direction they lacked with the addition of keyboardist/songwriter Ken Hensley. They would rechristen themselves Uriah Heep and find a home on Black Sabbath's record label, Vertigo, under the direction of manager and producer Gary Bron.

"I saw a lot of potential to do something very different. - Ken Hensley (Uriah Heep)

Due to the surprising appeal and positive reaction to the heavy music of Led Zeppelin and the release of BLACK SABBATH, Vertigo Records was looking for more hard rock bands to fill the new label's roster. The label was built to give hard rock and progressive acts a place to call home and Uriah Heep checked both boxes, joining Black Sabbath, Manfred Mann Chapter Three, Cressida, and a solo Rod Stewart.

Uriah Heep's early sound seemed to embody and incorporate the keyboard-driven elements of Deep Purple, the vocal heights of Led Zeppelin, and the pure heavy of Black Sabbath, but did things a bit more progressively, and at their musical core was harmony vocals. Oddly for Uriah Heep, their initial success wouldn't be in the UK or even the US... but Germany, Finland, Australia, and Italy, where their debut and subsequent albums would chart impressively high, giving the band large venues to play before UK and US uccess would find them.

"Deep Purple were rehearsing in the room next door to us. You can imagine that kind of racket we were both making between us." - Mick Box (Uriah Heep)

Ladies and gentlemen, boys and girls... I give to you the birth of Heavy Metal, The Original Big Four!

THE LEGACY OF THE GODS
(A VERY BRIEF HISTORY OF EVERYTHING METAL FROM THEN TO NOW)

Before we set out on the long, metal road with Ozzy, Tony, Geezer, and Bill, let's see what those first steps would culminate in for us as Heavy Metal fans. Within a few years of Sabbath's formation, we (as in the young music fans of the day, not me... I was just born) would see a major onslaught of hard rock and heavy metal bands from all over the world like UFO (UK/Germany), Thin Lizzy (Ireland), Blue Oyster Cult (US), Scorpions (Germany), Rush (Canada), AC/DC (Australia) and another band to emerge from Birmingham, Judas Priest. Most of these bands would take a couple of years, a few albums, and sometimes a line-up change or two to find their particular and soon-to-be trademark sounds, but all were influenced in one way or another by the Original Big Four! In turn, these bands would become the influencers for the next generation of Hard Rock/Heavy Metal bands moving into a new decade. Unfortunately for many acts who owned the 1970s like Aerosmith, Queen, KISS and Ted Nugent, the new decade (the Big 80s) saw them stumble out of the starting blocks and be lapped by the new and flashier bands they helped influence like Van Halen, Def Leppard, Iron Maiden, Quiet Riot and Motley Crue.

"We were influenced by Van Halen and Judas Priest as well as Black Sabbath, Led Zeppelin, and Uriah Heep." - Michael Sweet (Stryper)

The 1980s would be an interesting time of transition. We would also see members of the Original Big Four emerge from the shadows of their pasts and find success like Ozzy Osbourne, Robert Plant, The Firm (Jimmy Page), Whitesnake (David Coverdale), and Richie Blackmore (Rainbow). It was mostly younger fans that didn't know these artists did something before their 1980's success, let alone something as big as creating an entire genre. As Whitesnake's massive 1987 started its climb to sell 10 million copies worldwide, I remember that many friends did not know about Whitesnake's decade-long past, let alone David Coverdale being a part of Deep Purple! "Paul McCartney was in a band before Wings?" Yes, he was... and so were David Coverdale, Robert Plant, and Ozzy Osbourne!

Reunions would be popular and quite lucrative for some. In 1984, The Mark II line-up of Deep Purple (Blackmore, Paice, Lord, Gillan, and Glover) would reunite for the massive PERFECT STRANGERS, and, on July 13, 1985, we would see the original Black Sabbath and the surviving members of Led Zeppelin come together to help "feed the world" at Live Aid. With a few breaks here and there, Uriah Heep would consistently record and release new, and still very exciting and relevant music, and always be on the road, bringing their brand of rock to a concert stage near you.

"It's what we do, and, after all these years, still love to do it!" – Mick Box (Uriah Heep)

From the first post-Ozzy Osbourne release, 1980's HEAVEN AND HELL, Black Sabbath would continue to exist (as you will read in this history over the next couple of hundred pages), but it would be built with somewhat unstable line-ups around Tony Iommi. The band would still make amazing music but somehow could never recapture the success of the glory days, no matter how hard they tried. Their initial success with Ronnie James Dio gave fans a sense of hope and relief for the band's continued survival post-Ozzy, but when that all fell apart in 1983, Black Sabbath seemed to just become a band in name only, even though they still created some great music. Tony Iommi would watch most of his former vocalists, Ozzy Osbourne, Ronnie James Dio, Ian Gillan, and even Ray Gillen (with Badlands), all surpass Black Sabbath in sales, chart position, and good press when they left the fold.

"I was in a few versions and line-ups of Black Sabbath. The were members were changing even while I was in the band." - Eric Singer (Black Sabbath/Badlands/KISS)

For metal/music fans who grew up in the 1980's we would see a lot of bands fall under the Heavy Metal banner like Stryper, Dokken, W.A.S.P., and Ratt, who would kill the ozone layer with hairspray, puff and color their hair to epic heights, and make sure their image was on par with the music. As a bit of a rebellion against the so-called hair bands of the day, an underground movement was underway with four bands who took the hard and aggressive musical lessons of the past and cultivated a new sub-genre of Heavy Metal called Thrash Metal! Much like the Original Big Four a decade-plus earlier, Metallica, Slayer, Anthrax, and Megadeth didn't create Speed or Thrash Metal. What they did was take a sound from bands like Motorhead, Raven, Anvil, and Accept, mixed in a bit of Punk-Rock aggression and accessibility, and added subtle nods to the past, especially to Deep Purple and Black Sabbath. These bands worked out their amalgam of sound in the smaller clubs of California and New York, built up a steady and loyal following, and, finally, one by one, got signed to indie labels until the majors all saw this as a sellable/viable art form and begin to sign them all. Sound familiar?

First, Metallica released their debut in 1983, KILL 'EM ALL, followed a few months later with Slayer's SHOW NO MERCY. The following year, Anthrax would release their impressive debut, FISTFUL OF METAL, followed by Metallica's next, RIDE THE LIGHTNING, and Slayer's very heavy HAUNTING THE CHAPEL. In June of 1985, former Metallica guitarist/vocalist Dave Mustaine would unleash his band, Megadeth, and start their impressive, game-changing run of politically charged speed metal with KILLING IS MY BUSINESS... AND BUSINESS IS GOOD. There you see Big Four history repeating itself with heavy, challenging music, with some, like Slayer, featuring Satanic overtones. All four bands had a history with one another, supported each other, and helped create something that over the next few years would see many other bands like them like Testament, Nuclear Assault, and Exodus soon follow, creating that next wave.

"Metallica paved the way for the thrash metal bands." - David Ellefson (Megadeath)

Turning the clock back to begin our Heavy Metal journey at the beginning, it would be one of the bands from the original Big Four who would help take hard rock to the next level and the next decibel. Using thick, heavy, bone-crushing riffs, darkly imaginative and thought-provoking lyrics with an almost jazz rhythm underneath all that mayhem, you would get the true fathers of Heavy Metal... music from the darker side! THIS IS THE STORY OF BLACK SABBATH!

WHERE THE GODS ARE FORGED
BIRMINGHAM, ENGLAND

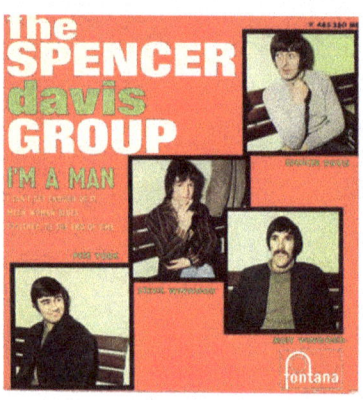 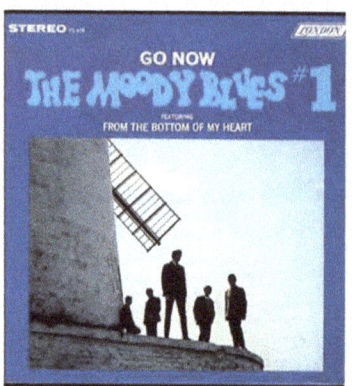 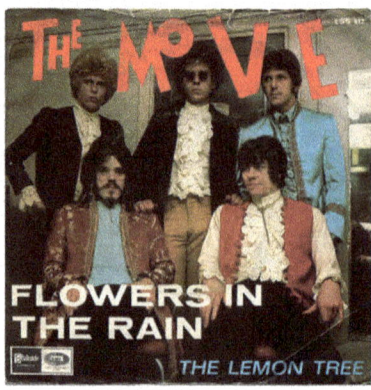

The Spencer Davis Group, the mystical The Moody Blues, and The Move were the early sounds that represented Birmingham, England

"For Americans to understand better, Birmingham was like your Detroit with its industry, but bleaker and with much less hope." - K.K. Downing (Judas Priest)

In the 1960s, the industrial city of Birmingham, England, was known musically for the R&B-influenced sounds of the Spencer Davis Group and the progressive music of The Move and the Moody Blues, much lighter than what would come, forged in the fires of industrial furnaces. Located in the heart of England (hence the Midlands name given to the entire region), Birmingham was still trying to recover from the destruction of World War II. Due to its vital and important industry, the city was a frequent target for German bombers during the Battle Of Britain, when Hitler's Luftwaffe tried to pound the British isle into submission. Birmingham played a major role in the development of the atomic bomb, the radar, and the jet engine, all major components in the Allies' victory over the Axis Power. Birmingham (from their work on radar) also was instrumental in the development of the greatest invention of all time, the microwave oven! Following the war, Birmingham would see a massive rise in population due to immigration both domestic and from abroad, by people looking for work no matter how hard it may have been. Despite the opportunities life was hard in the city, where a weekly paycheck didn't guarantee any sort of financial security. As one can imagine, the young of Birmingham became quite disillusioned at an early age and looked to music or sports to be their ticket out of town. For four young men living in the heart of the city who were forced to see, hear, and smell their future every time they passed a factory, growing up would be tough. All of them were living in poverty, surrounded by violence and mired in a sense of hopelessness.

"We all came from a pretty depressing area, and I think it came out in the music." - Tony Iommi

The soulful voices of Steve Winwood, Denny Laine, Jeff Lynne, and Justin Heyward would soon be replaced by a thundering tone that would change the face of music forever. Much of that thundering tone was born from an industrial accident that would befall a 17-year-old welder named Tony Iommi (born February 14, 1948) on his last day employed at a factory. As he worked a metal press, covering for someone who didn't come in that day, the press pulled his right hand in. In a natural reaction to pull his hand free, the weight of the press held the tips of his middle fingers, and when Iommi pulled back it took the tips clean off, leaving him with a bloody mess and almost ending this story before it began. With Iommi being a left-handed player and his right hand being used on the fretboard, the accident could have easily derailed the young musician's career. Full of doubt and anger, it was the factory foreman who told the recovering Iommi about Django Reinhardt, a jazz guitarist who sustained an equally horrible injury to his fretboard hand, leaving him with only two fingers to play.

Never one to give up, Iommi melted down plastic laundry soap bottles, fashioned tips for the fingers, and kept them on with strips of leather. Because of this, Iommi had to tune down his guitar and play with a lighter gauge of strings so he could push them down onto the fretboard. Now playing more riffs, the original sounds of Heavy Metal were born... but not just yet. Iommi would soon adjust to his new way of playing and find his way through a series of bands with one, Mythology, making some waves in the local scene. Another Brummie, drummer Bill Ward (born May 5, 1948), who Iommi knew from their time together in a band called The Rest, joined Iommi in Mythology and helped the band to get gigs out of Birmingham. The fun-loving Ward grew up heavily influenced by the Big Band sound of the 1940s and brought a large, very jazzy element to the band, giving Mythology a sound almost akin to Cream. Unfortunately for the band, a marijuana bust of all the members in 1968 brought an end to their time together, with no clubs or agents wanting to associate or hire a bunch of druggies and criminals. With no band, Iommi and Ward decided to work together to create their next project, a band that fused heavy blues and jazz rhythms.

"When we started playing in the local clubs of Birmingham, we were that grubby band that really nobody wanted." - Tony Iommi

Raised in a poor Irish-Catholic household, Terrence "Geezer" Butler (born July 17, 1949) read comic books, loved science fiction, and became influenced by the writing of British Satanist Aleister Crowley. Butler was the youngest of seven children in a decidedly non-musical family, although there was always music being played in the house. The youngest Butler did well in school, stayed out of trouble, and was spoiled by his entire family. At an early age, Terrence picked up the nickname "Geezer" because he used to call everyone Geezer, British slang for man. When the Beatles hit the charts and airwaves, music became Butler's passion. Wanting to be a Beatle, he was given a cheap guitar but wouldn't take it seriously until one of his brothers bought him a proper instrument. Butler formed his first band, Rare Breed (not to be confused with the US band, The Rare Breed) that featured vocalist John 'Ozzy' Osbourne (born December 3, 1948) who, like Butler, grew up in the Aston section of Birmingham. Osbourne grew up in a loving but very poor home. He struggled in school, was routinely bullied, and suffered from dyslexia, which went undiagnosed. Years later, Osbourne would bravely share the fact he was sexually abused by bullies at age 11. After leaving school at age 15, Ozzy moved from job to job... laborer, apprentice plumber and toolmaker, car factory horn tuner, and worked in a local slaughterhouse. The future madman was also arrested for burglary and spent six weeks in prison due to his father refusing to pay the fine to teach his son a lesson. It worked!

Rare Breed only lasted a few gigs before breaking up. Following its extinction, Iommi and Ward answered an advert that read "Ozzy ZIG Needs Gig – his own PA" in the hope of finding a vocalist for their new band following the demise of Mythology. Once Iommi discovered it was John Osbourne from school, he almost walked away because he hadn't like Ozzy when they were schoolmates and didn't like him now. But, and most importantly, Osbourne had his own and much-coveted PA system, purchased by his dad to help support his son's dreams. For the empty bassist slot, Butler would switch from guitar to bass and join Osbourne, Ward, and Iommi in their new band. As the smartest of the bunch, Butler would also handle the band's finances and other business matters.

Initially, the four were joined by guitarist Jimmy Philips and saxophonist Alan Clarke and called themselves The Polka Tulk Blues Band, until the two were let go and the band changed their name to the easier and more memorable Earth. Looking for gigs, the band encountered a local Birmingham musician named Jim Simpson who had recently opened a club, Henry's Blueshouse. Simpson asked Earth to play there.

The audience responded positively to their unique style and sound. Simpson began to manage the group as well as several other local bands including The Bakerloo Blues Band. He thought that Bakerloo would be his big band, having released an album and several singles as well as having supported Led Zeppelin in their London debut. History would show Bakerloo as nothing but a blip on the music radar but which provided some amazing players who saw success elsewhere like Dave Clemson (Humble Pie), Keith Baker (Uriah Heep), and John Hinch (Judas Priest).

Earth recorded a demo to help them get a record deal and more gigs, but as the band started to create a buzz in the Midlands, Ian Anderson of Jethro Tull would come calling. Following the departure of guitarist Mick Abrahams, Anderson reached out and offered Tony Iommi the guitar spot in his up-and-coming band. Knowing this was a huge break for his career, the band decided that Iommi should go, despite it meaning the end of Earth. Earth didn't look for another guitarist as Osbourne, Ward, and Butler assumed that it would be just another in a long line of failed bands. Making only two appearances with Jethro Tull, one being the televised ROLLING STONES ROCK AND ROLL CIRCUS, Iommi soon left Jethro Tull and returned to his friends. In his very brief time with Jethro Tull, Iommi struggled with the lack of camaraderie and the almost unapproachable status of bandleader Ian Anderson. He also acknowledged the many positive lessons he learned that he brought back to Earth.

Black Sabbath would sign with Philips Records, release their debut single with their subsidiary Fontana before finding a home on another Philips subsidiary label, Vertigo. Vertigo was created for bands that didn't fit the mold, like Black Sabbath and Uriah Heep.

With their guitarist back in the fold, the band continued right where they left off. While on tour in the UK, Earth discovered there was another band with the same name touring the UK. Following wrong bookings that put them in some tough situations, they decided to change their name to avoid any more confusion. The band wanted a name that would be representative of the darker, heavier music that they were writing. Their new name would come from the movie theatre marquis across from their rehearsal hall which was playing the 1963 horror classic, BLACK SABBATH starring Boris Karloff. Inspired by more than just the name, the band set to work on a song called Black Sabbath that featured horror-themed lyrics, satanic imagery, and the scariest riffs ever recorded!

In 1969, Black Sabbath played their first gigs with their new name and received a modest record deal with Philips Records to record a single. At the label's request, the band recorded *Evil Woman*, a cover of a song by an American band, Crow, that was a minor hit in the US and the UK. The single, backed with the original *Wicked World*, was released on the Philips subsidiary, Fontana Records. The song didn't chart but it did help get the band more shows, and, as a result, made them a much tighter unit.

Things were starting to happen for Sabbath, with the biggest thing of note at the time being their appearance on John Peel's Top Gear television show. In the late 1960s, there was no bigger champion of the counter-culture and good music than Peel, who would often rankle his BBC bosses with his music and lifestyle choices. On November 21, 1969, he helped introduce Black Sabbath to a national audience, performing *Black Sabbath, N.I.B., Behind The Wall Of Sleep*, and *Sleeping Village*. Even though *Evil Woman* failed to chart (and no one really even expected it to), there was a growing interest in Black Sabbath. With the game-changing success of the new Led Zeppelin and Deep Purple's luck in the US (two hit singles and two albums charting in the Top 40), every record label was looking for the next big and heavy thing... and Vertigo hoped they had theirs with Black Sabbath!

With Black Sabbath constantly on the road up and down the UK, they had to block a few days off to record a full album, assuming it would only take a few days. When the band finally had the opportunity to record with brand-new producer Rodger Bain for Vertigo Records, Black Sabbath was able to complete their debut album in one twelve-hour period. Following that historic session, they packed up their equipment and hit the road for more gigs. And now... our incredible journey begins...

Fans Tony Wheeler and Ray Paul standing on holy ground, the Mapledurham Watermill.

Super-fan Chris Pervelis made the pilgrimage while on tour in 2020. Chris is a founding-member and guitarist of the legendary NY Death Metal outfit, Internal Bleeding, the inventors and masters of slam.

Capturing two musical legends and icons with photographic realism, artist Maria Barnes can be found at Etsy (UK) at Marialouiseartworks

The Old Testament
BLACK SABBATH

The Book of Sabbath
Chapter 1

BIRTH 1:1

And it came from Earth, from the smoke, the fire, and the thunder,
four giants who would walk among the men, women and children.
Each giant, possessing something no one else possessed,
being gifts forged in flame and darkness.
These four would be treated like gods, and all their hands would be raised in tribute
to receive gifts of gold and platinum.

BLACK SABBATH (Vertigo/Warner Bros. Records)
Released on February 13, 1970 (UK) and June 1, 1970 (US)
Produced by Rodger Bain
Ozzy Osbourne (vocals), Tony Iommi (guitar), Geezer Butler (bass), and Bill Ward (drums)
All songs written by Butler, Iommi, Osbourne, and Ward (except where noted)

BLACK SABBATH
THE WIZARD
BEHIND THE WALL OF SLEEP
N.I.B.

EVIL WOMAN (Weigand, Weigand, and Wagner)
SLEEPING VILLAGE
WARNING (Dunbar, Dmochowski, Hickling, and Moorshead)

WICKED WORLD - US release, replacing EVIL WOMAN
WASP/BEHIND THE WALL OF SLEEP/BASSICALLY/N.I.B. - listed as one song on US release
A BIT OF FINGER/SLEEPING VILLAGE/WARNING – listed as one song on US release

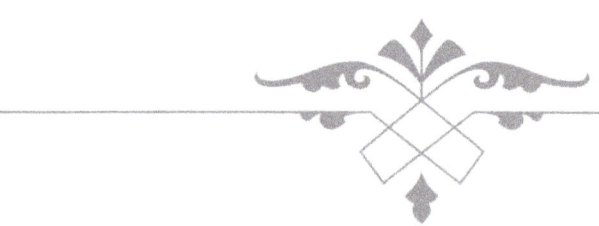

Following the recording of their classic debut album, Black Sabbath gigged everywhere and anywhere they could as they continued to develop their unique dark sound. With each original song worked on and perfected, covers like *Blue Coat Man, Early One Morning,* and *Knock On Wood* would be dropped from their setlist until it was almost all self-penned material like *Behind The Wall Of Sleep, Wicked World,* and *N.I.B.* The band's songs reflected and represented the hopelessness and negativity they all felt and hoped it would touch those who felt the same in post-war Europe and America, which was in the middle of the Vietnam War. Their sound was becoming the opposite of the mainstream, where love, peace, and beautiful people were filing the airwaves in ear-friendly bursts of three to four minutes. Black Sabbath was becoming a reflection of the horrors of the moment, like Vietnam and the Tate/LaBianca murders orchestrated by struggling-musician-turned-psychopath, Charles Manson, in sunny California.

Following a phone call from manager Jim Simpson, the band packed their gear into a van and drove from Birmingham to London. On October 16, 1969, Black Sabbath rolled into Regent Sound Studios in London or a recording session with producer Rodger Bain and engineers Tom Allom and Barry Sheffield. Allom had the most studio experience, having worked with Genesis in 1969 on their debut FROM GENESIS TO REVELATION, also recorded at Regent Sound. The studio wasn't up to the then-modern standards of recording, but five years earlier, the Rolling Stones recorded their debut album, THE ROLLING STONES, at Regent, so there was a coolness factor for the band. Before this project, Rodger Bain had no production experience but was a solid engineer and knew his way around the studio. His job was to keep the four-track tape machines running and keep the band on schedule since their recording budget was incredibly limited, secured by a $1,500.00 loan taken out by Simpson. It is also reported that every producer except for Bain asked to oversee the sessions refused. For Black Sabbath, their goals were very simple; fulfill their dream by making an album and try to out-heavy Led Zeppelin!

"Nobody gives an unknown group a lot of money to make an album with." – Ozzy Osbourne

Not knowing what to expect and with no idea about the process of recording an album, Bill Ward, Geezer Butler, and Tony Iommi set up in one room and Ozzy Osbourne was isolated in a smaller room. With Bain rolling tape, Black Sabbath tore through their entire set live with every song being captured on either a first or second take. Some double-tracked guitar solos and sound effects (the bells, rain, and thunder sound from the title track) were overdubbed... and that was it! When the sessions were completed some twelve hours later, the band packed up their gear and made their way to yet another gig. For Black Sabbath, the recording session wasn't anything special or out of the ordinary. It was just like a rehearsal between gigs but with the tapes running. What would be captured on tape by Bain and his engineers would change the world of music forever.

Fontana Records, who'd released the first Black Sabbath single, *Evil Woman*, in January 1970, were stunned when manager Jim Simpson showed up at their offices with an entire album worth of music already recorded and paid for, since they had not signed the band to record an album. Black Sabbath was signed to Vertigo Records, the new imprint set up by Philips Records to handle more progressive, album-oriented rock and challenging acts like Colosseum, Manfred Mann Chapter Three, and Rod Stewart. As with many artists of the day, the deal that Black Sabbath signed was horrible, giving the band a modest advance and a bad rate for royalties. To make any money they would have to hit the road and tour constantly.

Looking back, it is remarkable what Black Sabbath and Rodger Bain were able to accomplish in such a short time, with so little money and no experience. Like their heroes the Beatles and their then contemporaries Led Zeppelin, extra time in the studio means nothing. When you hear PLEASE PLEASE ME (recorded in 13 hours) and LED ZEPPELIN (36 hours over two weeks), you hear the raw energy, pure talent, and great songs. Compared to the band Boston, it took them 10 years to record three albums, let me correct that, three amazing and brilliant albums.... but wow! Most local/garage bands in the 1980s could record with better equipment than Black Sabbath had, but with more time and more money, would the album have been better? Probably not.

"We just went in the studio and did it in a day. We played our set and that was it." - Tony Iommi

Fan photos from the Mapledurham Watermill in Oxfordshire, England. Thank you to I-O and Johan BS for taking the trip I wanna take.

What Is This That Stands Before Me?

The music that Black Sabbath made on their debut album needed the perfect cover art to make the package complete. With no involvement at all in the process, the band didn't get to see the finished product until their manager showed them the printed copy. The band thought that they would use a group photo for the cover as was the norm back then, but the record label went in another direction.

Photographer Keith McMillan (professionally known as Keef) took the iconic photo at the Mapledurham Watermill, located on the Thames River in Oxfordshire, England. In this normally scenic and beautiful locale, the fallen leaves, the dull colors, and the woman dressed in black turned this into the stuff of nightmares. The model on the cover, Louisa Livingstone, adds an incredibly spooky element and despite knowing nothing about the band or the music, captures the tone and mood perfectly. At first, McMillan tried to create a bit of sexuality by having the model wear nothing under her black cloak, but this was taking away from the mood he was trying to create.

"Any kind of sexuality took away from the more foreboding mood. But she was a terrific model. She had amazing courage and understanding of what I was trying to do." – Keef

Fans were treated to a gatefold album, a rarity for a band's debut. Inside, there were inverted (upside down) crosses and a poem written by Roger Brown. With none of the art or packaging needing approval by the band, it may have been the only time non-band involvement worked. Despite the dark lyrics and mentions of Satan, the band was concerned that true Satanists would interpret the album's art and stylings as them being devil worshippers... and it did! But the band loved what they were given and so would the fans.

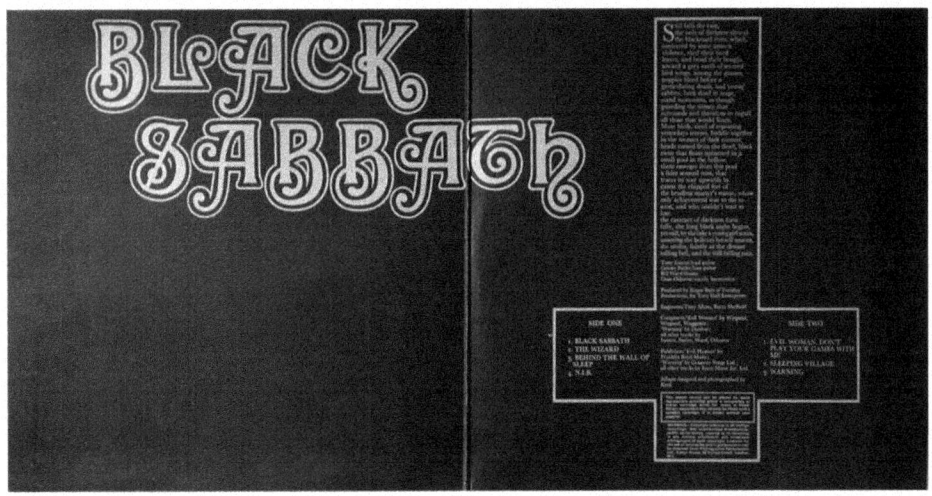

The inside of BLACK SABBATH with the upside-down cross featuring the album's credits and a poem written by Roger Brown.

WORDS THAT GROW READ NO TOMORROW?

With the album recorded in October of 1969, it would be four months until the disc was released to an unsuspecting world. As a fitting and perfect marketing plan, BLACK SABBATH saw its UK release through Vertigo Records on February 13, 1970, Friday The 13th! Following the release, an unexpected thing happened... the album became a massive hit, going to #8 on the UK charts, just two spots behind Led Zeppelin's first release, showing that there was a market and desire for heavy music slightly over the edge. Its success was quite impressive, considering there was so little hype about the band and no big financial push that a major record label could provide. It would be eight months later before BLACK SABBATH would see a North American release. After seeing the chart success in the UK, Black Sabbath was signed to Warner Bros. Records by VP Joe Smith, knowing he could sign them on the cheap. Smith was looking to expand the Warner Bros. roster with diverse musical acts, especially one that could compete with Atlantic Records' Led Zeppelin. With their doom and gloom sound, many worried the US music-buying public would run screaming from the album, but on October 16, 1969, BLACK SABBATH would become an unexpected hit, going to #23 in the US and remaining on the charts for a year, selling over a million copies.

"Jim Simpson rang me the night before and asked if I heard the news... your album has entered the British charts? I was speechless!" – Ozzy Osbourne

The US version would differ slightly from the UK, with *Evil Woman* being omitted and replaced by *Wicked World*, a song written while listening to and being influenced by Led Zeppelin. Several songs were also blended into a longer medley style to give the illusion of more songs and to possibly getting a now shorter one, like

N.I.B. released in single format.

Despite the chart success and surprising sales, the critics all lined up to shoot down the band! Rolling Stone magazine said "just like Cream! But worse" and The Village Voice called it "bull$&#t necromancy" and "the worst of the counterculture." Small press, especially in the UK, was just as harsh about the release but some would find at least something positive to write about amidst the criticism.

With the success of BLACK SABBATH on both sides of the Atlantic, manager Jim Simpson was now becoming a bit overwhelmed with his duties, with Black Sabbath no longer being a local band, but now an international act. Moving in for a takeover of the band's fortune was London-based manager/gangster, Don Arden. Arden sent one of his people, Patrick Meehan, to speak with the band and make an offer to manage them. Meehan had decided to break away from Arden. Another one of Arden's associates, Wilf Pine, would also leave the mogul and set up shop on his own, stealing away Black Sabbath from Arden. This was a deed that would not go unpunished by Arden and sadly begin the trend of bad representation and care for the band.

"You are superstars, and I am going to make you a million dollars." – Don Arden

The many faces of BLACK SABBATH – The Japanese release, the American version on 8-Track, the back of the US cassette with song titles and running order, and a much-forgotten format, Reel To Reel. Thank you to Matt Sabbath (Austin, TX) for sharing his collection.

The Sea Began To Shiver

With a gentle rain, rolling thunder, and a bell ringing in the back, *Black Sabbath* (the song, the album, and the band) officially began. With a chaotic crash, the band kicks into a groove that is led by Tony Iommi's most evil riff ever, known as the dark tritone or the Devil's Interval. The vocals of Ozzy Osbourne are nothing spectacular compared to some of the era's best singers, but no one could have sung this song with the emotion and conviction he does here. The song is quite simplistic in structure but so brilliant and exciting in its execution. When the song begins to pick up the pace towards the end, it becomes a whole new beast with great soloing, pounding drums, and Geezer Butler's bassline holding it all together. A new era in music had begun.

Starting with a harmonica blast, *The Wizard* is another jazz-influenced song featuring some great musical play between Butler and Ward with some nice riffing by Iommi. Featuring harmonica by Osbourne, this one isn't as dark a song as the previous track, with its lyrics based on Gandalf, the wizard from the **Lord Of The Rings** book series, a favorite of Butler. It has become a classic that has never been a favorite of mine, but it was a favorite of Blue Oyster Cult, who took parts of it for their song, *Cities On Flames With Rock And Roll*.

When I listen to this song now, I realize how underrated Bill Ward is as a drummer.

"That was our first attempt at imitating Black Sabbath. And of course, we stole the riff from The Wizard. It's well documented." – Albert Bouchard (Blue Oyster Cult)

Possibly my favorite on the album, *Behind The Wall Of Sleep* is very psychedelic and trippy with some great blues bass by Butler and some solid playing by Ward, who leads the song in and out of different styles. The song was inspired by the H.P. Lovecraft story of the same name, and has a unique vibe which separates it from the other songs on the album. There's a great drum solo within it that I wish had kept going... and going... and going. Great musical interplay here. It's interesting that Ward's drumbeat in this song has been sampled by many rappers, including Too $hort on the 1995 song *Paystyle* and A Tribe Called Quest's *We The People* in 2016, who won a Grammy in 2016 for the album that features the song.

WE GOT IT FROM HERE...THANK YOU FOR YOUR SERVICE

"It was totally spontaneous in the studio (bassically) because I had just gotten a wah-wah pedal and I was playing about with it." – Geezer Butler

Following a bass solo leading into the song called *Bassically* (you get it. I get it. we all get it.), Geezer Butler leads us into the bass lead with *N.I.B.* Despite Butler getting much of the spotlight in this song, it's Osbourne who really gets time to shine here vocally. For many bassists, this was the song that introduced them to the power of the 4 strings and its use as a lead instrument, not just something to hold the song together. I love how every time this song begins to go on a tangent, it comes back full circle.

Despite not wanting a cover on the album, the band gave into label and manager pressure and recorded *Evil Woman*, a song that was recorded in 1969 by the band Crow. Crow brought it to #19 on the US Singles Chart and the song fit the mood and style of what Black Sabbath was all about. Despite the band hating it, they did a great job making it their own and creating a mood that fits in with the album. Since the song wasn't a hit for the band, it was able to be dropped and forgotten, rarely to be heard from again. The band's rendition is close to what Deep Purple would evolve into in a few years. It isn't a bad song. It just isn't really Black Sabbath.

"I didn't like the song!" – Bill Ward

A real surprise on the album is *Sleeping Village*. In comparison to the rest of the album, this is the oddball, but it is a great song. It's a shorter one that starts off acoustic and then transforms into the Black Sabbath sound, with Butler and Ward filling in the space between the Iommi riffs. Then suddenly... jazz breaks out! For many, this is not only their favorite on the album but their favorite Black Sabbath song ever.

The final song on the album is another cover called *Warning*. Unlike *Evil Woman*, this one is a much better fit for the album and the mood the band created. It's a long one and really has a Zeppelin vibe to it. When you listen to the full-on blues (about the 1:30 mark) you would think it was Page, Jones, and Bonham performing. Originally recorded by the Aynsley Dunbar Retaliation in 1967, the song is the longest on the album (originally under 4 minutes) and certainly could be considered a jam song with everyone getting their moment in the spotlight. For me, this is the song I would play if I were trying to prove how truly talented Black Sabbath was and how they were so much better than... Led Zeppelin. There I said it, OK?

For the US version, *Evil Woman* was replaced by *Wicked World*, a song that is quite jazzy at the start but then turns into a quite heavy song riff-wise. Ozzy's voice is higher here than normal, making the song less monotone than the rest. As I mentioned above, the US version blended songs together to create a song of greater length, possibly to appeal to long-form music fans. *Behind The Wall Of Sleep* is mixed with *N.I.B.*, features two introductions to the songs, and it works pretty well unless you know the songs individually. The second side features a 14-minute epic joining *A Bit of Finger, Sleeping Village*, and *Warning* as one track.

"I love the album because it is so raw, primitive, and heavy, especially given the time and what came before it. To me, I think it's really the first metal album and the reason it's so good is that it still holds up today and the songs are still the most evil sounding rock songs ever written. The sound of the tuned-down guitar to accommodate Iommi's prosthetics also add to the guttural guitar sound that make this album and most of Black Sabbaths songs so great." – Christian Dancy (Massachusetts fan)

LOOK INTO MY EYES, YOU'LL SEE WHO I AM

Although Black Sabbath never quite got off the road, the official tour in support began on February 5, 1970, at the Cardiff Arts Center Project, a charity show that also featured Pink Floyd on the bill, when they were also a band just trying to find their musical way. Since many of the shows had been booked before the album's release and subsequent success, Black Sabbath was making far less per show than they should have, as little as $50.00 a performance. They would honor those deals. Black Sabbath played any gig in the UK they could get and found themselves with some interesting opening acts like Family, Uriah Heep, Deep Purple, Traffic, and a festival appearance with The Crazy World Of Arthur Brown.

When the album was finally released in the US in July of 1970 (five months after its UK release), a proposed 20-plus-show tour was planned, tickets were sold (and sold very well, too) including multiple dates at the Filmore West in San Francisco, where Led Zeppelin kicked off their American invasion a year earlier. The tour would be canceled/postponed due to concerns that Black Sabbath would somehow be lumped in with the high-profile trial of the psychotic Charles Manson and his "family." With Warner Bros. Records really pushing the perceived Satanic angle for the band, the timing couldn't have been worse, considering Manson proclaimed himself to be a real-life Satanist. Sadly, rock music played a major role in the murders, especially the Beatles, whose song *Helter Skelter* apparently told Manson to take innocent lives. On the door of one of the murder scenes, the word "PIG" was written in blood, not a great coincidence with Black Sabbath featuring a new song in their set called *War Pigs*. Before the band could hit a US concert stage, the plug on the proposed tour was pulled... a good move for the band's longevity. It wouldn't be until October 30, 1970, that Black Sabbath would finally get to play their first show in the U.S. at the Glassboro State College in New Jersey.

"Why blame it on me? I didn't write the music." – Charles Manson

FINAL THOUGHTS...50 YEARS LATER

Many bands take years and careers to find their signature sound, but not Black Sabbath. The formula was there from the start and all you need to do is listen to every other Black Sabbath album to hear this. It doesn't matter who was (or wasn't) in the line-up, the dominant sound, and the overall feel was established here on their very impressive debut album. Heavy riffs, lyrics that make you slightly uncomfortable, and an odd sense of melody. My overall rating for BLACK SABBATH is a solid 7.5 out of 10 scary women dressed in black! The complete presentation (cover art, band performances, and production) is absolutely fantastic, especially for a first effort, but it loses points for me because the songs (in my opinion) are either amazing or mediocre... nothing in the middle to keep it flowing properly. Ranking the entire Black Sabbath catalog of 19 studio albums I put BLACK SABBATH as my #10 favorite album and it is one that I go back to time and time again, mostly in the Fall for some reason. Among the members of the Black Sabbath Facebook family, BLACK SABBATH is their #2 favorite album with so many awesome reasons given as to why. In their 100 Greatest Heavy Metal Albums, KERRANG magazine ranked BLACK SABABTH at #31.

To me, it is so important to note how unexpectedly successful this album was on both sides of the Atlantic! The year before, Led Zeppelin, another band with Birmingham roots (Robert Plant and John Bonham) had similar success with their debut album LED ZEPPELIN (Atlantic Records released January 12, 1969) going to #10 in the US, #6 in the UK and #11 in Canada and helped usher the way for hard rock bands to not only make it on the road but sell lots of albums along the way. Led Zeppelin also put out another album in October of 1969, LED ZEPPELIN II, an album much heavier than their debut that also did incredible usiness... going to #1 in the US, UK, and Canada. This helped pave the way for Black Sabbath and other heavy bands like Deep Purple, who were now noticing that loud sells, with guitarist Richie Blackmore beginning to transform Deep Purple from a pop to a hard rock band, starting with the dismissal of vocalist Rod Evans and bassist Nick Simpler.

ROCK AND ROLL'S ORIGINAL MADMAN, ARTHUR BROWN!

On March 29, 1970, Black Sabbath played a festival in Victoria Park in London that featured The Crazy World Of Arthur Brown, quite possibly rock's first true real madman! As a member of CWOAB during the time of the hit single, Fire, Carl Palmer learned what a character Brown really was. Now almost five decades later, Arthur Brown recently performed with Carl Palmer's ELP Legacy on the Royal Affair Tour also featuring YES, ASIA, and John Lodge. Meeting him was a huge thrill for me and discovering that he still is the same crazy guy he was way back when was just the icing on the cake. He still is the "God Of Hellfire... and he still brings you, Fire!"

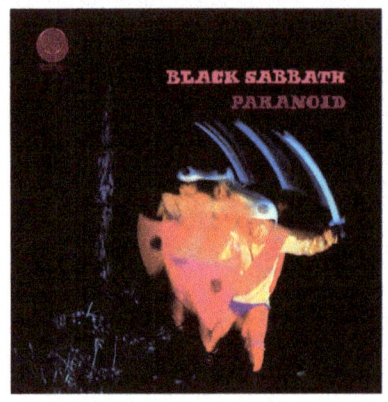 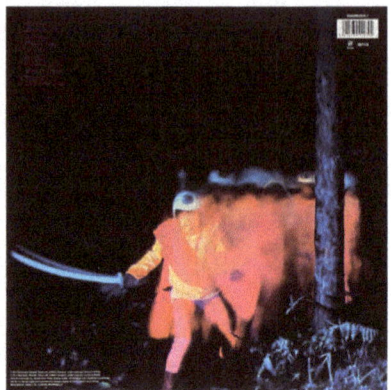

PARANOID (Vertigo/Warner Bros. Records)
Released on September 18, 1970 (UK) and January 1, 1971 (US)
Produced by Rodger Bain
Ozzy Osbourne (vocals), Tony Iommi (guitar), Geezer Butler (bass), and Bill Ward (drums)
All songs written by Butler, Iommi, Osbourne, and Ward

WAR PIGS
PARANOID
PLANET CARAVAN

IRON MAN
ELECTRIC FUNERAL
HAND OF DOOM
RAT SALAD
JACK THE STRIPPER/FAIRIES WEAR BOOTS

"I knew we were doing something different because everybody hated us." – Bill Ward

"DEATH AND HATRED TO MANKIND"

As the band prepared to record album number two, they found themselves in the same situation as the year before, still on the road, always on the road, and never coming off the road. But that is what bands did to make money and spread the message of their music, especially the bands that didn't have a radio-friendly sound. Behind the scenes, Black Sabbath, needing more international and proven management, was fearful of signing with Don Arden but decided to sign with one of his now-former associates, Patrick Meehan. Former manager Jim Simpson would receive the news in the form of a telegram relieving him of his responsibilities when it came to representing Black Sabbath. The band was not happy about how this all happened and felt bad for cutting Simpson loose so callously and with little discussion, but the band's fortunes were on the rise and they needed bigger and better representation to handle it all. Despite missing out, Don Arden would always have his eyes and ears on the business of Black Sabbath, waiting for just the moment to get involved.

"The letter said they were leaving because I hadn't been doing my job right. Yet when they left me, they had an album on the charts in Britain and America. And I haven't been doing my job right?"
– Jim Simpson (manager, Black Sabbath)

Despite never having a proper tour to support their debut album, the band spent almost six solid months on the road. Many of the shows were booked before their debut album's success and the band honored those deals, including the much lower pre-arranged fee. As the year went on, the shows got better, the crowds got larger, and the band got tighter and more professional. Needing more music to fill their setlist, Black Sabbath began to work on some new songs, including an epic track called Walpurgis that had the same musical feel and lyrical content as the song Black Sabbath and another that started life as Iron Bloke.

Following a show in Cambridge, UK, Tony, Ozzy, Geezer, and Bill took their new songs, almost all of them worked out on the stage (actually played or worked out in soundchecks) and began sessions for the new album on June 16, 1970, only 16 days after their debut was released in the US. Because of the success of BLACK SABBATH, and a solid rapport, Rodger Bain was brought back to produce along with engineers Tom Allom and Brian Humphries, to keep the original team intact. Taking slightly longer than their first, the album now titled WAR PIGS would take a week to record. The band would utilize two studios, one being a return to Regent Sounds and also the much superior Island Studios in London. This made the band quite happy to finally be recording in the same studio as their friends and rivals, Led Zeppelin. The upgrade in studios and much stronger material really pushed the band to create a true classic.

"Critics hated us. Audiences loved us." – Bill Ward

Lyrically many of the songs that started out one way ended up taking a turn somewhere else, most noticeably War Pigs. Originally about a Satanic Christmas, the lyrics now shifted toward a very anti-war and ageless sentiment, about rich politicians creating a war for profit and sending the poor into fight and die in it. With the American involvement in Vietnam escalating and being viewed every night on the news, people were growing sick and tired of it. Hand Of Doom was another anti-war song, dealing with the problem of US soldiers returning from war hooked on drugs, and Fairies Wear Boots was a lyric written by Osbourne about a fight he and the band had with a bunch of skinheads.

As the sessions finished, Bain informed them that they were about four minutes short of a complete album (about 40 minutes) and needed just one more song. According to Iommi, twenty-five minutes later Paranoid was born. Lyrically, the song deals with depression, an issue Butler knows all too well. For a song just thrown together to fill space, Black Sabbath created a true masterpiece and one that became their calling card.

"I said to Tony 'It's too much like Zeppelin, we can't do that.' To me, Paranoid is like a remake of Communication Breakdown." – Geezer Butler

The band's composition style was really created here with Iommi coming up with the riff, Osbourne coming up with the vocal melodies, Butler the lyrics, and the beat by Ward driving the song. When this formula happened, nothing could stop the band, who split songwriting credits four ways, giving each member an equal share and avoiding the big issues of whose songs would get on an album or be released as a single.

A few firsts happened on the album with other instruments being brought into the instrumental song Planet Caravan, with Iommi playing flute, Ward playing congas, and engineer Tom Allom playing piano, creating a new sound for the band.

Several UK posters featuring Black Sabbath from 1970. The first two announcing the arrival of Black Sabbath's second album, PARANOID, and the third for a May, 1970 show. As always, Black Sabbath did their work on the road.

With the album set for release and cover art shot (more on this in a few paragraphs), Warner Bros. in the US objected to the album's title WAR PIGS. This was because of the anti-war message of the song and because of the word "pig" in the title. As mentioned in the last chapter, the word "pigs" was written in blood at the site of the Manson Family Murders and the fear was the public outrage would unfairly hit Black Sabbath. In marketing, there is good controversy that sells a lot of albums and bad controversy that just pisses people off, and this would have been bad controversy. With the album now being called PARANOID, Black Sabbath packed their gear and headed to Frankfurt, Germany, for Rock Circus '70, a festival featuring Deep Purple headlining the 16-act show including Family, The Byrds, and Chuck Berry.

"Lyrically it was a genuine anti-war song that spoke directly to a generation of young Americans then facing the draft to Vietnam." – Geezer Butler

STARS SHINE LIKE EYES

In the first of many Black Sabbath album cover miscues, the cover to PARANOID is a pure Spinal Tap moment. With the album done and named WAR PIGS, photos were taken at Black Park in Buckinghamshire, England, by Keef who did the amazing art on the debut. On the front cover, a model is jumping out from behind a tree wearing a helmet, a sash, and a weird uniform with sword drawn high and a shield for protection. The image was draped in pink with the sword an almost neon blue. For effect and to show plural (WAR PIGS) the image is laid out three times. A bit weird and trippy, but when you first see it you may be thinking that Black Sabbath and the graphics team were looking to make some grand statement with art... but nope! The warriors were to represent war pigs, how I don't quite know, but that was the plan. When the album's title was changed, the art would remain the same. I am not saying that this is a bad cover at all because even before I knew the story, I thought it was pretty cool-looking and quite eye-catching. The back cover has the same warrior(s) in a slightly different pose jumping out from behind the same tree on the other side.

"What the f#& does a bloke dressed as a pig got to do with being paranoid?"* – Ozzy Osbourne

Inside the gatefold, there is a black-and-white picture of the band outside. As a massive Doors fan, this picture always resonated with me, with the band's poses and being in the outdoors, like WAITING FOR THE SUN. A solid visual representation for the album, despite the name change. I always thought the warrior on the cover was a paranoid vision representing the lyrics of the song. Nope... it was a war pig!

YOU NEED SOMEONE TO HELP YOU

With BLACK SABBATH still on the charts in the US and still doing great business in the UK, PARANOID was released in the UK on Vertigo Records on September 18, 1970. Before the release, the label released the single *Paranoid* in August, and, just like that, Black Sabbath had a hit single. The song reached #4 on the UK singles charts and would be a worldwide smash, providing the band with an appearance on the popular British music show, Top Of The Pops! The album would also be a huge hit, going to #1 in the UK. When the album was finally released in the US in January of 1971, it would go to an astonishing #12, making the very unassuming Black Sabbath one of the biggest bands in the world!

"We saw people dancing when we played it and we decided that we shouldn't do singles for a long while to stay true to the fans who'd liked us before we'd become popular." – Tony Iommi

Despite the hit single and amazing chart positions on both sides of the Atlantic, critics were once again not very kind to the band and the masterpiece they had created. Many reviewers not only put down the music and the band but also the fans who bought the music and went to see Black Sabbath in concert. It is incredibly unfortunate that most failed to hear the amazing music inside and just posted their rambles based on their misconceptions. In the US, *Iron Man* would be released as a single and see a massive push from Warner Bros., taking it to to #52, nine spots higher than *Paranoid*. Considering the song's length and pure heaviness, it is a shock it went that high and an even bigger shock that *Iron Man* would be Black Sabbath's highest US appearance on the Billboard Hot 100.

Despite doing everything they could to avoid real controversy, Black Sabbath made national news when an American nurse committed suicide, and, on her turntable, PARANOID. There was an inquest, but it was decided that Black Sabbath was not responsible for the young woman's tragic death. This would be a theme that would rear its ugly head in several high-profile cases in the 1980s, one featuring Ozzy Osbourne and another with fellow Brummies, Judas Priest.

"It was taken to court saying it was because of the album that she killed herself." – Tony Iommi

ALL DAY LONG I THINK OF THINGS

Like on their debut, PARANOID starts off with an epic song, *War Pigs!* This one is quite long and tells a story... a brutal but incredibly truthful one for the time then... and certainly, for now, about the horrors of war! As a lover of history and someone who saw friends of my dad come home from Vietnam not the same way as they left, the protest spoke to me. As the years went on and I began to discover what I liked about certain styles of music, I really became attracted to the openness of the song. With Black Sabbath, not every second had to be filled with a cacophony of sound, but the song could grow organically and have time to breathe.

If people consider *Black Sabbath* the first metal song, then I consider *Paranoid* the first Punk Rock song. This has more jammed into its almost 4-minute time than anything else at the time. It has a riff that drives the song and a steady beat provided by Bull Ward that points the song in the proper direction. Like the British Punk bands of the mid-1970s, Ozzy's voice isn't anything spectacular, yet it is the perfect voice for the song. Throw in Johnny Rotten and it would be a Sex Pistols song.

"I don't think any one of us even knew what 'paranoid' meant." – Tony Iommi

Planet Caravan is so mellow. It should bring the album to a complete stop but it doesn't because it's so cool. Bongos by Ward, flutes by Iommi, piano by engineer Tom Allom, and Ozzy's synthesized voice create a real atmosphere unlike anything else Sabbath had done in the past. This is another song I can hear a definite Doors influence on and a weird one. Tony Iommi playing his best George Benson.

Although a great and historic song, *Iron Man* has never been a favorite of mine and I don't like *Iron Man* comic book characters, but still, this has "classic" written all over it and with good reason. Again, the mood is created with a heavy Iommi riff and an almost wall of sound created by Butler and Ward. Here is a perfect example of sound helping to tell the story with the distorted guitar parts and single drum creating the walking motions of a man of iron. Behind the mayhem, Butler follows the riff with his heavy bass work and Ozzy really helps to tell the tale, singing perfectly. But the best moment is in the middle of the song when the guitar solos, bass, and drums pick up at breakneck speed, which also happens again at the end of the song.

Another trippy and psychedelic song, *Electric Funeral* starts with some seriously distorted riffs before Ozzy launches into some horrific nuclear holocaust lyrics. For a band that was tagged as one-dimensional and only singing about the Devil, the band, and this song especially, were tackling a heavy subject, the death of humanity. I never thought this song got the credit it truly deserved.

Hand Of Doom is a deep, dark, and very menacing song, especially lyrically. Musically, this is typical Sabbath, heavy playing, jazz drum fills behind the wall, and Ozzy's voice really setting the tone and sending a message. This dark and moody track is about how many US soldiers came back from Vietnam addicted to drugs and the fact that the drugs may have been the only way to live with the horrors they experienced. On this song more than most, Sabbath really shows off what superb musicians they really were.

"We continued to tour the world. We'd done nothing but live in our hotel rooms." – Ozzy Osbourne

I'm not a fan of instrumentals but *Rat Salad* is a real good one. So good, Van Halen started out their musical career as *Rat Salad*, before changing it to Mammoth and then Van Halen. The highlight of this song is the Bill Ward drum solo in the middle.

Based on a story about a real fight between the members of Black Sabbath and some skinheads, *Fairies Wear Boots* is the dark horse on the album. Maybe saving the best for last, we start with a nice Iommi riff that leads into an extended jam with an almost swing vibe. The main riff and melody have an almost jazz drive which gives a simple song about a fight with a lot of different feels and colors.

  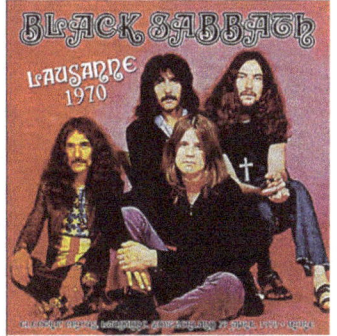

As the band was now a major concert attraction, they also became the target of bootlegged albums and tapes. These were recordings that were illegally made at a show back in 1970, this wasn't an easy thing to do considering the bulkiness of the equipment to record.

TIMES CAUGHT UP WITH YOU

Following the recording of PARANOID, Black Sabbath would hit the road to support the album. Sure, it was incredible that the demand was so high for the band, but the members were already beginning to burn out and drug use was becoming more and more common. At the time of the release of PARANOID, most of the band members were still living at home although hardly ever there. The band's setlist added new songs *Paranoid, Hand Of Doom*, and *Fairies Wear Boots* to their already lethal set that had been featuring *War Pigs* and *Iron Man* since the last tour.

On September 24, 1970, Black Sabbath would make an unexpected and quite emotional visit to Top Of The Pops, the top music show in the UK at the time. There the hottest bands would lip-synch the biggest singles in the UK, something Black Sabbath now had with *Paranoid*.

The tour started in Swansea, Wales, in September and wouldn't finish up until April of 1971, only stopping to record another album. This tour would finally see Black Sabbath play in the States, headlining their own shows, being supported by YES and Manfred Mann Chapter III to name a few of the odd pairings, or supporting bands like Jethro Tull, Rod Stewart & The Faces, Emerson Lake & Palmer, and The James Gang. Despite their growing fame and status, Black Sabbath would play a stretch of 20 shows in 10 days, making a hefty payday but at a serious cost to the band's overall health. The band members were now doing more than just drinking and smoking pot, with cocaine becoming the band's drug of choice to help keep them going.

"If you're a student of music, then go listen to YES." – Bill Ward

With new management in place that could help them break internationally, it is sad to see now what was going on then, record and make money, tour and make more money and repeat. Instead of taking care of his band or at the least, his assets, Manager Patrick Meehan was constantly sending the band out on the road and keeping them in enough drugs and money to not think that anything was wrong. Throwing the band little financial crumbs and keeping them in spoils, they were getting a small fraction of what they were really earning, they just didn't know it. People were getting quite rich off the backs of Black Sabbath.... and it wasn't Ozzy Osbourne, Tony Iommi, Geezer Butler, or Bill Ward.

FINAL THOUGHTS... HALF A CENTURY LATER... AND STILL PARANOID!

As I began to work on this chapter and rediscovered the majesty of PARANOID, I made an incredible discovery, a collection called PARANOID SUPER DELUXE! Released in 2016 on Rhino Records, this four-disc set contained a lot of great stuff like two live shows from 1970, a remastered version of the classic album, and a hardbound book, containing pictures, interviews, and so much cool information. But for me, the biggest gem in this collection was the Quad Mix of the album originally done in 1974. If you don't know what 'Quad' or Quadrophonic sound is (or was), it was a process that would split a recording into four distinct channels for four speakers. Each speaker would play something the other speaker wasn't giving you since it wasn't all mixed together. An easy way to think about it is this.... vocals in one speaker, bass in another, guitar in yet another, and drums in a final speaker. Other sounds would share a speaker (or channel) and would give the music much more depth and create almost a live concert feel. This was first tried in the late 1960s and despite the cool idea of being surrounded by music, the process was very expensive, too much for the target audience, and the equipment was quite problematic.

As for my thoughts on PARANOID, this is a seriously mature album for a band that hit the mark on their first try and followed it up with an even stronger album. The songs contained on the album are all solid with some being real classics, but the pure joy of the album comes from the overall flow and consistency of the record. The band's performances are all top-notch, the production has a bit more life to it than their debut, and the overall presentation is a bit better than the first. When you think about the pressure to follow up a classic, Black Sabbath and Rodger Bain were certainly up for the task. To give it a rating, PARANOID is a solid 7.5 out of 10, making it my #6 favorite Black Sabbath album and an instant classic! My friends that are part of the Black Sabbath Facebook communit rated PARANOID #3 out of the band's 19 studio albums. In 1989, KERRANG! magazine placed it at #39 in their 100 Greatest Heavy Metal Albums Of All Time in their reader poll.

EASY LIVING WITH MICK BOX (URIAH HEEP)

Mick Box on stage at the Wolf Den at Mohegan Sun in Uncasville, CT on 2/23/2018 WHERE Uriah Heep played to an incredibly enthusiastic crowd. Mick backstage (with yours truly) was an incredibly kind and funny guy who didn't have a bad thing to say about anyone and is thankful for everything Uriah Heep has given him. Despite being around for over half a century, the band and Mick show no signs of stopping or even slowing down. If you don't know much about Uriah Heep, shame on you, and go pick up a Greatest Hits.

www.uriah-heep.com

MASTER OF REALITY (Vertigo/Warner Bros. Records)
Released on July 21, 1971
Produced by Rodger Bain
Ozzy Osbourne (vocals), Tony Iommi (guitar), Geezer Butler (bass), and Bill Ward (drums)
All songs written by Butler, Iommi, Osbourne, and Ward (except where noted)

SWEET LEAF
AFTER FOREVER (Iommi)
EMBRYO (Iommi)

CHILDREN OF THE GRAVE
ORCHID (Iommi)
LORD OF THIS WORLD
SOLITUDE
INTO THE VOID

"Previously, we didn't have a clue what to do in the studio and relied heavily on Rodger. But this time we were a lot more together, understood what was involved, and were more opinionated on how things should be done." – Bill Ward

ALL YOU CHILDREN OF TODAY...

There is an old perception that a band has forever to write their debut album and just months to write their second. This is because a band, from the day they get together until they get to first record an album, can write and perfect those first songs. For a second album, there isn't the time or attention to detail due to touring commitments and days only containing 24 hours no matter how hard a band works. Since many of the songs on PARANOID were written, arranged, and brought to the stage, in some cases, before the band recorded their first album, the pressure was on to have songs ready for a new album, all coming from scratch. With the pressure on, how would Black Sabbath respond?

The tour to support PARANOID officially ended in London on April 26, 1971, but studio work began for the new album in early February, while the band was between gigs. With a few months off, the band were able to catch their breath a bit and enjoy the fruits of their labors. The band now had money whenever they needed it (for the first time in their lives) and were able to buy houses and cars and help set up their families. Unfortunately, not knowing how much money the band actually earned to this point made them unaware of how much they actually brought in and how the things they purchased were not bought in their name, but on behalf of their management team, WEA. Whenever someone in Black Sabbath needed something, they got it, so there was never a reason to question anything. Patrick Meehan kept the band working, wanting for nothing and keeping them in drugs, as well, something that stopped the questions being asked.

Again, Black Sabbath entered the studio with producer Rodger Bain and engineer Tom Allom, keeping the team together that created magic and two huge-selling albums to show for it. With their successes, the band was able to work out of a much nicer and more up-to-date studio, Island Studios in London. Another luxury was the time allotted to record, before having days to record the band was now given a few months in the studio, spread out of course between gigs, so the band would always be working.

"We could take our time and try out different things." – Bill Ward

As the songs began to come together, the Satanic angle was not as prevalent, but the doom and gloom lyrics and heavy music began to get thicker and quite a bit darker than on the previous two albums. One of the main factors was guitarist Tony Iommi having to tune down his guitar to reduce the tension on the strings, meaning the looser they are on the fretboard, the more comfortable they were to play due to his injured fingertips. To match the new guitar tones, bassist Geezer Butler also tuned down, creating a much heavier sound that was easier for Ozzy Osbourne to sing along to. Also introduced to the sessions (and songs) were lots of drugs, mostly marijuana use, that would result in the classic *Sweet Leaf*, a song introduced by a coughing Iommi who was having trouble holding the smoke from a rather large joint Osbourne brought to him.

As the music became much heavier, the songs and lyrical content became more varied and progressive, less one-dimensional. Lyrically, the song *After Forever* features spiritual lyrics that take on the conversion or religious awakening of someone who has changed their ways. Quite a departure for Black Sabbath, but that's why it works so well on this album. Even though the band was writing and recording some of the best songs of their career (including *Children Of The Grave*), the number of pure songs wasn't quite there so many songs were given longer intros, more soloing, or just dragged out a bit more than usual.

With more time to record, the band members would spend a little more time fine-tuning the material, giving it less spontaneity with more overdubbing than before. This isn't a bad thing. It was just that the band had time on their hands to actually record and spend time making MASTER OF REALITY the best album they possibly could.

COULD IT BE THE END OF MAN AND TIME?

Lacking an image or photo to help cultivate feelings, emotion, and expectations, MASTER OF REALITY is as simple as it could possibly be... the band's name and the album's title... nothing more, nothing less! The original print run of the album contained no color, just the words embossed in an open-top cover and containing a poster of the band outside in the forest, between two trees and a slight fog in the back, taken by Keef. Later versions would feature the band name in purple with the album title in gray. The back of the album contained the lyrics to all the songs below a purple Black Sabbath logo, giving people the actual words to the tunes, making it impossible for interpretation or so you would think. Many thought the lyrics to After Forever were referring to God being the Devil and someone just embracing the evil.

Since not much can be said about the cover, you can look at the poster (that hung in my room for most of my teen years) and see how visual and artistic the band could be. Keef did an incredible job capturing the band in an odd locale by darkening the color pallet and bringing out a cold, almost fall feel. Osbourne would refer to the poster as the band's BEATLES FOR SALE moment, four tired musicians with the spark in the eyes now gone due to too much work and a realization that things would have to change or it would all fall apart. For the Beatles, the only way to slow it all down was to get off the road to focus just on studio work, an option that was not available to Black Sabbath.

The album cover wouldn't receive any awards or kudos for creativity, but it served the purpose and gave the buyers the thought that if the cover is different, the music inside must be different, too... and it certainly was.

"Slightly Spinal Tap-ish, only well before Spinal Tap." – Tony Iommi

A few unique versions of MASTER OF REALITY from over the years, two cool and very different picture discs and a mini–Japanese CD.

YOU THINK YOU ARE INNOCENT, YOU'VE NOTHING TO FEAR

MASTER OF REALITY would finally see a same-day release date in the US and UK, July 21, 1971 on Warner Bros. Records and Vertigo, respectively. As was expected, the album hit the charts with a vengeance, going to #5 in the UK and #8 in the US, and going gold on pre-order sales alone, something very few bands were able to do at the time. The single, *Children Of The Grave*, failed to chart but US radio, especially the now growing FM format, was looking to fill its playlist with longer, heavier, and more challenging music and gave it a home. There would be differences in the song listings on the US release to give the illusion of more songs, 11 to the UK's eight, much like was done on the debut album. The outro to *Children Of The Grave* was given the title *The Haunting*, the intro to *After Forever* was called *The Elegy*, and the intro to *Into The Void* was called *Deathmask*. Reissues of the US version would remove three of the titles and list the proper tracks.

By the time of the release of MASTER OF REALITY, Black Sabbath was already three weeks on the road in the US, including a 4th of July show in Detroit, MI, called the Outdoor Rock Fest. Here, Black Sabbath shared the bill with local Michigan heroes The Amboy Dukes, featuring a pre-gonzo Ted Nugent, and Brownsville Station.

As expected, the fans loved the album, and, of course, the critics hated it! Sick of always being destroyed by the press, Black Sabbath pulled a Led Zeppelin move and began to refuse to do interviews, especially if they weren't going to be supported. It wasn't like the band needed the press to sell records and concert tickets. They were receiving most of their business from hard work and the word of mouth of their loyal fanbase. Mainstream reviews called the album monotonous, a waste of time, and dim-witted. With platinum sales in the US and Canada, MASTER OF REALITY was Black Sabbath's highest-charting album in the US ever... until 2013.

"We've done well in America, the gold discs and all that." – Tony Iommi

THEY ARE GONE

Starting off with a cough, *Sweet Leaf* opens the album with a typical heavy riff by Tony Iommi and Ozzy Osbourne's "All Right Now!" Album number three has begun with one of the best Black Sabbath songs ever. Osbourne's voice is as upfront as before and slightly higher than before as the band seems to be playing deeper and lower than before. Midway into the song when Iommi, Geezer Butler, and Bill Ward get to go off on a tangent, they keep it really interesting with so many things going on, especially Ward, who is as good as John Bonham or Ian Paice but doesn't get the credit for it.

As a teen listening to this album, I had a bit of trouble wrapping my head around Black Sabbath recording a song like *After Forever*. I was amazed that Ozzy was singing about accepting God because I was and still am a Jesus guy. It was confusing because I bought into the Satan-worshipping thing they were selling, especially when Ozzy's solo career first started. Musically, it is challenging in all the right ways and finds the band in that sweet groove

"I consider "After Forever" the first Christian Rock song ever recorded." – Michael Sweet (Stryper)

Embryo is a short instrumental that just has an evil feel to it. Every time I listen to it I think I won't feel uptight about Iommi's weird minstrel show sound, but I still do.

Children Of The Grave is my second favorite Black Sabbath song ever because it is just plugged in, gets the groove going, has everyone join in, and then... classic! The track gallops at a fantastic pace and really shows the skills of Sabbath and producer Rodger Bain to not overload the music with tons of overdubs, giving it time to move, breathe, and be heard. Isolate the drums and you hear another Bill Ward clinic. Osbourne's voice never sounded better! In the US, the weirdness at the end was given a title... The Haunting, complete with Friday The 13th Jason chi-chi-chi noises... years before the films were made.

Another instrumental, *Orchid*, really shows another side of Tony Iommi. Yes, we know he can create massive riffs and blistering solos, but did you know he could just grab an acoustic guitar and craft beauty?

Lord Of This World is a great song but the one on the album I never got into, possibly because it is way too bluesy. The song has some great moments and featured a very inspired and enjoyable vocal, but it never hooked me in. It has a great rhythm going on in the middle section with the Butler bass leading the way over Iommi leads.

"Our music is aggressive. People get off on it." – Ozzy Osbourne

Much like *Planet Caravan* from the last album, the slow and very hippy-sounding *Solitude* begins the album's winding down in a big way. It is slow and very haunting with Osbourne's voice being softer and more personal than ever before. Along with Iommi's flute and Ward's sleigh bells, the song is a radical departure for this album and the band. You could call this one a Led Zeppelin moment.

Ending the album as awesome as it started, *Into The Void* is pure Sabbath, but certainly one of their more challenging songs. Lyrically, Osbourne had a lot to spit out and Ward had to work with some crazy time changes. Butler's bass helps make this the heaviest song on the album and the blueprint for the grunge movement of the 1990s.

THROUGH THE UNIVERSE IN THE ENGINES WHINE

Barely having time to catch their collective breath, Black Sabbath hit the road for another long run, this time ten months, starting in the US in July, leaving for Europe for three festivals in September, returning to the US until October, the UK until February, and a final run through North America ending in April. The fanatic non-stop pace would catch up to the band in November 1971 with almost a dozen shows in the UK being canceled due to the illnesses of Tony Iommi, Geezer Butler, and Bill Ward. Surprising that Ozzy Osbourne would be the only one not get sick, considering his unhealthy living on the road. Only two new songs would be added to the setlist, the expected *Children Of The Grave* and *Sweet Leaf*.

"It's all so horrible! Flying around and around, landing again." – Ozzy Osbourne

With the success of the album, shows became much bigger and better, seeing Black Sabbath headlining in the biggest arenas. Support for the band would come from many bands, including Nazareth, Humble Pie, Wild Turkey, Black Oak Arkansas, and Alice Cooper. Some interesting and historical bills that happened in 1971 featured the band playing with progressive legends YES, future superstars REO Speedwagon, and, for two dates in New York (Syracuse and Rochester), Black Sabbath opened up for their friends and rivals, Led Zeppelin. On September 4, 1971, Black Sabbath was part of a massive festival in Speyer, Germany, that featured pop stars Rod Stewart and the Faces, the progressive Family, a fairly new band called Fleetwood Mac, rocker Rory Gallagher, and Sabbath rival Deep Purple. The name of the event? British Rock Meeting!

FINAL THOUGHTS...ON REALITY

This was a great deal of fun for me to really spend some quality time with MASTER OF REALITY, an album I admit I never gave much attention to in the past beyond a few songs. What I love about this album is the sheer heaviness of the songs, yet still there is some solid growth and maturity between this one and PARANOID, like there was from that one and their debut. Black Sabbath was beginning to stretch their experimental musical boundaries while managing to keep their devoted fanbase happy... never an easy thing to do. Not a big fan of the cover, but I am a fan of the songs and the overall flow and feel. For all the good I can also see its faults, such as the many instrumentals that to me just fill up space that could be filled with a few more real songs. Overall, I give MASTER OF REALITY a solid 7.5 out of 10 and rank it my #7 Black Sabbath album of all time. What did the Sabbathheads of the Black Sabbath Facebook community collectively think of this one? We were pretty close in our rankings with those guys and gals placing it #8 out of 19. In 1989, KERRANG! magazine placed MASTER OF REALITY at #53 in their 100 Greatest Heavy Metal Albums Of All Time poll.

 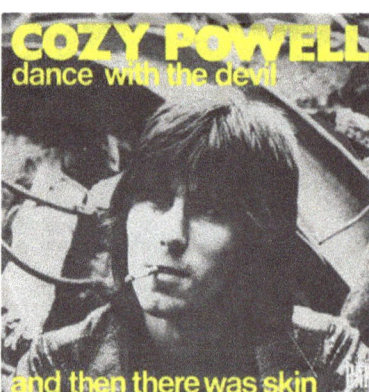 

In 1971, two future members of Black Sabbath (both drummers) made names for themselves with big projects. Jeff Beck Group's ROUGH AND READY featured Cozy Powell and The Electric Light Orchestra with Bev Bevan began their quest for gold and platinum!

"It was the rock 'n' roll music of my childhood inspired me – Elvis Presley, Little Richard, Ray Charles, Eddie Cochran." – Bev Bevan

WITH STEVE HOWE THE ANSWER IS ALWAYS YES...AND ASIA

When I first discovered that YES did a lot of shows with Black Sabbath in the 1970's it didn't make much sense to me musically. But, back in the old days, putting the heaviest band in the world with the most progressive group on Earth sort of made sense for ticket sales and introducing their music to each other's audiences. In 1971, YES was riding high as the flag bearers of the growing Progressive Rock movement and scored big with THE YES ALBUM and FRAGILE, the first two YES releases to feature the brilliant Steve Howe.

www.yesworld.com

VOL. 4 (Vertigo/Warner Bros. Records)
Released on September 25, 1972
Produced by Black Sabbath and Patrick Meehan
Ozzy Osbourne (vocals), Tony Iommi (guitar), Geezer Butler (bass), and Bill Ward (drums)
All songs written by Butler, Iommi, Osbourne, and Ward

WHEELS OF CONFUSION
TOMORROW'S DREAM
CHANGES
FX
SUPERNAUT
SNOWBLIND
CORNUCOPIA

LAGUNA SUNRISE
ST. VITUS DANCE
UNDER THE SUN

"The band started to become very fatigued and very tired." – Bill Ward
(Oh, really? Both? -Editor)

Lost In Happiness I Knew No Fears!

Looking in from the outside, Black Sabbath were all very rich, world-famous, and everything they touched turned to gold, silver, and platinum. They were living far beyond their wildest dreams and all this was accomplished in a very short time. To show how popular Black Sabbath was at this particular moment when MASTER OF REALITY was released, both BLACK SABBATH and PARANOID were still on the charts, another Beatles moment for the band. They were selling out the biggest venues in the world and becoming the spokesmen for the disillusioned or disenfranchised youth who were putting their albums high on the world album charts. This was with no support from the media and very little from radio. Behind the scenes, the picture was a lot less rosy with the members of Black Sabbath all working and struggling with spiraling addictions (alcohol, cocaine, and heroin), exhausted from the non-stop touring they had no control over, and, although bringing in millions of dollars in revenue, the band was only seeing a fraction of it. As burned out as they were from drugs and the road, they never thought to investigate their finances and what exactly manager Patrick Meehan was doing with them. What he was doing was getting very rich off the backs of the band.

The members of Black Sabbath look back at this point in their career and consider this time when the band began to really fall apart and lose sight of what was important. Being a member of Black Sabbath, with all it entitled, stopped being fun. With a bit of time off, the band and Meehan decided to get out of the UK to record the new album, becoming tax exiles, and hoped that a change of scenery would inspire the boys to create another million-seller. Not making the trip to sunny California would be producer Rodger Bain and engineer Tom Allom, who would not be asked to be a part of the production of the new album. Instead, the band and Patrick Meehan would produce the new record, although Meehan's involvement in the decision-making was somewhat exaggerated... by Meehan himself. The band felt they could do Bain's job since his producing style was incredibly hands-off. Bain and Allom would resurface a few years later and work with another Birmingham band, Judas Priest. Engineering Sabbath's new album would be Colin Caldwell and Vic Coppersmith-Heaven, who previously worked with Cat Stevens.

"Previously we had Rodger Bain as a producer, and although he's very good, he didn't really feel what the band was doing." – Ozzy Osbourne

Deciding on a studio, the band chose the modern and newly built Record Plant in Los Angeles, California. The band (and the entire management team) would rent the Bel Air mansion of millionaire John du Pont and move into their home/rehearsal space in the early summer of 1972. This month-long residency would see the band encounter some very lofty highs and some deep, dark lows as well as some practical jokes gone horribly wrong. While writing and rehearsing, the band turned their (until now) casual cocaine usage into full-on addictions, devoting much time and over half the album's financial budget on, as the band described it, "speaker boxes full of cocaine." To make it easier, and more dangerous for the band, it would all be delivered right to the band and paid for indirectly by their record labels. The mansion would soon become the hang-out and party spot, yet somehow the band would still be able to create new music.

Despite the abuse and paranoia that came with the drug usage, Black Sabbath was somehow able to write and record some of the best and most challenging music of their careers. Wanting to be known for more than the heavy doom and gloom of their previous three albums, Black Sabbath began to really broaden their musical horizons and open their sound up quite a bit. After all, if a heavy band like Led Zeppelin could do it, why not Black Sabbath? Their lyrics had become less about the Devil and the darker side of life, while musically they became far more colorful. At the Record Plant, the band found an amazing atmosphere, the most up-to-date equipment, and a new sense of freedom to do whatever they wanted to do, and surprise, it was cheaper than most other recording studios. As on the last album, new instruments were brought in to create something multidimensional, especially piano. In their rented house, Tony Iommi discovered a piano and wrote the music for the tender song, *Changes*.

As things progressed for the most part without incident, there came an incredibly tense time surrounding the recording of the challenging song, *Cornucopia*. For some reason, drummer Bill Ward was having a difficult time catching the needed groove and the more frustrated the band became with him, the more of a mental block developed. As a result, Osbourne had decided Ward wasn't serving any purpose in the studio and decided he should just go home. The ultra-sensitive Ward didn't even have a home to go home to, so he got it together and recorded the needed drums, but the situation tells a dark tale of where the band was in their interpersonal relationships.

"That was the very first indication that there was a change because that had never happened before. It was the first time a band member had been rebuked. It hurt." – Bill Ward

With writing, recording, and overdubs being completed in about a month, Black Sabbath presented to Vertigo Records and their American label Warner Bros. their new album called SNOWBLIND. The labels loved the music and expected it to be another big hit, but said absolutely "NO" to the chosen title, knowing exactly what it meant. It may seem a bit hypocritical, considering the number of drugs being used by record label execs and how cocaine was a form of industry commerce, but this is what they wanted and it's exactly what they got. With nothing else to name it, the band took a page out of Led Zeppelin's "no title, just a number" branding and would just call the new album VOL 4.

While the sessions created a closeness with the band, when it was all over bad feelings began to creep in. When the recording was completed, the band minus Tony Iommi went back home to their personal lives. Iommi went to London to finish the production and mixing chores, and, for him, resentment began to set in, feeling he was doing more than the rest of the band. Osbourne began to feel disillusioned with the band. His time away from his young family made him wonder if he should just walk away from it all. The soft-spoken Butler was beginning to get angry at Osbourne because he felt the singer was relying too much on him to create the lyrics he would sing, as well as the public assuming that Osbourne wrote all the lyrics. With everyone in full-on abuse mode, it was Bill Ward who bypassed his bandmates to become a full-on junkie.

"On drawing power and album sales we can compare with groups like Led Zeppelin and The Who, although we seldom get recognition for that fact." – Tony Iommi

The World Will Still Be Turning When You're Gone

Keeping the album's art simple but not as simple as the previous album, Keith Macmillan (going by Keef) took a now-iconic shot of Ozzy Osbourne at a hometown gig at the Birmingham Town Hall in 1972. With Ozzy at the mic in full control of the crowd, whose hands are in the air flashing peace signs, the image was colored with a mustard yellow on a dark black background. On the top and sides in white block letters are the words BLACK SABBATH VOL 4. Incredibly simplistic in design but very effective visually, especially if this album is on the sales rack trying to catch your eye. On the back, the jacket is the same thing (kind of boring, yes, and not too original) and printed very small under the number 4 is the song listing. If you bought the 8-Track cartridge or cassette, you were treated to the color scheme being reversed, yellow background with black Ozzy. The change was quite effective and really caught the eye.

"There was no Volume 1, 2 or 3, so it's a pretty stupid title really" – Bill Ward

When you opened the album up (ripping the clear plastic wrapping off) you would have a gatefold sleeve with a page in the middle, creating a page for each band member. It would feature solo shots of each member (again captured by Keef at the same gig as the cover photo) presenting some very cool pictures of the band live on stage, especially Bill Ward's photos. The record labels would spend the extra money on gatefold sleeves and photos because, for them, a Black Sabbath album just had to exist to sell and they would make their money back tenfold. Future editions of the album would skip the page and give you a gatefold picture of Geezer and Tony, no Bill or Ozzy. Very confusing if you didn't know the history of the release. I just thought they were mad at Bill Ward. Also slipped in was a thank you to the great COKE-Cola, an obvious reference to the drug, not the soda.

My Eyes Are Blind But I Can See

Before the album's release, the single *Tomorrow's Dream* b/w *Laguna Sunrise* would be released, and, like the previous two singles, it would fail to chart, proving that Black Sabbath was not a singles band. Black Sabbath's fourth album, VOL 4, would see a worldwide release on September 25, 1972, and do the standard business on the charts, #5 in the UK and #13 in the US. Despite it being Black Sabbath's fourth straight platinum-selling album in the US and their best seller in the UK, chart positions were down from their previous two releases, instantly creating a bit of a panic for the band, management, and the record labels. Could VOL 4 become Black Sabbath's first failure? And if so... how can a million-plus selling disc be a failure? Chart positions were a slight letdown (to the labels), reviews were still bad, BUT... many of the mainstream media outlets praised the album and the band for the new style of music they were creating. To prove you can't please everyone, those same critics who blasted the band's heavy and dark sound were now condemning the band for changing things up. You can never win!

"By the time we got to Bel Air we were totally gone." – Tony Iommi

This Is Where I Feel I Belong

VOL 4 starts off with an almost Led Zeppelin song at first, then turns right into classic Sabbath. *Wheels Of Confusion* is led by a typical Tony Iommi riff, cleaner but incredibly heavy. When Ozzy Osbourne begins to sing you notice a highness in his voice, creating another new depth to the song. Midway through the song, the music and tempo change up into something completely different and wonderful. Apparently touring with YES rubbed off a bit on the band, especially on this track, with its progressive feel and beautiful lead solos. The 8 minutes just fly by.

For the second track, *Tomorrow's Dream*, Black Sabbath craft one of their greatest songs ever. With this one, you understand that the vocals are slightly different (and multi-tracked for real effect) and the musicianship is getting better, but the band may be moving away from the pure doom and gloom. I love how on this performance you hear every Bill Ward cymbal crash, giving the song some extra bounce.

Going completely in another direction altogether is the beautiful and haunting *Changes*. I remember hearing it for the first time as a kid and really feeling the pain Osbourne was going through in this song. However, I didn't get it because Sabbath was supposed to be heavy all the time. With piano and strings creating the mood, this one seems to get a bad rap. Black Sabbath tried to expand their musical horizons and met with some resistance from the fan base but, oddly, not the critics. This song resonates with so many people for so many different reasons.

FX is an instrumental that I always thought of as just filler until I understood what Iommi was trying to do, which was hitting the strings with his cross to create a weird experience and a nice lead-in to the next track.

It is hard to imagine what the band could have accomplished in the studio if they weren't all messed up when you hear the pure brilliance of *Supernaut*. Starting off with a melody right out of a 70's cop show TV theme, the band just rip into this one and never let go. The star of this one is drummer Bill Ward as he leads the way with some of his heaviest, most intricate fills and a calypso moment in the middle break. There is a reason this was John Bonham's favorite Sabbath song, because it is very Led Zeppelinish, from drums to riff, from funky bass to Osbourne's soaring vocals.

The almost-title track for the album, *Snowblind* is the theme for the cocaine generation… or Black Sabbath 1973. Lyrically, there isn't any hidden meaning or agenda… it's just a plug-in and play cut with Ozzy singing about the band's white powder of choice. But wow, what another amazing song… pure energy and aggression. If you ever thought the song was about snowfall in a winter wonderland… just keep thinking that. Amazing with more underappreciated drums by Ward.

"Yeah, that's what it was, cocaine!" – Geezer Butler

Evoking the spirit of old Sabbath, *Cornucopia* is a heavy, driving, just-put-your-head-down-and- go moment. This was never a favorite of mine and always felt it was the first real stumble on the album, not because it was bad, but because it seemed out of place with the music that came before it. However, I have to give extra points for Ward's work here.

Written by Iommi after watching the sunrise on Laguna Beach, the obviously titled *Laguna Sunrise* is a thoughtful instrumental that has a very classical flavor and another Led Zeppelin vibe to it. Black Sabbath was influenced by their friends but a little jealous that they and their music were never taken seriously. This is sad because people may have missed out on some amazing music because of not understanding just how much Sabbath had to offer.

I know this may seem like a broken record, but *St. Vitus Dance* is another track that has a heavy Led Zeppelin influence to it, especially in the opening/introduction. This is another one that isn't a favorite, but is still a very interesting song that sounds like Sabbath trying to go old school Country and Western.

Under The Sun/Every Day Comes And Goes is heavy… heavy… heavy!!! For all the light on the album, the band finishes in the darkness with a great and very underrated song. There is so much to love here, especially Osbourne's voice and inflections as he sings along with the rhythm. Some great guitar moments as the song changes tempo and becomes two songs.

"I was putting so much of the stuff up my nose that I had to smoke a bag of dope every day to stop my heart from exploding." – Ozzy Osbourne

I've Opened the Door, Now My Mind's Been Released

As usual, Black Sabbath was rushed back on the road in the United States starting in July in Wildwood, New Jersey, before VOL 4 would be released. While on the road in America, the band would begin to encounter people and situations that made them resentful of touring, and, in the case of Osbourne, began to resent America. In an interview with Circus magazine, Osbourne complained about the never-ending hotel rooms, being scared of American audiences, and being so far away from his family. The article, called "Why Black Sabbath Hate America" was less an attack on the USA as it was a cry for help from the singer, who, like his bandmates, was beginning to become unhinged. New songs added to the setlist were *Tomorrow's Dream, Under The Sun, Wheels Of Confusion, Cornucopia,* and an early version of *Killing Yourself To Live*. Sharing the stage with the band would be Blue Oyster Cult, who just released their debut album, the up-and-coming J. Geils Band, and Gentle Giant, a progressive rock/jazz band co-managed by Patrick Meehan and YES manager Brian Lane. Gentle Giant had a hard time winning over the Sabbath fans, being booed and heckled most nights, and it soon became violent. Following a show at the famed Hollywood Bowl, a cherry bomb was thrown on stage, exploded, and caused the band to exit the stage rather urgently, but not before vocalist Phil Shulman unleased a justified verbal tirade at the crowd.

"I'll never forget it."- Derek Shulman (Gentle Giant)

Several shows were canceled due to Osbourne losing his voice because he had been unable to get a few weeks off to just rest and let himself heal. Black Sabbath would play almost 30 shows in the US before the speed-of-sound pace finally caught up to them. It wasn't just the Gentle Giant tirade at the Hollywood Bowl show that made it memorable. It was Tony Iommi's body, mind, and soul that had just had enough. Following the last song of the set, Iommi walked off the stage of the legendary venue and collapsed. Due to exhaustion brought on by the tour schedule, not sleeping or eating right, and yes, cocaine, the guitarist's body just shut down. The doctor told him, "Go Home!" Because of this, the final dates of the US tour would be canceled, and a second leg, scheduled to begin in April 1973, was also canceled. Not good news for record sales, considering the band would be off the road when the new album was finally released.

Black Sabbath would pack up for a run of dates in Australia in January 1973 and Europe in March. Looking at the success of Deep Purple's double-live MADE IN JAPAN release (see below), the plan was to record a live album of their own reportedly to be called FIRE ON THE MOUNTAIN, and have it ready to release before the band's proposed (but now canceled) US tour. Two UK shows were recorded: Manchester (3/11) and London (3/16), but the label said no due to their displeasure with the band's performances and the recording's quality. These tapes would resurface in a spite move in 1980 as the album, LIVE AT LAST. By now the Black Sabbath bubble had sadly begun to burst and the narrative changed into a sad story of survival, mismanagement, and lost opportunities.

Final Thought...Part, or Vol. 4

For me, this is where it all came together as a Black Sabbath fan. Although I didn't discover this album until a decade after its original release, I can still hear, respect, and understand what the band was trying to say and do musically on this album. As huge fans of the Beatles, Black Sabbath knew the Fab Four didn't want to get locked into one sound and style and become stagnant, so they grew... and here, so did Black Sabbath. I don't care if it was the massive amounts of drugs or just original creativity that fueled this project, but VOL4 is a real gem. In hindsight, it gives us the ability to see where this musical change would culminate on the next album. Unlike their partners in crime Led Zeppelin and Deep Purple, Black Sabbath wasn't praised for trying to change things up and add something new to their music. They were just expected to be heavy and one-dimensional. Since I am a huge fan of The Beatles, I liken VOL4 to RUBBER SOUL, the point in time when things changed musically.

"That whole period was one of the most enjoyable times ever." – Tony Iommi

For their wanting to take chances and step out of the doom and gloom, retain the expected quality, and be true to themselves, I give this album an easy 7.5 out of 10 and rank VOL 4 my #9 favorite Black Sabbath album out of their 19 studio releases. The collective known as the Black Sabbath Facebook groups think highly of the album as well, ranking it an impressive #7 out of 19 studio releases. The respected publication, KERRANG! magazines poll of the Top 100 Heavy Metal Albums Of All Time put VOL 4 at #48.

"Before every album, it's really hard to get back into it after you've been off the road for two or three months." – Geezer Butler

A Clash of Titans...Iommi vs Page

I believe Tony Iommi is a better guitar player than Jimmy Page.
There. I said it. Historians of music know what a polarizing comment this is, and I fully understand the passion Led Zeppelin fans live with and the respect that Jimmy Page has, but... it had to be said. The more I began to listen to Black Sabbath and Tony Iommi in particular, I discovered that he is so much more than just thunderous heavy riffs. Yes, he is that, but he can play anything the song or moment needs. Most of Page's signature creations are based on (and sometimes stolen as history has shown) blues riffs and to me the plagiarizing charges (guilty in court or not) sour Page's originality. This is not saying he isn't a brilliant player and if it wasn't for his vision of Led Zeppelin, we may not have had a Black Sabbath or the entire Original Big Four movement. I always thought there was a bit of sloppiness to Page's playing that I think made him a bit more human than the god-like status he has. Truth be told, I prefer his playing in The Firm to his work with Led Zeppelin.

Tony Iommi and Jimmy Page! Art by Black Sabbath fan and dear friend, Rusty Brown.

Both are pure legends and visionaries, but picking one over the over for me is easy. Despite working at a disadvantage physically, I always looked at Iommi as one of the best players ever who could play anything from heavy riffs, to psychedelic rock, to the short pop song, filling it all in with blistering leads yet somehow managing to make it all sound so good. I just think the image of Black Sabbath took away from everyone appreciating his pure talent, while Page's image and his band cultivated the guitar god mythos.

"We were really good mates with Led Zeppelin, especially Robert Plant and John Bonham who came from the Midlands. They had wanted us to be on Swan Song, but we couldn't make it work out." – Tony Iommi

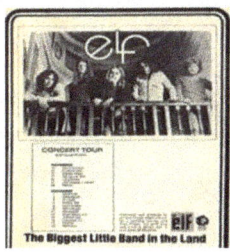  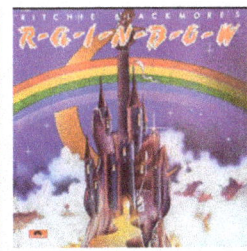 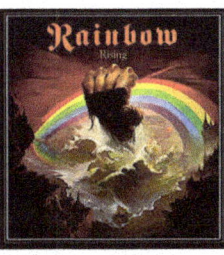

Elf had the good fortune of opening for Deep Purple, not only putting them in front of thousands of fans each night but making a huge impression on the members, especially Richie Blackmore who would take ¾ of Elf and form the first line-up of Rainbow in 1975.

Elf on the shelf...Ronnie James Dio

Discovered, signed, and produced by Deep Purple's Ian Paice and Roger Glover, Elf was a blues/boogie band from Cortland, New York, that was led by a short bassist/singer/trumpeter with a massive voice named Ronald Padavona, but would go by the name Ronnie James Dio (born July 10, 1942). Elf would release their self-titled debut album on Purple Records in (1972) and would find themselves in a very coveted spot, opening for Deep Purple on several world tours. Musically, Elf had more in common with Rod Stewart's early solo albums than the power of Deep Purple, but Dio (now just singing) made quite an impression on guitarist Richie Blackmore. In 1974, Elf released CAROLINA COUNTY BALL, and while on the road Blackmore asked Elf to back him on a solo project he was working on. Unknown to Elf at the time, Blackmore was planning on leaving Deep Purple and forming his own band called Richie Blackmore's Rainbow with the members of Elf (minus guitarist Steve Edwards) being recruited as the band's first of a zillion line-ups. By the time Elf's third album, TRYING TO BURN THE SUN, was released, Elf had already been broken up for several months.

On August 4, 1975, RICHIE BLACKMORE'S RAINBOW would be released and see solid sales and chart action, going to #30 in the US and #11 in the UK. In 1978, the classic RAINBOW RISING was released (#48 US and #11 UK) and would be followed by the double live ON STAGE in 1977. In 1978, amid strife and turmoil, Rainbow released LONG LIVE ROCK 'N' ROLL (1978), an album containing one of the greatest songs ever, *Gates Of Babylon*. Following the tour to support the album, Dio would leave Rainbow, tired of the constant line-up changes, battles with Blackmore and drummer Cozy Powell, and the compromises to the music. Blackmore wanted hits where Dio wanted integrity. In 1979, Dio would receive a call from a desperate Tony Iommi.

"I've always felt it was better to remain a bit untrained to maintain your individuality." – Ronnie James Dio

Too hot to handle...Phil Mogg

In the rock 'n' roll version of Six Degrees Of Separation, UFO (vocalist Phil Mogg above) and Black Sabbath may have never shared band members, but many UFO'ers spent time with Black Sabbath guys in other bands, some a few times. Ready? Neil Carter, Neil Murray and Cozy Powell (with Gary Moore), Pete Way (with Ozzy Osbourne), Michael Schenker and Paul Raymond with Cozy Powell (Michael Schenker Group), Laurence Archer and Neil Murray (with Grand Slam), Aynsley Dunbar and Neil Murray (with Whitesnake), Simon Wright and Ronnie James Dio (DIO), Jason Bonham and Glenn Hughes (in Black Country Communion), Michael Schenker and Neil Murray (MSG). UFO and Black Sabbath have similar histories, and both mean so much to me, but musically, they aren't even close!

www.ufo-music.info

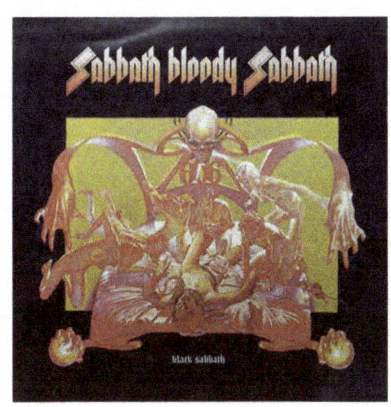 

SABBATH BLOODY SABBATH (Vertigo/Warner Bros. Records)
Released on December 1, 1973 (UK) and January 1974 (US)
Produced by Black Sabbath
Ozzy Osbourne (vocals), Tony Iommi (guitar), Geezer Butler (bass), and Bill Ward (drums)
All songs written by Butler, Iommi, Osbourne, and Ward

SABBATH BLOODY SABBATH

A NATIONAL ACROBAT
FLUFF
SABBRA CADABRA
KILLING YOURSELF TO LIVE
WHO ARE YOU?
LOOKING FOR TODAY
SPIRAL ARCHITECT

"SABBATH BLOODY SABBATH was really the album after which I should have said goodbye because after that I really started unraveling. Then we ended up falling out of favor with each other." – Ozzy Osbourne

you bastard!

With their first real break in almost four years, the members of Black Sabbath were able to escape the rat race and tried to live as normal a life as they could, that is until the cycle would begin all over again. But it appeared that the band who were so burned out and miserable from the constant touring couldn't relax when they were off the road and were just as miserable. Tony Iommi was beginning to recover from his exhaustion, got married (with best man being Led Zeppelin's John Bonham) but oddly, didn't come up with any new riffs or song ideas. Ozzy Osbourne and Geezer Butler tried to settle into family life as best they could with mixed results, and Bill Ward found himself spiraling more and more out of control with drugs. Once the bell rang, the band packed their bags, kissed their families goodbye, and headed back to the du Pont Mansion and the Power Plant Studio in California to begin work on a new album. Considering the debauchery and destruction that happened the last time the band rented the house from John du Pont, it was a shock they were let back in... but apparently all was forgiven... or at least reimbursed.

"We had such a great time doing VOL 4 in Los Angeles, and we wanted to recreate the experience for what would become the next album." – Tony Iommi

Many things were going on in Black Sabbath's world, and most of it was bad! Musically, the band was excited about the prospects of building on the growth and musical expansion started on VOL 4, but the record labels and band management didn't want what they saw as another failure from the band. They just wanted the heavy. Everyone who had a financial stake in the band was looking to recoup lost revenues that canceling the last US tour caused. The record labels (Warner Bros. and Vertigo) also wanted theirs, feeling they lost massive sales when the second leg of the US tour was canceled following VOL 4's release. To show how out of control everything had become, Black Sabbath played about 30 shows without an album to support, and when the album was finally released and certified gold, the band managed only a small European tour before it was all shut down.

Wondering how they could owe anyone any money or have to worry so much about financial losses, the band members began to ask questions to WEA (their management company) about their finances, and the more they investigated, the more shocked, frustrated, and upset they became. For starters, their homes, cars, and all their assets, which they thought they owned, were owned by the management company and the band was actually renting from themselves. The more the band began to question, the more Meehan and company pulled away. To keep the band away, Meehan hired accountants to answer their questions, keeping himself away from the band. Yes, this blocking move was being paid for by the band. This began to have a major impact on the band members, and for Iommi, this manifested itself into serious writer's block.

"Everybody was sitting there waiting for me to come up with something. I just couldn't think of anything. And if I didn't come up with anything, nobody would do anything." – Tony Iommi

The band settled into the mansion and the Power Plant to work out new songs, but nothing was coming from the guitarist except frustration. In the Black Sabbath songwriting model, Iommi comes up with the riffs,

Osbourne comes up with the vocal melody to sing to, Butler provides the lyrics for Osbourne, and Ward builds the rhythm and drive of the song. Four working as one, possibly more than any other band ever has, but, as you can see, without riffs... nothing! Another big problem was trhat the studio that they loved the previous year had some drastic changes in it (a huge synthesizer left by Stevie Wonder), ruining the flow and disappointing the band, ultimately really causing more issues with Iommi's fragile psyche.

Another unfortunate incident that would have a lasting consequence on the band was a physical altercation (yes, it was drinking-related) between Osbourne and Butler that became a bit more than expected when Iommi intervened and punched Ozzy in the face. For the already insecure Osbourne, this brought up a lot of bad feelings about being picked on and bullied (by Iommi and others) in their school days. It also began to really upset Osbourne how Iommi always tried to control him. After a month of wasted time and money, the band opted to return to the UK and find a different environment to write, and, hopefully, record.

"I became the bully again, which I didn't want to be." – Tony Iommi

Needing a particular atmosphere to create, Black Sabbath chose Clearwell Castle in Gloucestershire, England, to live in and put the music together. They would then use Morgan Studios in London to record it. Trying to make the magic happen, Iommi spent time in the castle's dungeon searching for inspiration... and he certainly did, creating the riff that saved Black Sabbath!

"Once Tony came out with the riff for 'Sabbath Bloody Sabbath' we went... We're back!" – Geezer Butler

Once the riffs returned to the master, the songs began to flow, much of it challenging their own boundaries and musical expectations. Was it the castle and its gothic atmosphere that inspired the band? Was it the ghosts the band claimed to encounter all over the castle? Was it the drugs and constant (and sometimes out of control) pranks the band played on each other? Whatever it was that got the creative juices flowing, it worked, and Black Sabbath was off and running again. According to the band, they got themselves so wound up and scared that they would often work until late into the night and then take the long rides back to their houses just to get some sleep. Unable to get any lyrics completed in the castle, Butler would often leave for the day, finding it easier to write at home and not have to worry about being set on fire by Osbourne.

As the sessions began to move along at a nice pace, guests like John Bonham (Led Zeppelin) and Rick Wakeman (YES) made their way into the studio, with Wakeman finding himself on the album, playing keyboards on *Sabra Cadabra*. In fact, Bonham wanted to play drums on the same song, but Black Sabbath preferred to keep all the playing of the main instruments by members of the band. Wakeman's involvement happened because his band, YES, was recording their latest, longest, and most indulgent album, TALES FROM TOPOGRAPHIC OCEANS, in the studio next door and Wakeman wanted to hang out with people who lived more like he did. Wakeman was a meat eater and alcohol drinker while the rest of YES were vegetarians, which caused personal riffs between him and his bandmates. Wakeman would go so far as eating curry on stage during a show, publicly expressing his displeasure with YES and their music at the time. There was a rumor circulating that Wakeman would join Black Sabbath, but that was probably never more than just the drink talking. Not wanting payment for his services, Wakeman was paid in beer and was quite happy with that.

"I loved Black Sabbath. I loved them musically and loved them as people." - Rick Wakeman

Speaking of keyboards, Black Sabbath brought in more instruments to fill out their new sound. Noticing the change in music and success with the above-mentioned YES, Pink Floyd's DARK SIDE OF THE MOON, and the Who's QUADROPHENIA, the band wanted more from their music and felt they were finally allowed the opportunity to do so. Unfortunately, many diehard fans didn't agree and wanted their Black Sabbath to be that of the first three albums. Osbourne played Moog synthesizer on two tracks, *Killing Yourself To Live* and *Who Are You*, a song the singer wrote on his Moog. Always looking to add more, Iommi brought in acoustic guitar, harpsichord, organ, flute, and bagpipes yet still tried more. His plan was to bring in a sitar.

One of the most noticeable differences you hear right away on the new material is the pitch and range of Osbourne's voice, how high he is singing. To compete with Ian Gillan, Robert Plant, Roger Daltrey, and Jon Anderson, the singer had to change up his approach to singing and how it was recorded. Osbourne's voice adds another amazing level to the songs, cutting through the music and making them that much better. There is multi-tracking of his voice on several tracks and a lot of the new voice was created in the studio, but bottom line, on vinyl, cassette, reel to reel, or 8-Track, his voice sounds amazing.

love me 'til the end of time

By far the best Black Sabbath album cover. Yes, this one scared the Hell out of me as a kid (and still does as an adult) but it is a brilliant piece of art, especially in conjunction with the back cover that really tells yet another part of the same story. If you just look at it for what it is you will see in blazing crimson is a man on a bed with a demonic headboard come to life, reading 666, and naked people on top and on the sides of him. If you look closely, you will see the bed covered with rats. When you let the cover speak to you see it represents someone on their death bed wrestling with their past demons and pretty much heading to Hell as they die an incredibly horrible and quite emotional death. The back cover with its softer color palette is the absolute opposite... a passing surrounded by the people that care for him and the animals that are protecting his soul as he leaves this world in peace bound for the next one. Replacing the Satanic evil headboard is a male and muscular figure (torso only) with outstretched arms representing God's open, welcoming, and comforting arms.

The artwork was done by Drew Struzan, who was working for Pacific Eye & Ear, a company that created album art worthy of the music inside. From Aerosmith to The Doors, the company created almost 200 album covers with Struzan illustrating two of their best, SABBATH BLOODY SABBATH and Alice Cooper's WELCOME TO MY NIGHTMARE (Atlantic Records). In 1977 Struzman would help create the 1978 re-release posters for STAR WARS and continue to create visual art for dozens of movies, including BACK TO THE FUTURE, E.T., and THE GOONIES. The gatefold picture inside features a transparent band, naked (but nothing showing) standing in front of a bed like the cover, just minus the headboard. Brilliant all over and for the first time since their debut album, the artwork outside actually matched the art inside.

"I f@#$%^g love that cover!" – Ozzy Osbourne

don't delay you're in today

On December 1, 1974, in the UK (slightly later in North America) Black Sabbath unleashed their strongest album to date, SABBATH BLOODY SABBATH. With a solid mix of really heavy and progressive/mature songs, the band seems to strike the perfect balance between their old and new sound. Now competing with newer bands like Judas Priest, UFO, and Bad Company, Black Sabbath was able to create an album that fits in perfectly with the best releases of 1974, BAD COMPANY, BURN (Deep Purple), and PHENOMENON

(UFO). Without a hit single to precede the release and get everyone ready, SABBATH BLOODY SABBATH still received very positive reviews from those who were always over critical. Rolling Stone, for example, called the release "an extraordinarily gripping affair," finally giving the band the adulation they always wanted and certainly deserved. Always looking for the same respect given to Led Zeppelin, Tony Iommi looked at this masterpiece with pride.

The album was an immediate hit in the US and became the band's fifth consecutive platinum-selling album. It was also the first to attain Silver certification status in the UK for sales of over 60,000 units. On the charts, SABBATH BLOODY SABBATH went to #11 in the US and #4 in the UK, making it the band's best-charting album next to PARANOID. Following the release and all the accolades, Black Sabbath could at last feel like they achieved exactly what they wanted. They took their time, fought through adversity, substances, and each other to create an album they would all be proud of, one that would stand the test of time.

"SABBATH BLOODY SABBATH was really the album after which I should have said goodbye because after that I really started unraveling." – Ozzy Osbourne

sadness kills the superman

One of the greatest albums kicks off with one of the greatest songs ever, *Sabbath Bloody Sabbath*. For all the sensitivity and experimentation of the previous disc, this track starts off with power and serious fury, broken up with some softer moments only to explode once again in power. Osbourne's vocals are once again in a higher range (this possibly being the highest) and really add so much to the musicianship behind him. The song has a lot of time changes but always remains true to itself. Brilliant!

"It's very personal and I wouldn't like to embarrass the person it was written about." – Ozzy Osbourne

A National Acrobat has a bit of a funky side to it, with Iommi and Butler playing in unison and Ward blasting under them with Osbourne really singing his heart out. The song's true magic and what makes it so different is the chorus. Here the song changes up a bit with multi-tracked vocals and guitars that have a lot of cool effects put on for a great song. Completely underrated!

Fluff is a beautiful acoustic guitar piece Iommi wrote for his wedding and is a perfect counterbalance to the album's power and drive. Having a Rod Stewart feel to it, the song would have the distinction of being played after almost every Black Sabbath concert as the house lights went on and everyone got up to leave. Named after BBC disc jockey Alan "Fluff" Freeman, until a few years ago I thought the song was called "Pluff."

  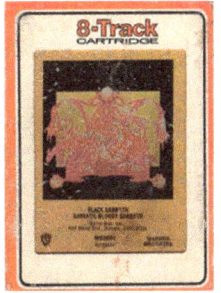

Another tale of three formats for SABBATH BLOODY SABBATH, the UK cassette inlay, the Japanese vinyl and the American 8-Track

"We weren't so much the Lords of Darkness as the Lords of Chickens***."- Ozzy Osbourne

Although I loved the title *Sabbra Cadabra*. It was and still is a song that I never got into because it was just a straight-ahead boogie song with nothing special for me to hold onto. Again, not a bad song, just one that doesn't do much for me, except the middle break before the solo. The song does feature the piano wizardry of YES's Rick Wakeman, who was next door with his band recording the epic TALES FROM TOPOGRAPHIC OCEANS.

Side two kicks off with *Killing Yourself To Live*, thus setting the bar quite high for the rest of the album. I always loved the almost muddy guitars playing lively riffs and the drums falling behind them. When the song begins to pick up and go, it is led by a great rhythm and a steady pace. Osbourne is again hitting some really high notes, adding to the almost desperation of the song. One of their most underrated songs... but I will say that about two of the next three as well.

"We were all happy with SABBATH BLOODY SABBATH." – Ozzy Osbourne

Starting off with some cool synths (another YES influence?) Who Are You? Is a very slow song that, again, sees Black Sabbath moving away from the hard-rock craziness that they are known for. Safe to say, it won't get a pat on the back for taking chances musically. Not a favorite, but a nice break, and I certainly enjoy what the band was trying to accomplish.

Next to the title track, here is my favorite song on the album. *Looking For Today* is just a great song that has so much to hold onto. The well-placed acoustic guitars and flutes of Iommi in the chorus really showcase Ozzy's vocals and give a lot of room for Butler's bass to keep things going with Ward just being Bill Ward!

"We rehearsed in the dungeons and it was really creepy, but it had some atmosphere, it conjured up things, and stuff started coming out again." – Geezer Butler

Right or wrong I tend to look at the last song on an album as the last one written or recorded. Does it match the first song? Is it better or worse? The last song here, *Spiral Architect*, has a lot of Moody Blues moments especially in the beginning with its acoustic guitar and drum patterns. It isn't a fast song or an intense burst of emotion. It is just a great song and a nice way to end the album, complete with strings.

"There are many gems on this album that call on the band's roots in blues, Jazz...and their improvisational abilities. The magic of Ozzy's vocals is he can take you on a magic carpet ride of audio emotions from high to low. I feel this album is above all in the original line-up's discography, it was their SGT. PEPPER!!! This album not only gave you, the listener, all you'd expect from a Black Sabbath album, but it also allowed the band to think outside the box to follow new musical paths that the listener was only too happy to tag along on." - Rob Smith (guitarist - Kiss Forever)

now I found you out

For the first time in the band's history, their latest album would be released and then a tour would begin. The new album was out by the time the band played the UK and Europe in December and January with a return to the States on January 31, 1974 (with Blue Oyster Cult) and would finish in late February. Supporting Black Sabbath in the US would be Bedlam (featuring drummer Cozy Powell), with Bob Seger, Spooky Tooth, and The James Gang opening for them on select dates.

The setlist would see several new songs added... *Killing Yourself To Live*, *A Natural Acrobat*, and *Sabbra Cadabra*. Some shows would feature an early version of *Megalomania*... yet not *Sabbath Bloody Sabbath*. More than likely, the vocal rage the song was recorded in would have been impossible for Osbourne to hit night after night, so it was never added.

"Everything is so beautiful and peaceful and no hassles." – Ozzy Osbourne

The highlight of the tour happened on April 6, 1974, at the Ontario Raceway in front of 250,000 fans, the fabled California Jam! This historic concert also featured Earth, Wind & Fire, Rare Earth, The Eagles, Black Oak Arkansas, Seals & Croft, and co-headliners Emerson Lake & Palmer and Deep Purple. Black Sabbath played an amazing hour-long set in the early evening, showcasing the well-oiled machine they had become on stage. But behind the scenes, a battle was brewing with Deep Purple, who refused to take the stage until it was dark. This caused a huge delay and created tensions with ELP, who were fearful the crowds would leave due to it getting so late. Deep Purple's power play would turn into a memorable performance featuring their newest members, David Coverdale (vocals), and Glenn Hughes (bass/vocals), which ended with a broken TV camera (thanks to Richie Blackmore's temper tantrum) and an on-stage explosion gone horribly wrong.

"Then an almighty row broke out between Deep Purple and ELP about who was going to close the show. They were trying to involve us as well." – Tony Iommi

Following Cal Jam, the band had a few weeks off and then would resume their tour in the UK in June with Black Oak Arkansas. Following an unheard-of six months off the road, Black Sabbath would tour Australia with a young up-and-coming band called AC/DC. When it was all said and done, Black Sabbath performed fewer shows on this tour than ever before... with no arguments from Osbourne, Iommi, Ward, and Butler.

final thoughts on sabbath bloody sabbath

Many people consider this one to be the pinnacle of their career and I agree to an extent. Yes, SABBATH BLOODY SABBATH is almost a perfect release, with every song invoking a new emotion. But to me, a pinnacle implies a fall on the other side, and despite some lean times and unsuccessful albums coming up shortly, the band is far from peaking here. The music on the disc offers so much maturity without losing what made the band so great and original. As much as I love the title track, it's *Looking For Today* that really gets me going and shows the development of the band as not only amazing performers and brilliant writers, but as producers and arrangers. Amazing is the fact that I didn't discover this song until a few years ago when I took a real deep dive into the grooves.

Of the 19 Black Sabbath studio albums that will be released, SABBATH BLOODY SABBATH ranks as my #4 favorite with a rating of 8.5 out of 10. I always thought that the album suffered from being taken seriously by the casual music fan because of the cover and the title. The cover (as awesome as it is) is not a reflection of the music inside and I hope that people don't dismiss it as just another "Satanic Black Sabbath release," because there is some seriously good music here. As far as the fans go, the album is also incredibly popular with the crowd at large, agreeing with my assessment and also putting it at #4 out of 19.

all we are saying is give appice a chance
– Vinny Appice

Making his uncredited debut on John Lennon's WALLS AND BRIDGES album and Appice's band that Tony Iommi was a fan of, Axis!

Not very many performers get to make their recording debut with John Lennon. Unfortunately for him, his work went uncredited, but drummer Vinny Appice (born September 13, 1957) gets to have the memory of adding his handclaps to *Whatever Gets You Through The Night* from Lennon's 1974 release, WALLS AND BRIDGES. The younger brother of Vanilla Fudge's legendary player Carmine Appice, Vinny would be influenced by his brother (of course) and Led Zeppelin's John Bonham. Appice developed his loud, thick style by holding his sticks backward, listening to who he worked with, and absorbing every experience to make them his own. His big break would come when he began to work with Rick Derringer for several years and two albums (DERRINGER and LIVE IN CLEVELAND), before starting his own band, Axis, with guitarist/vocalist Danny Johnson and bassist/vocalist Jay Davis. Axis released an exceptional debut album in 1978 for RCA Records, called IT'S A CIRCUS WORLD, that unfortunately didn't do anything as far as sales, but it put Appice out there. When Axis broke up, sadly, before a second album, Appice recorded the album VOLUME for Ray Gomez while looking for the next project to sink his teeth into.

"So, we went downstairs…and there's John Lennon in the control room! So, we did handclaps on the song "Whatever Gets You Thru the Night" — that's me and my band. We were freaking out. I mean, I was in high school — I was going to high school the next day." – Vinny Appice

"I called my brother and told him I got this offer to join Ozzy Osbourne in England. Is this guy crazy? He said yeah... he's real f@#$%# nuts." – Vinny Appice

The first call Appice got was from manager Sharon Arden asking if the drummer would be interested in traveling to the UK to work with Ozzy Osbourne, who was starting to put together his BLIZZARD OF OZ album and band. After getting sage advice from his brother, Appice declined the offer but a few months later received a call from Black Sabbath about a vacancy on the drums with the departure of Bill Ward. Sabbath guitarist Tony Iommi met with the drummer, told him how much he enjoyed his work on the Axis album and would he be interested in helping the band finish their current tour. Black Sabbath would get together with Appice, jam on Neon Knights, and the rest was history. The original plan was to have Appice fill in until Bill Ward (hopefully) returned behind the kit, but for the immediate future he'd have the gig. In a few short days, he had to learn their entire set for a show in Hawaii. No pressure.

symptom of the universe
– James Pulli (Impellitteri)

Bassist James Pulli is both a fan of Black Sabbath and Uriah Heep (note the shirt) and is heavily influenced by the late Gary Thain but considers Geezer Butler to be his main influence. As a member of the legendary band Impellitteri, James was excited to cover Symptom Of The Universe for the band's 2018 release, THE NATURE OF THE BEAST. When forced to pick a favorite Black Sabbath song... he picked two, Hole In The Sky and Fairies Wear Boots. His favorite album by the band is the next one we cover, SABOTAGE!

www.impellitteri.net

NO OBLIGATION
To Buy Anything Ever!

BRAND NEW HIT LIST!

MORE GREAT HITS

Title	No.
LONDON CHUCK BERRY	6882
GODSPELL Movie Soundtrack	7914
ERIC CLAPTON At His Best 2 LPs & 2 Tapes	0901
BEETHOVEN Symphony No. 5	7252
AROUND THE WORLD WITH THREE DOG NIGHT 2 LPs & 2 Tapes	0760
STEPPENWOLF 16 Greatest Hits	1214
THREE DOG NIGHT Seven Separate Fools	1404
SHA NA NA Golden Age Of Rock And Roll 2 LPs & 2 Tapes	0729
URIAH HEEP Magician's Birthday	2014
ERIC CLAPTON Clapton	5355
2001 A SPACE ODYSSEY	9050
NEWPORT FOLK FESTIVAL	3152
TEMPTATIONS Masterpieces	6619
GRASS ROOTS 16 Greatest Hits	1198
JAMES TAYLOR The Original Flying Machine	3707
GRAND FUNK Phoenix	4606
CURTIS MAYFIELD Superfly	5959
STEVE MILLER BAND Anthology 2 LPs & 2 Tapes	0117
BEETHOVEN Three Piano Sonatas	7047
HISTORY OF THE GUESS WHO?	9324
URIAH HEEP Look At Yourself	2022
URIAH HEEP Live 2 LPs & 2 Tapes	0208
THE DIONNE WARWICK STORY 2 LPs & 2 Tapes	0273
ARTHUR FIEDLER & THE BOSTON POPS Bacharach-David	9371
RIGHTEOUS BROTHERS 14 Greatest Hits	9373
CHOPIN Polonaise in C Sharp Minor	7054
MAMAS & PAPAS 20 Golden Hits 2 LPs & 2 Tapes	0612
ISAAC HAYES Shaft 2 LPs & 2 Tapes	0638
THE VERY BEST OF BILLIE HOLIDAY	9209
LOBO Of A Simple Man	7322
MANDRILL Composite Truth	5306
FIFTH DIMENSION Living Together, Growing Together	7850
DR. ZHIVAGO Movie Soundtrack	9345

GREATEST OFFER EVER

Other record and tape clubs make you choose from just a few labels. They make you buy up to 12 records or tapes a year. And if you don't return their monthly IBM cards, they send you an item you don't want and a bill for up to $8.38. But Record Club of America has BANISHED "AUTOMATIC SHIPMENTS FOREVER! You'll never receive an unordered recording again.

SEE HOW YOU SAVE

Join now and get with your introductory recordings incredible "BUY 1, GET 2 FREE" offer on 100's more Top Hit LPs and Tapes! New SUPER-DISCOUNT offer every 28 days. Imagine paying $1.69 average price for $5.98 Stereo LPs... $1.99 for $6.98 Tape Cartridges and Cassettes. Yet that's exactly the Sale Offer mailing now to members even as you read this!

LOOK WHAT YOU GET

- 6 LPs or 5 Tapes for 99¢! • Lifetime Membership—with NO OBLIGATION to buy anything ever! • Giant Master Discount Catalog of all readily available records and tapes! • Free subscriptions to Disc & Tape Guide magazine and the WAREHOUSE Catalog! • Your order computer processed for Express Service Delivery! • 100% Moneyback Guarantee!

Artist / Album	No.	Label
MOODY BLUES Days Of Future Passed	5020	Deram
CAT STEVENS Matthew & Son / New Masters (2 LPs & 2 Tapes)	0885	Deram
ROD STEWART Every Picture Tells A Story	2055	Mercury
THE BAND Rock Of Ages (2 LPs & 2 Tapes)	0101	Capitol
BLACK SABBATH Sabotage	4689	Capitol
STEELY DAN Can't Buy A Thrill	101	ABC
THE BEST OF THE JAMES GANG	100	ABC
ROD STEWART Never A Dull Moment	2154	Mercury
FIFTH DIMENSION'S GREATEST HITS ON EARTH	7823	Bell

© 1973 Record Club of America

RECORD CLUB OF AMERICA
CLUB HEADQUARTERS / YORK, PENNSYLVANIA 17405

V15

YES — Rush me my Lifetime Membership Discount Card, Giant All-Label Master Discount Catalog, plus subscriptions to Disc & Tape Guide Magazine and the WAREHOUSE™ Catalog. Also send me the 6 LPs or 5 Tapes of my choice indicated below (sets marked 2 or 3 LPs or Tapes count as 2 or 3 selections) with a bill for the Club's standard mailing and handling fee. I enclose my $5 Lifetime Membership Fee plus 99¢ for my recordings for a total of $5.99. I am not obligated to buy any records or tapes ever — no yearly quota. If not completely delighted, I may return above items within 10 days for an immediate refund. IMPORTANT: selections marked with ✱ are not available on tape.

ENTER 6 LP OR 5 TAPE NUMBERS BELOW—Sorry, No Mixing

IMPORTANT! YOU MUST CHECK ONE: ☐ LP or ☐ 8 TRACK or ☐ CASSETTE

Mr. Mrs. Miss _____

Rt RR RD SR _____ Box or P.O. Box _____

Street _____ Apt _____

City _____ State _____ Zip _____

APO & FPO ADDRESSES, PLEASE FILL IN YOUR SOCIAL SECURITY NO.

CANADIANS mail coupon to above address. Orders will be serviced in Canada by Record Club of Canada. Prices and listings may vary slightly.

The Old Testament
Black Sabbath

The Book of Sabbath
Chapter 2

Fall 1:2

Behold, as the seasons change,
deception plagued the land of the giants each time the bird flew.
As the giants looked to the east and the west,
the keeper of their riches turned to magic and alchemy
to deceive them, leaving them with no protection.
As the bottom-feeders began to eat of the fallen treasures,
the giants began to stumble and bicker, creating
a path for those to take advantage of, and, ultimately, destroy!

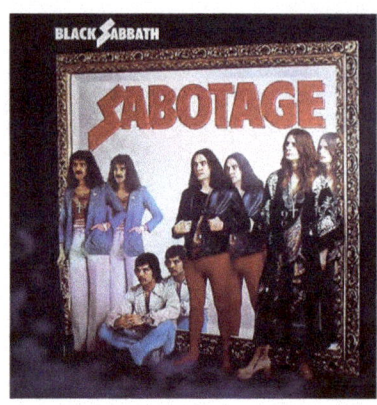 

SABBATH BLOODY SABBATH (Vertigo/Warner Bros. Records)
Released on July 28, 1975
Produced by Black Sabbath and Mike Butcher
Ozzy Osbourne (vocals), Tony Iommi (guitar), Geezer Butler (bass), and Bill Ward (drums)
All songs written by Butler, Iommi, Osbourne, and Ward

HOLE IN THE SKY
DON'T START (TOO LATE)
SYMPTOM OF THE UNIVERSE
MEGALOMANIA

THE THRILL OF IT ALL
SUPERTZAR
AM I GOING INSANE (RADIO)
THE WRIT

I'M GETTING CLOSER TO THE END OF THE LINE

It was reported in the press that before Black Sabbath would record another album, vocalist Ozzy Osbourne would possibly record and release a solo album. But this plan would fall by the wayside as the band got hit with the horrible reality that their financial situation was far worse than they thought.

This should have been the best time in the life and times of Black Sabbath! Their last album, SABBATH BLOODY SABBATH, erased any bad memories of the perceived failure of VOL4 and was being hailed by almost everyone as the best release of their career. Unfortunately, the band members would soon discover all was not what they thought or were being told. First, in 1969, when Black Sabbath signed their record deal with Vertigo, they were just another collective of musicians who basically sold their soul to the devil and signed a horrible deal, possibly the worst ever. A bit later when the band signed with Warner Bros. in the US, it wasn't the best deal as far as the band was concerned but they didn't know any better. As the band became more and more successful, there was no management support to renegotiate a better deal, something that could have really helped Black Sabbath. Next, manager Patrick Meehan and his company, WWA (World Wide Artist) were taking a bigger chunk from the band's earnings than they should have. Keeping them on the road, on drugs, and with enough creature comforts to stop them from asking any questions, the band were being robbed snowblind without even realizing it. As the band started to pay attention to their finances, Meehan started to pull away and put underlings between him and the band while he focused on other things. With no other options available to them, Black Sabbath fired their manager and looked to get out of their unfavorable contract. This would not be as easy as anyone thought.

"It was like the more you found out, the less you wanted to know. It was horrible!" – Geezer Butler

Hoping to build on the momentum of the previous album and a shorter tour schedule, the band entered Morgan Studios in London in February 1975. Their intention was to take the frustrations of their situation and create another musical masterpiece. The band, with co-producer Mike Butcher (who previously engineered The Kinks) and engineer Robin Black (engineer for Paul McCartney and Jethro Tull) would work primarily in the middle of the night, giving the band time to create. This way Sabbath could avoid the lawyers and collection agencies from calling or being served papers from whoever was suing them today. Without management, there were the day-to-day things that needed to be done. Drummer Bill Ward stepped up and began to take on the financial burdens of the band. Unfortunately, the band members' working-class backgrounds never gave them any training to handle the sheer volume of money that was coming in and going out.

"Management never let us realize how big we were." – Ozzy Osbourne

To add to the situation, Ward's drinking began to interfere with his playing, his mood, and his relationship with the band, causing more undo stress. But the band soldiered on with what they knew best... making music. For Iommi, he began to see Sabbath's sound much bigger than before and was incorporating more and more textures like acoustic guitars, heavy keyboards, and even an English Chamber Choir. Geezer Butler and Osbourne began to question if keeping the band together was even worth it, knowing now that all their hard work would go unrewarded. There were more frustrating moments that didn't help at all, such as when tape operator David Harris accidentally ruined finished recordings (he receives a playful credit as 'Saboteur') forcing the band to re-record entire songs. With everything going against them, Black Sabbath was able to put together a solid album, but lyrically most of the songs were veiled attacks on Meehan and everyone suing them because this was the band's sad reality.

"During this period, the band began to question if there was any point to recording albums and touring endlessly just to pay the lawyers?" - Ozzy Osbourne

    If you are reading this and wondering why this section about making SABOTAGE has less to do about the process of creating the album than the legalities going on behind the scenes... imagine how Osbourne, Iommi, Butler, and Ward felt. To try to right the sinking ship, Iommi reached out to manager Don Arden for help, knowing if anyone could help them out of their current situation it was Arden. Fortunately for the guitarist, Arden had a soft spot for Black Sabbath and always wanted to manage them, so any past slight was forgotten. For Arden, he saw Black Sabbath as a band primed to have success in America, something he had not been able to make happen despite a very talented stable of acts. In 1968, Arden signed The Move, another Birmingham-based band that saw moderate UK success, but it was the two bands formed out of the ashes of The Move, Wizzard and The Electric Light Orchestra, that would bring Arden success, especially ELO.
    Don Arden and his daughter, Sharon, took on Black Sabbath with their first order of business being to get the band's record labels to give them much-needed advance money. This would help them finish the new album and promote it on the road where the band could make money for themselves. With the life-saving funding in place, the band was able to finish up and set their new album, SABOTAGE, for a summer release.

"I wanted something new out there that they did earn royalties from." – Don Arden

SWIM THE MAGIC OCEAN

    To me, it has always been amazing that such a visual band could never seem to get it together for album cover visuals. For album number six, we are given another head-scratcher, especially when you consider the brilliant art for SABBATH BLOODY SABBATH. The cover shows the band facing you while standing in front of a mirror that shows the same image. The back cover features the band facing the mirror and facing away from us with "Sabotage" spelled backwards across the top. The band's name is in the top left corner with the title in the mirror in a large red font. Again, we are seeing the use of the stylized 'S' that gives the title an identity.

"I think the shots hilarious to be honest with you." – Bill Ward

    The cover art and graphics (conceived by Bill Ward's drum tech Graham Wright) is a cool idea in concept, and, for the most part, the execution, but where people tend to fall out with it is the clothing the band is wearing. As the story goes, the band thought they were going to a test photo shoot where black suits would be provided. When they got to the shoot... there were no clothes, so the band was forced to wear what they were wearing (Butler and Iommi) or what they could find, with Ward wearing his wife's red tights and Ozzy's underwear, and the singer in a kimono, platform shoes, and no underwear, because Ward was now wearing it. That makes sense, right?
    The original concept had the band wearing black suits (like rock and roll vampires) standing in front of a castle with a portal leading somewhere else. THAT sounds cool! But what we got was what many have called the worst album cover ever created, not just the band's... but for anyone, EVER! I don't think it's that bad...

"A lot of journalists hated the sight of us. I think we became the band they liked to pick on from day one because we'd gone against all the things we were supposed to be." – Tony Iommi

THE JOKE IS ON ME

Never thinking the album would ever be finished let alone given to the public, Black Sabbath released SABOTAGE on June 28, 1975, on Vertigo (UK) and Warner Bros. (North America) to the usual and instant results. The album would peak at #7 in the UK and #28 in the US but wouldn't have any staying power on the charts like previous albums and slide away rather quickly. 1975 would be an exciting time for hard rock music with the charts, magazine covers, and airwaves dominated by new(er) North American bands like KISS, Aerosmith, RUSH, Ted Nugent, and European groups like Thin Lizzy, UFO, Queen, and Scorpions positioning themselves for success. Instead of riding the wave as leaders, Black Sabbath would sink beneath the waters, and the band for the most part didn't even care.

Despite the not-so-stellar chart performances, the album would see some great reviews by the mainstream media with Rolling Stone calling it their "best record since PARANOID. It might be their best ever." SABOTAGE would go gold in the US, an amazing accomplishment, but this would be the first Black Sabbath record not to go platinum, and was the lowest-charting Black Sabbath album in the states. SABOTAGE would be the last Black Sabbath album to make any significant chart impact for a long, long time.

"To me, SABOTAGE beats the last one..." – Ozzy Osbourne

EVERY DAY I SIT AND WONDER

The festivities begin with the heavy *Hole In The Sky*, a song that certainly begins where the last album ended. Osbourne's vocals are again in a high register, soaring above the rest of the band. Despite its more colorful music, it really does follow the classic heavy riff, thumping bass of the past, but less depressing. For me, the song never resonated like it has with other fans and made the album an upstream struggle for me to get into.

"Technology had changed and I think it shows on SABOTAGE" – Bill Ward

Don't Start (Too Late) is a short acoustic instrumental that doesn't help me to get a strong grip on the album. It is more of an introduction to the next song, but it really isn't helping to create an overall vibe.

I've heard people say that they regard *Symptom Of The Universe* to be the first Thrash and/or Progressive Metal song, and I will certainly agree with that. The riff from Iommi and the drumming of Ward is machine gun-paced but still maintains a sense of melody and isn't fast for the sake of being fast. The song changes pace a few times and moves in and out of levels of heavy, a blueprint that bands would copy in the coming years. One of the better songs on the album, but still not getting me where it counts.

"That has been described as the first progressive metal song, and I agree." – Tony Iommi

The epic *Megalomania* is another fan favorite, but one that to me just plods along without anything substantial to pull me in at first. Musically, the almost ten-minute-long cut really tries to do something. I just don't know what it is. It isn't until the middle, when it almost becomes another song completely, that I become interested. The riff, the cowbell, and the bass underneath are very reminiscent of old KISS, something that makes you move your feet, not something Black Sabbath-y.

A slower-paced song, *The Thrill Of It All*, is quite heavy but it doesn't get interesting until the keyboards come in and make it a better song. With a very blues feel to it, Osbourne does have time to really sing the hell out of this with fire and conviction. The second half is much bouncier and has more life than the beginning with the elevating keyboards and a much faster pace.

Another instrumental and one of the best songs on the album, *Supertzar* has some great playing by Ward, Butler, and Iommi, and is given a level of spookiness with the addition of the English Chamber Choir. A great song to hit the stage with.

The best song on the album, *Am I Going Insane (Radio)*, features lyrics written by Osbourne and not Butler. What makes this song so good and stand out miles above everything else on the album is the structure of the song, the odd guitar tones, and the heavy droning of the bass. The song actually has a chorus that is almost hypnotic and gives the listener something to return to. The band's performances are top-notch and Osbourne's vocals are electric. Sad that this one didn't become a hit single.

Written about the countless lawsuits the band was part of, *The Writ* is a song that just spits anger and fire. The title comes from a written document or the slang 'writ' that kept being served to the band while recording the album. The lyrics are justifiably venomous and pointed at now-former manager Patrick Meehan who if you only know the story from the song, isn't a very good person. "Are you Satan are you man"? Wow...

"I wrote most of the lyrics myself, which felt a bit like seeing a shrink." – Ozzy Osbourne

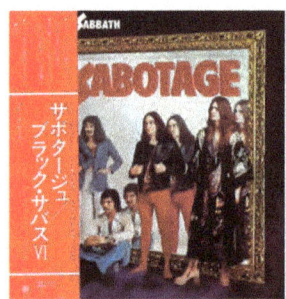

The album cover that made everyone (including the band) say...what? Pictured above are two different Japanese pressings (both re-releases) and the US cassette inlay. Despite the growing popularity of cassettes in the 1970s, it would take ten-plus years before the labels would create a better overall presentation.

WON'T YOU HELP ME, MR. JEU?

Well-rested for one of the first times in their entire career, but now exhausted and feeling the stress of the never-ending legal issues, Black Sabbath hit the road in the US in July. The band would only play a handful of dates before the release of SABOTAGE, finally giving the band a product to promote in a timely manner. Brought on the road to augment their growing live sound the band had created in the studio was fellow Birmingham native, keyboardist Gerald 'Jezz' Woodroffe, who would play offstage out of the view of the audience. Bringing a keyboardist on the road was a controversial move for the band, but with the addition of several new songs to their set, including *Hole In The Sky, Symptom Of The Universe, Megalomania*, and an early version of *Rock & Roll Doctor*, it was much needed.

Black Sabbath would spend the next three months in North America playing with a who's who of 70's artists including The Faces, KISS, Brownsville Station, and Mahogany Rush. They would continue in October and November in Europe before spending two weeks in December back in the States playing shows with Aerosmith, Peter Frampton, KISS, and Kansas, four acts on the verge of breaking it big! On the SABOTAGE tour, Black Sabbath would play for the first time (I believe) the Springfield Civic Center in the city of my birth, Springfield, MA, on August 10, 1975. With the addition of Springfield, MA as a viable tour stop, bands like Black Sabbath now had a place to play between gigs in Boston and Hartford/New Haven, on their way to New York City.... or in reverse.

"On a couple of dates, we had KISS supporting us. Their show was really interesting to watch. I couldn't believe what was going on." – Tony Iommi

A major highlight on the tour was being filmed for the pre-MTV network music showcase, Don Kirshner's Rock Concert. For the first time ever, Black Sabbath was invited into the homes of fans and enemies alike, looking to win over a new crowd. On the popular show, the band performed five songs (including *Hole In The Sky*) with blistering intensity with a vocally controlled Osbourne and a constantly smiling (maybe because he was high) Tony Iommi. Watching that performance, you would think that in the world of Black Sabbath, everything was fine. The end of the tour would be postponed due to a motorcycle accident that injured Ozzy Osbourne. All November UK shows would be made up in January, but Osbourne would be ready for the December gigs in the States.

FINAL THOUGHTS ON SABOTAGE

Well, if there is a time that I will probably piss off my fellow Black Sabbath family... it will probably be right now. When I first discovered Black Sabbath, and this album in particular in the early 1980s, it never was a favorite of mine but I did try very hard to like it. In fact, I never liked it very much, and, as I researched this book, I think I like it even less. Before you get too upset with me, let me say it isn't a bad album, just not a favorite. Yes, I do love the Iron Maiden moment in *Symptom Of The Universe*, the anger of *The Writ*, and the sing-a-long chorus of *Am I Going Insane (Radio)*, but the rest just doesn't get me going. Despite having a few good moments, it isn't an album I will ever just put on to listen to, ever. For my ears, it lacks anything that I can grab onto and emotionally bond to. But... for many fans I know, they feel the absolute opposite.

Of Black Sabbath's 19 studio albums, I rank this one way down at #17 and rate it 3.5 out of 10 because I feel there is only one good song on the album and nothing more than some fragmented ideas with flashes of coolness. I know I'm gonna get it from the fanbase because the Black Sabbath Facebook family ranked it #5 out of 19, with so many of you really expressing your love and support of SABOTAGE, and that is great. Music is art and art can be subjective, so please don't hate me or try to beat me up.

WEARING A MASQUE • RICH WILLIAMS (KANSAS)

In 1975, Kansas were touring to support their third album, MASQUE, and opened for Black Sabbath on December 5th at the Indianapolis Convention Center. Kansas were still an album away from finding their sound and the top of the charts when they opened for Black Sabbath but were one of the hardest working groups on the circuit... and still are! There since the beginning, guitarist Rich William

www.kansasband.com

WE SOLD OUR SOUL FOR ROCK 'N' ROLL (Vertigo/Warner Bros. Records)
Released on December 1, 1975
Produced by Rodger Bain, Mike Butcher, Patrick Meehan and Black Sabbath
Ozzy Osbourne (vocals), Tony Iommi (guitar), Geezer Butler (bass), and Bill Ward (drums)
All songs written by Butler, Iommi, Osbourne, and Ward (except where noted.)

(1) BLACK SABBATH / THE WIZARD / WARNING (Dunbar, Dmochowski, Hickling and Mooreshead)
(2) PARANOID / WAR PIGS / IRON MAN
(3) TOMORROW'S DREAM / FAIRIES WEAR BOOTS / CHANGES / SWEET LEAF / CHILDREN OF THE GRAVE
(4) SABBATH BLOODY SABBATH / AM I GOING INSANE (RADIO) / LAGUNA SUNRISE / SNOWBLIND / N.I.B.

I FEEL SO HAPPY...I FEEL SO SAD

Normally, a compilation or greatest hits collection wouldn't receive its own chapter, but the story behind this one, in particular, is sadly so important to this story and the unraveling of Black Sabbath.

If you could put your finger on a particular moment that would signal the end for Black Sabbath, the release of the greatest hits package, WE SOLD OUT SOUL FOR ROCK 'N' ROLL is that one defining moment. Before the compilation's release, Black Sabbath had gotten out from under the questionable dealings and mismanagement of Patrick Meehan at a huge financial and emotional cost to the band. When they confronted Meehan on their plans to leave, he didn't say a word or try to put up a fight.... he just let them go. It is easy to see that with Black Sabbath beginning to implode and not having the success they previously were used to, Meehan thought the band's best days were behind them. Little did the band know, Meehan owned the very soul of the band... their entire back catalog.

According to Tony Iommi, the situation got so much worse when the band tried to sue Meehan and the courts told them they didn't have a legal leg to stand on due to the contracts they signed. Then, to add insult to already so much injury, Meehan returned the favor and sued the band.... and won! To put this event into one horrible statement, Black Sabbath had to pay a lot of money to get out from under Meehan, who already made (stole) millions from them and looked to cash in on the band's back catalog anytime he wanted to. You think it couldn't get any worse, surprise! Black Sabbath also had to pay original manager Jim Simpson for financial losses due to them signing with Meehan back in 1970. With the crushing financial fallout(s), the band was beginning to unravel more than ever before.

Although critically acclaimed, Black Sabbath's last two studio albums failed to match the success and praise of their previous four and were seeing each album sell less and their chart positions drop. SABOTAGE went to #28 in the US, which is not a bad placement, but it was 16 spots lower than SABBATH BLOODY SABBATH the year before. Many at their respected labels (Vertigo and Warner Bros.) felt their time had passed and were beginning to wonder if the Gold and Platinum well had finally run dry.

As Black Sabbath was on the road supporting SABOTAGE (and still doing great business at the box office), behind the scenes Meehan (who owned the back catalog of Black Sabbath through the company NEMS) was looking to cash out on the band, possibly for the very last time. With Meehan's consent and support, Vertigo and Warner Bros. Records help to put together the two-album compilation, WE SOLD OUR SOUL FOR ROCK 'N' ROLL, just in time for the Christmas/Hanukkah record-buying seasons.

"I was handed an album by a fan to sign while on tour and didn't recognize it." – Tony Iommi

The release of the album proved to the band how NOT in control they were of their own careers, something they worked so hard on. It also wasn't lost on the band that their own record label(s) did this behind their backs, because they could. Black Sabbath started to feel that their best years were now behind them despite some of the triumphs they were having on the road. As the miles piled on, more bad feelings and heavier drug use began to permeate their once brotherly bond. Current manager Don Arden told his band to forget about all of it and just tour.... and tour.... and tour.

Two Japanese versions of WE SOLD OUR SOUL FOR ROCK 'N' ROLL, the first released in 1975 and the other a recent release. The cassette inlay is from the Columbia Record And Tape Club version that carries the 'CRC' on the top of the spine, above the WB logo.

WE SOLD OUR SOUL FOR ROCK 'N' ROLL was released conveniently a few days before the start of the last leg of the SABOTAGE tour, starting with a big show at Madison Square Garden In New York City with Aerosmith (December 3), Indianapolis Convention Center in Indiana with Kansas (December 5) and in Syracuse, New York (December 12) with KISS.

The tour would end and 1976 would begin with five make-up dates in the UK, rescheduled from November due to Ozzy Osbourne's motorcycle crash. The final show would take place on January 13, 1976, with opening act Brandy Legs, a Birmingham band that would soon change their name to Quartz.

The quite unsettling inside gatefold sleeve for WE SOLD OUR SOUL FOR ROCK 'N' ROLL, still the stuff of my nightmares, maybe yours?

Now for the inside... wow! When you open the gatefold sleeve you are in for a complete and unexpected shock! Inside the center spread is a coffin that you are looking down into that contains the body of a young woman who is holding a big, bright cross. At this time in my life (around 1981), I had never gone to a funeral and didn't know anyone who died, so this image creeped me out with its slightly out-of-focus fuzziness and the deathlike stare from the young woman in the coffin. As I look at it now for research, it still conjures up some unsettling feelings that made the 14-year-old me throw the album away one night. As a young Christian kid growing up and trying to balance my faith with my music, I always struggled to own this album because of what the title implied and what was pictured on the inside cover, but never because of the music. Not long after throwing it away, I realized that as a completist I had to have the album to be able to lay claim of owning every Black Sabbath album. So I bought it again. I just never opened it up since I had all the songs!

THE SUN NO LONGER SETS ME FREE

WE SOLD OUR SOUL FOR ROCK 'N' ROLL was released through NEMS in the UK on December 1, 1975 (Vertigo) and in the US on February 3, 1976 (Warner Bros. Records), missing the US Holiday sales but apparently hoping to capitalize on the big Easter Rock Album holiday. You may laugh, but my sister and I used to always get albums for Easter. Currently, the album has sold over 2 million copies in the US alone, but at the time...not so much. This would block any chance for a band authorized greatest hits that would have the band's input and reward them financially. Despite not being authorized and quite unhappy about it, Black Sabbath was still affected by the poor chart positions, feeling like it was the end of the road.

Complete BUT Obsolete

One of the strangest Black Sabbath releases during this time of everyone selling everything thanks to Patrick Meehan, was a German release called REFLECTION on Fontana Records (remember them?). Released in 1975, REFLECTION features the best of SABOTAGE and SABBATH BLOODY SABBATH, all wrapped in a bizarre album jacket that looked more like a Bay City Rollers sleeve. First, the album itself contains seven songs, *Sabbath Bloody Sabbath, Who Are You?, Looking For Today, Killing Yourself To Live, Hole In The Sky, Thrill Of It All,* and *Megalomania*, called *Symptom Of The Universe/Megalomania* accidentally on the sleeve and record label. The collection of songs are brilliant and make for an incredible listen, taking the best of the band's last two releases, but it just showed how Black Sabbath's music could now be sold and packaged to anyone as long as Meehan was paid and not the band!

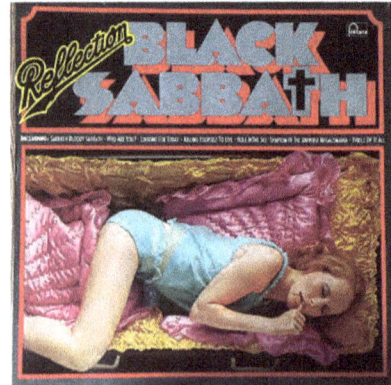  

I bought REFLECTIONS at an import record shop in Northampton, MA, not knowing what it was or the history surrounding it. Containing my favorite songs from SABBATH BLOODY SABBATH and SABOTAGE, I was just excited to just be getting a great album.

Speaking of the packaging, the cover contains a very generic logo with a young girl laying in a wicker basket/coffin lined with a pink blanket and sucking her thumb. This alone makes the cover creepy in a not-cool creepy way because the young girl is scantly dressed and the thumb sucking implies she is young! The cassette version has a slightly different variation of the girl with her face showing more and her arm resting behind her head. With the covers the German band Scorpions were putting out at the time for their releases IN TRANCE and VIRGIN KILLER, it appeared the Germans were less sensitive about the sexuality of their albums.

FINAL THOUGHTS ON SELLING MY SOUL

For many young (and old) music fans, WE SOLD OUR SOUL FOR ROCK 'N' ROLL was our introduction to the classic world of Black Sabbath! As young kids with limited budgets, this was the best and cheapest way to get more music for a reasonable price. I remember that having this album added instant street cred with my older sister's friends because it was so mature. When you know the full story, it is so sad how Black Sabbath made nothing off of this one as well as the millions of compilations that would soon follow. When you think of how betrayed the band must have felt with their labels endorsing, pressing, and promoting this release, it is even more upsetting to think about.

In 2014, Rhino/Warner Records released an incredible remastered version of WE SOLD OUR SOUL FOR ROCK 'N' ROLL that is a must-have... or at least a serious must listen. Every song sounds fresh and alive like they were brand new and gives the listener a different experience as you get to hear new sounds, textures, and flavors, without ruining the heart and soul of the songs.

ANOTHER 'OZ' GETS INTO BLACK SABBATH
OZ FOX (STRYPER)

www.stryper.com

Stryper guitarist Oz Fox is a huge Black Sabbath fan! "The first time I heard them was when I was in school. Iron Man! After that, I had to get some money together and I bought WE SOLD OUR SOUL FOR ROCK N ROLL and wore the grooves out of it." When you listen to Oz's play, you can hear the influence Black Sabbath has had on his playing as well as Stryper's overall sound. One of the coolest guys I know, Oz is still the same kid he was when he saw Black Sabbath live with Journey, Sammy Hagar, and Van Halen, just a bit older.

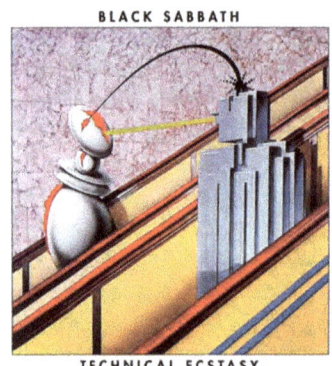 

TECHNICAL ECSTASY (Vertigo/Warner Bros. Records)
Released on September 25, 1976
Produced by Black Sabbath
Ozzy Osbourne (vocals), Tony Iommi (guitar), Geezer Butler (bass), and Bill Ward (drums)
Additional musicians - Jezz Woodroffe (keyboards)
All songs written by Butler, Iommi, Osbourne, and Ward

BACK STREET KIDS
YOU WON'T CHANGE ME IT'S ALRIGHT
GYPSY

ALL MOVING PARTS (STAND STILL)
ROCK 'N' ROLL DOCTOR
SHE'S GONE
DIRTY WOMEN

"Punk was massive then and we felt that our time had come and gone." – Geezer Butler

IT'S ALRIGHT...YES, IT'S ALRIGHT

Following one of the best and worst times in the band's career, Black Sabbath was now trying to figure out their place in the changing musical landscape. Where once the band led the way, they were now in danger of being swallowed up by debt, substance abuse, and the burgeoning Punk Rock movement in the UK. With bands like the fantastic Sex Pistols, The Damned, Generation X (featuring a young Billy Idol), and The Clash now capturing the imagination and spending money of the disenfranchised British youth (like Black Sabbath had done years prior), the old guard was now considered dinosaurs and the worst word in the music business... "irrelevant." Legally, the band finally had representation with Don Arden, who at the time was watching the Electric Light Orchestra become a massive success in North America. Arden had a reputation for getting things done, just not always legally. Black Sabbath always looked at Led Zeppelin and saw how their larger-than-life manager Peter Grant protected his band and made them all very rich. Black Sabbath wanted that for themselves. Unfortunately, it was becoming too late for any of that.

"I started to lose interest and kept thinking what it would be like to have a solo career." – Ozzy Osbourne

Also, and possibly most important, the band members weren't seeing eye to eye on anything anymore. Up until this point, the guys would rely on each other and keep a united front in the wake of adversity, but the legal battles, now including a massive US tax bill, was making the band question if they even wanted to continue. The music business didn't seem to want them, and they didn't want each other anymore. There began to be a massive split in the foundation, certainly not helped by the massive amounts of cocaine and alcohol.

Outside the Sabbath family, most of the band's personal relationships were beginning to crumble under the stresses and strains, especially Iommi, who would see his eight-year marriage come to an end. Iommi began to write songs, but he was now bouncing ideas off Jezz Woodroffe, the keyboardist who Black Sabbath toured with the previous year. This was giving the normally hard-edged music Iommi created a softer and smoother sound that when presented to the band would create some ruffles. Osbourne didn't like this one bit because he wanted to continue with the heaviness of the past albums, the element that brought them success.

Ozzy was beginning to seriously not want to be part of Black Sabbath anymore, but, like everyone else, was caught in the cycle of recording and touring and all the excesses that came along with it and didn't know how to get out. Osbourne began to wear a shirt he'd made that said "Blizzard Of Ozz" which was featured in some photos from this period. For the singer, the seed had been planted. Outside the band, Osbourne would have a series of incidents (including shooting a coop full of chickens) and checking himself into the Stafford Country Asylum in an attempt to help his fragile mental state, although he ended up not staying for very long.

"Tony was always saying, 'We've gotta sound like Foreigner or like Queen. But I thought it was strange that the bands we'd once influenced were now influencing us." – Ozzy Osbourne

As Black Sabbath put together the songs for their next album, the members were not in love with the music they were writing yet did little to fix any problems. They were looking at Led Zeppelin and Deep Purple, who were able to shift their sounds and do what they wanted without (for the most part) much fan backlash, and they wanted that credibility, that ability, and that right. As Sabbath looked to go into the studio, Arden suggested the members record outside of the UK and become tax exiles, a way to limit their time in the country and lower what could be a hefty tax bill. The band decided to move operations to Miami, Florida, and the new home studio of Eric Clapton and the Bee Gee's, Criteria Sound. The band would enjoy the warm weather, sun, and almost unlimited supply of cocaine, but Tony Iommi would become incredibly resentful at his bandmates, feeling he was doing the bulk of the work in the studio while the others enjoyed the amenities, and he was absolutely right. Not that Iommi was clean during all of this. He would just do his drugs while producing in the studio, never getting to see the sun outside.

For a month (June of 1976), a frail and damaged Black Sabbath would record eight new songs of different styles, tones, and textures for the album they now called TECHNICAL ECSTASY. The music would certainly be a radical departure from their past albums and sound like a band that may not have lost its direction but was making a sharp left off the road. Despite finally having legit management with their finances at least somewhat back in order, the band ran out of money while recording. It's fair to say the money wasn't needed for studio time, but their massive drug bills. When the band reached out to Don Arden for help, he was nowhere to be found, upsetting the already fragile band who thought the management problems and trust issues were over. The band eventually got Warner Bros. Records to send some much-needed relief and the recording of the album continued.

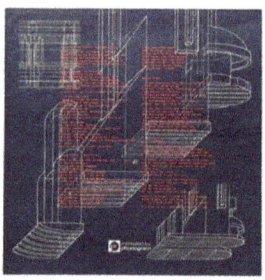 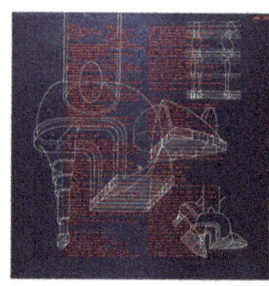 

The inner sleeve for TECHNICAL ECSTASY continues the concepts of the front and back covers, trying to create a concept with the entire packaging of the album. The Japanese pressing of the single, It's Alright, the amazing John Lennon-sounding song sung by Bill Ward.

To explain a bit of the financials of the recording process, the record label will give a band a certain and predetermined amount of money to record an album. The money should go into paying the studio and producer for the time spent recording. This should help with scheduling and set up goals to finish on time. Unfortunately, the majority of funds here were used for drugs and when the money ran out, the band was on the hook and forced to ask for more. Another negative of the band/record label system at the time was bands and artists had to pay back the money the record label gave them to record. If you had a bad record deal, to begin with (like Black Sabbath did), it became an impossible cycle to get ahead of. When you hear of bands going into debt during recording (like Def Leppard did recording HYSTERIA in 1984-1987), this is why and how it happens. The longer you spend recording, the more you owe and the more albums and concert tickets you have to sell. When they were finally done recording (after about a month), Black Sabbath had their seventh album ready to go. The Eagles and Fleetwood Mac were recording career-changing albums in the same studio at the same time, while Black Sabbath was struggling to make it out of the studio a still-functioning band.

"That was the beginning of the end, that one." – Geezer Butler

HEAR WHAT I SAY!

If fans and critics would struggle with the music inside the detailed album sleeve, then they would be drawn over the edge by the album's quirky cover. Created by Hypgnosis, the art studio that created thought-provoking album covers for Pink Floyd, UFO, and Led Zeppelin, the cover for TECHNICAL ECSTASY is certainly more at home for Pink Floyd, being artsy and open to interpretation. The image has been described over the years as two robots having sex on an escalator and well...okay. I think one of the first noticeable differences is not necessarily the images, but the color palette used for this cover. To this point, Black Sabbath album covers were usually very dark, quite mysterious, and for the most part, simplistic. For TECHNICAL ECSTASY, there are colorful objects with yellow escalators on a bright white frame, with an ordinary font used for the album's title and band name. Did I mention robot sex?

"We're very fond of that cover. It's love at first sight, but I felt robots wouldn't do it like humans would do it, so instead they're squirting lubricating fluid at one another" – Storm Thorgerson

Despite the bad feelings for the art, I loved the cover... because of most of the criticisms. When you would (or at least I would, and still do) lay out all of Black Sabbath's albums on the floor, or just study them in order, TECHNICAL ECSTASY is one that people either love or hate, mostly hate... but not me. I can see and completely understand what the band was trying to do and say. with this statement and wanting to make their album art reflect the changing styles of the music. Unfortunately, Black Sabbath wasn't given the chance to change like other bands. They underestimated their fans' loyalty to accept change.

 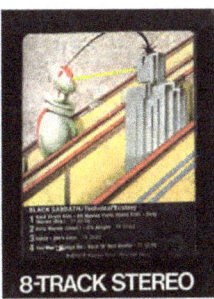 

TECHNICAL ECSTASY, the Vertigo cassette inlay, the Warner Bros. 8-Track, and a later issued CD with a different back cover.

TECHNICAL ECSTASY was released to the world on September 25, 1976, by Vertigo Records all over the world and Warner Bros. Records in North America. Most of the reviews were very negative due to the change in the Black Sabbath format. Not that bad reviews were anything new. These hit harder because of the fragile psyche of the group. It wasn't lost on Black Sabbath or fans when you saw reviewers who once criticized the doom and gloom sound now complaining that the album was lacking the traditional Black Sabbath sound. As usual, the band couldn't win for losing. TECHNICAL ECSTASY would be the worst-charting Black Sabbath album ever, going only to #51 in the US and #13 in the UK. On the charts, the placement would be a shocking 23 spots lower than the last release, SABOTAGE. Thoughts must have crept into the members' heads about the successes with Patrick Meehan and now without him.... nothing.

"If we had stayed the same, people would have said we were still doing the same old stuff. We tried to get a little more technical, and it just didn't work out very well." – Tony Iommi

LISTEN TO THE MUSIC

TECHNICAL ECSTASY was released to the world on September 25, 1976, by Vertigo Records all over the world and Warner Bros. Records in North America. Most of the reviews were very negative due to the change in the Black Sabbath format. Not that bad reviews were anything new. These hit harder because of the fragile psyche of the group. It wasn't lost on Black Sabbath or fans when you saw reviewers who once criticized the doom and gloom sound now complaining that the album was lacking the traditional Black Sabbath sound. As usual, the band couldn't win for losing. TECHNICAL ECSTASY would be the worst-charting Black Sabbath album ever, going only to #51 in the US and #13 in the UK. On the charts, the placement would be a shocking 23 spots lower than the last release, SABOTAGE. Thoughts must have crept into the members' heads about the successes with Patrick Meehan and now without him.... nothing.

"If we had stayed the same, people would have said we were still doing the same old stuff. We tried to get a little more technical, and it just didn't work out very well." – Tony Iommi

On a side note, while Black Sabbath was recording TECHNICAL ESCATSY, both Fleetwood Mac and The Eagles were recording their new albums at Criteria Sounds as well. Unlike Black Sabbath, Fleetwood Mac turned their inner band turmoil and fractured relationships into the classic RUMORS. RUMORS would go to #1 everywhere on the planet and be the top album in the US for an amazing 31 weeks, spawning four hit singles and sell over 10 million copies worldwide in the first month of its release alone. The Eagles would find similar success with their fifth studio album, HOTEL CALIFORNIA, the first with new guitarist Joe Walsh. Another pure 1970's classic, HOTEL CALIFORNIA would also go to #1 in the US, have 3 hit singles (including one of the greatest songs ever, *New Kid In Town*) and sell 6 million copies in the first year of its release. Currently, RUMORS is the 8th biggest-selling album of all time with almost 40 million confirmed copies sold and HOTEL CALIFORNIA is the 16th biggest of all time, selling over 31 million copies. TECHNICAL ECSTASY comes in just a little.... well, a lot.... a crap-ton shorter than those milestones.

Another interesting tidbit, the final song on HOTEL CALIFORNA, The Last Resort, had to be recorded multiple times due to Black Sabbath's sounds bleeding into their sessions.

"The Eagles were recording next door, but we were too loud for them. It kept coming through the wall into their sessions." – Tony Iommi

GOTTA GET MYSELF TOGETHER

The album starts with the rocker *Back Street Kids*. Here, Ozzy's voice is in the higher range like it was on Sabbath Bloody Sabbath with a driving beat behind it. Iommi's guitar tones are much lighter and have some great dancing bass lines courtesy of Butler. Musically, the song sounds and feels like a RUSH track minus the vocals. An amazing song that ends super-fast... so fast I always thought my album skipped.

You Won't Change Me begins with a moody and scary intro until it breaks into some serious Led Zeppelin chords, very Dazed And Confused until the keyboards kick in above the Michael Schenker-like leads and riffs. I think this song has always appealed to me because it sounds like UFO circa the LIGHTS OUT/OBSESSION era. If Phil Mogg was singing, this would be a brilliant UFO song, not an underrated Black Sabbath song.

"We need a new direction." – Geezer Butler

Here is where many longtime Sabbath fans fell apart! Fact is, *It's Alright* is a brilliant track sung with passion and conviction by Bill Ward and feels like a lost John Lennon song. When this was first heard, the fanbase screamed for blood, but over the years the song has become appreciated for its simplicity and brilliance. This song is so good. Axl Rose used to perform this (at the piano) during Guns 'N' Roses heyday, and it made it on the album LIVE ERA '87-93.

Starting with a Bill Ward drum lead, *Gypsy* is another song that has so little to do with the Sabbath sound of doom and gloom and musically is more in line with 1970's KISS, and that isn't a bad thing. The song has some real soaring moments that are broken up with piano, which ushers in a 10CC moment, before returning to a somewhat familiar sound. Ozzy shows a lot of versatility on this one.

"It was enjoyable to make, well... Tony enjoyed it." – Ozzy Osbourne

Very funky, almost Blue Oyster Cult-ish, *All Moving Parts (Stand Still)* took me a long time to get into, but again, another of my favorites. For many fans listening to the album, they never bothered to turn the disc over and missed this one, which is another great Geezer Butler moment. Also, the song has a bit of a Ted Nugent feel with the lead and riff tones, very Motor City Madman, but with more control.

Rock 'N' Roll Doctor pays tribute to those who serve the band so well, the drug dealers! Like the Beatles Doctor Robert or much later, Motley Crue's Dr. Feelgood, this one is a real rocker, complete with timey-wimey piano by Jezz Woodroffe. If it wasn't for Ozzy's voice you may think it's Mountain or BTO.

"By TECHNICAL ECSTASY we were pretty much war veterans." – Bill Ward

She's Gone gets an amazing amount of hate because of its acoustic guitar, strings, and slow ballad style. What you really have here is typical Black Sabbath lyrics where the voice is lamenting for something out of reach. It just happens to be a woman... not death or the devil. Get over it, folks. This is one of Ozzy's finest moments. I could listen to this song forever on a continuous loop.

  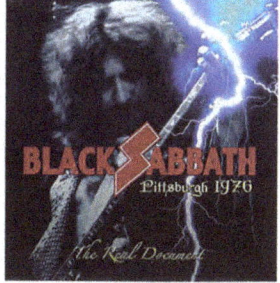

The program (or programme) for the TECHNICAL ECSTASY tour. Two bootlegs from the 1976 tours, the first from Fresno, CA, and the second are from Pittsburgh that was recorded for a radio broadcast. This is where many bootlegs would get their source material from.

The album ends with *Dirty Woman*, a tribute to the ladies of the night, a weird one following the tender *She's Gone*. But, if there were less of these, there may have been hope for the relationship. Vocally, Osbourne's tones and multi-tracking give him a sound much like he would have on his first two solo albums, but I'm jumping ahead. The solo by Iommi is typical and classic, despite not being all doomy and gloomy!

THE DAYS ARE PASSING SLOWLY

Black Sabbath would hit the road in support of an album that the fans were rejecting. The band's setlist included four new songs, *All Moving Parts (Stand Still), Gypsy, Dirty Woman*, and *Rock 'N' Roll Doctor*. While on the road, the band would be augmented once again by Jezz Woodroffe on keyboards (behind the stage, of course). The band would have an incredibly basic stage set, except for Bill Ward's massive drum kit that would sit in the middle of a big shell. The tour would begin on October 22, 1976, in Oklahoma, and wind down at the end of April 1977 in Sweden where sold-out crowds in the biggest arenas would greet them enthusiastically. One of the make-money plans for the band on the road devised by Don Arden was to package Black Sabbath with other acts that in his words "sell-out half the house themselves." This is one of the band's shorter tours, in which Black Sabbath had Journey, Bob Seger, Ted Nugent, Heart, and Boston supporting them. Boston was riding high on the charts with their massive selling epynomous debut album and a huge hit single, More Than A Feeling. In Europe, AC/DC, who were the rising stars in the hard rock world were the opening act, promoting their greatest album ever, DIRTY DEEDS DONE DIRT CHEAP. According to everyone involved, there was no love lost between the two bands, especially Geezer Butler and the always volatile Malcolm Young.

Joining the bill in Germany would be the Ian Gillan Band, the former Deep Purple vocalist's first attempt at a solo career. The Ian Gillan Band would see only moderate success and would disband following these shows, to be replaced by a much more hard-rocking (and more wanted), Gillan.

"Parents can take their kids to our shows now." - Geezer Butler (sarcastically)

Things on the road were not good, especially for Osbourne. Among the self-abuse he put himself through, he was feeling the daggers thrown by Iommi, making the already fragile singer only angry and very confrontational. Iommi always felt that his band was never given the respect of the two bigger Original Big Four bands, Deep Purple and Led Zeppelin. He also felt the band was never given their full due because of Osbourne's limited vocal abilities, always comparing him (and quite unfairly) to Robert Plant, Ian Gillan, and David Coverdale. By the time the band got off the road, Osbourne had had enough and wanted out!

The cover to the unauthorized (by the band) BLACK SABABTH GREATEST HITS that didn't scare me although it should have!

FLOGGING A DEAD HORSE (PART ONE)

When Black Sabbath walked away from Patrick Meehan, their former manager decided the best way to get back at the band is to show who owned their recordings, and sadly, he did! In yet another (and certainly not the last) crappy move that didn't help the band at all financially or legally, NEMS released BLACK

SABBATH GREATEST HITS in 1976. The album was exactly as promised, the ten greatest hits of Black Sabbath, pulled from their first five albums with no frills at all, just the music.

I remember buying this one in the mid-1980s as an import (and a very cheap one, too) at the Ingleside Mall in Holyoke, MA, and being excited at the low price, especially for an import. I was also a little weirded out by the album's cover, a painting of what I interpreted as Hell. Called *The Triumph Of Death*, the art depicts a scary skeleton army just destroying and tormenting an old town on a river. (Fun! -Editor)

The painter, Peter Brugel the Elder, painted this work around 1562, and little did he know (how could he) it would fit this collection of Black Sabbath hits so perfectly. When you look deep into the cover (or painting), there are Biblical references like a man being thrown into a river with a millstone on his neck to weigh him down (Matthew 18:6) and commentary on then-contemporary society, especially the fact that no matter your class or social standings, you will all die at the hands of skeletons... it's just that simple. In the painting, peasants, soldiers, and even a cardinal and a king are being tormented by these horrific creatures. Pure stuff of nightmares, but a fascinating study of society and art.

I do remember vividly getting a cut in my palm and fingertips on the sharp edges of the vinyl. Where an album's edges were usually smoothed down, this one was like razor blades. It was also contained within a very flimsy cardboard jacket. But, at $5.00, I didn't care. I would apparently bleed for Black Sabbath.

FINAL THOUGHTS WHILE ON ECSTASY

There is obviously a real issue with fans and TECHNICAL ECSTASY and I can see both sides of the argument. Since I was a bit too young for this when it was originally released, I can completely understand how and why long-time Black Sabbath fans reacted this way! This album was not PARANOID or MASTER OF REALITY at all. What it had were eight songs that were all too much like the progressive sounds of the previous two albums and for long-time fans that was eight too many. This album rocks, but more like UFO rocks than '*Children Of The Grave* rocks! I love this album because of all the amazing textures and colors the band brings to the table as they tried to adapt to a changing music scene in danger of leaving them behind. I love how the music is a bit brighter with less doomy chords and downer vocals and I LOVE Bill Ward's ode to John Lennon, *It's Alright*. The only thing I'm not a fan of is the slightly muddy production that sounds like what punk bands The Clash and Damned were producing at the time, but I don't think that was the intention.

If you give this album a chance and really listen to it for what it is, not what it isn't, you will find a very enjoyable and fun album. I rate the album an easy 9 out of 10 with a point being lost to the production. Of the 19 Black Sabbath studio albums released, I rank TECHNICAL ECSTASY very high, my #3 album of the entire catalog. The Black Sabbath Facebook community ranks it much less, but it did receive some love, putting it at #15 out of 19!

ANOTHER ONE GOES OVER THE RAINBOW

Bob Daisley would enter the music scene as the bassist of Chicken Shack, Mungo Jerry and Widowmaker before joining Richie Blackmore and Rainbow in 1978 for LONG LIVE ROCK 'N' ROLL. Like many, his time in Rainbow would be short... very short

With Black Sabbath struggling to keep it all together, Widowmaker was seeing their star on the rise... well, sort of. Formed by guitarist Luther Grosvenor (Ariel Bender from Mott The Hoople), the band also featured a young Australian bassist named Bob Daisley (born February 13, 1950), the band would release two solid albums WIDOWMAKER (1976) and TOO LATE TO CRY (1977) to critical acclaim (but not financial) before Daisley would audition for Richie Blackmore and Rainbow and get the gig. Daisley came in late to the recording sessions and played on only three of the songs on LONG LIVE ROCK 'N' ROLL (1978), one of them being the wonderful Gates Of Babylon. Daisley would join Blackmore, vocalist Ronnie James Dio, drummer Cozy Powell, and keyboardist David Stone on tour to support the album.

Following the tour, Daisley and vocalist Ronnie James Dio would leave on their own, and keyboardist David Stone would be fired. In October 1979, Daisley would meet Ozzy Osbourne and guitarist Randy Rhodes, who were looking to start up Osbourne's solo career. Daisley was hired to not only play bass but be a major songwriting partner, and contribute to the overall feel for the material on the first two Ozzy Osbourne solo albums.

"I liked Bob immediately. He was a proper rock 'n' roller, he wore denim jackets with gut out sleeves and had his hair blown out." – Ozzy Osbourne

THE ALMOST BLACK SABBATH VOCALIST BRIAN HOWE (BAD COMPANY)

One of the most recognizable voices in rock, I was introduced to Brian Howe when he was the vocalist on Ted Nugent's PENETRATOR album. Following his time in 'Gonzoland', Howe guided Bad Company through the mid-1980s and '90s with a run of platinum-selling albums and hit singles. Brian told me in 2019 about seeing Black Sabbath as a teenager and how he was running back and forth in the front, following Ozzy Osbourne, yelling to him to let him on stage and sing with him. Waiting for a great finish to the story, Brian ended it by telling me, "yeah... he didn't." That was Brian Howe's dry sense of humor, which I loved. Sadly, a few days after adding this section to the book, Brian passed away on May 6, 2020. You will be missed...

NEVER SAY DIE! (Vertigo/Warner Bros. Records)
Released on September 28, 1978
Produced by Black Sabbath
Ozzy Osbourne (vocals), Tony Iommi (guitar), Geezer Butler (bass), and Bill Ward (drums)
Additional musicians - Don Airey (keyboards)
All songs written by Butler, Iommi, Osbourne, and Ward

NEVER SAY DIE!
JOHNNY BLADE
JUNIOR'S FARM
A HARD ROAD

SHOCK WAVE
AIR DANCE
OVER TO YOU
BREAKOUT
SWINGING THE CHAIN

"It's a combination of what we've all been through in the last ten years" – Ozzy Osbourne

A VICTIM OF MODERN FRUSTRATION

Following disastrous sales and chart placement for a really good album followed by a successful tour, Black Sabbath found themselves in a horrible position yet again. Being handcuffed by bad management and then surprising, very hands-off management, the band continued to go from one horrible financial situation to the next, including a lot of debt and taxes owed, with the taxman looking to collect, NOW! Like last time for TECHNICAL ECSTASY, it was recommended that they record their next album and live outside of the UK for a bit, to keep the government away. Trying to keep things afloat, the band chose Sound Interchange in Toronto, Ontario, Canada, during the winter months.... never a good plan. Odd the band didn't return to the sun and fun of Criteria Studios in Florida, instead opting to go way more up North in the dead of winter. Before jumping back into work with Sabbath, Tony Iommi would take a quick break and produce the debut album by another Birmingham band, Quartz. The self-titled album was released on Jet Records and is a solid release that featured fellow Brummie Geoff Nicholls on keyboards and guitar. While working with the band, Iommi would see a lot of potential in Nicholls and the two would become close. He was someone outside the world of Black Sabbath Tony could trust and bounce ideas off. Interesting to point out that the album's first song, Mainline Riders, includes a bass line and a riff that sounds a lot like Heaven And Hell, a song a few years away from being recorded.

Before Black Sabbath could pack up and fly to Canada, Ozzy Osbourne suddenly left a rehearsal and quit the band, something always expected but catching the band off guard at that moment. Personally, Ozzy wasn't happy at all with the Sabbath situation and was emotionally falling apart, abusing drugs and alcohol more than ever before. His marriage was falling apart and becoming somewhat violent. To add to the misery in his life, Ozzy's beloved father, John Thomas Osbourne, was dying from cancer.

"Losing my parents had always been my worst fear, ever since I was a little kid." – Ozzy Osbourne

Sadly, personal dysfunction was the case for everyone in Black Sabbath, dealing with pressures and expectations that went along with being a major band on the decline. As expected, these issues were made much worse because of the drug and alcohol abuse that surrounded everything the members did on and off stage.

In his place, the band brought in singer David Walker, another Midlands musician who Iommi and Ward knew from their days in Mythology. At that time, Walker was living in San Francisco looking for his next project. Iommi liked that he had a very rich, bluesy voice and was an easy-going guy, something the band desperately needed. Walker made a name for himself in Savoy Brown (along with a pre-UFO Paul Raymond) and in an early version of Fleetwood Mac where he recorded the album PENGUIN in 1973. Upon his arrival in the UK, Walker would spend the next few months writing and recording new music with the band for their new album. The vocalist was told to bring a lot of lyrics for all the songs the band had written. Upon his arrival, Walker discovered they had no songs written, just a lot of bits and pieces. Before Walker's hiring was even made official, Black Sabbath made an appearance on a Midland's TV show called LOOK! HEAR! where Walker fronted Black Sabbath, performing the classic *War Pigs* and a new song, an early version of Junior's Eyes. Walker's rough, blues-based vocal style had passing resemblances to Ozzy, but with a bit more range and depth.

"I didn't think I was cut out for their style of music. I thought I'd give it a try." – Dave Walker

How would Dave Walker fit in for the long haul with Black Sabbath? It's hard to know with such a small, almost nonexistent sampling. It was during this time that Ozzy would return to the fold, slightly battered and bruised emotionally and spiritually. In the time the band was working with Walker, there was absolutely no contact with Ozzy until he reached out to them and asked to come back. According to both Iommi and Osbourne, the singer's words were "I'm sorry, can I come back?," and so he did. It may have made perfect sense for Osbourne's return, but everyone knew this reunion was only going to be a temporary situation because Osbourne was in seriously bad shape and didn't really want to be back. It was a comfortable, familiar thing thing to grab onto.

"We never wanted him to leave, but no one would tell the other how they felt." – Tony Iommi

I don't want to admit that I bought the Shawn Cassidy CIRCUS magazine because of Shawn Cassidy... but, I did. That's rock 'n' roll...

With Ozzy now back in the band, he understandably wanted nothing to do with any of the lyrics written by Walker, so the band lost precious time having to rewrite all the songs with (and for) Osbourne. Unfortunately for Ozzy, his beloved father had passed away, leaving the singer in even more of a fragile state considering his father was always a strong supporter of his son and the band. Once songs were worked out, the members traveled to Toronto where they were rehearsed and fine-tuned in an old and very cold cinema. Sabbath found themselves recording in a studio that didn't give them the sound and feel they needed. While in isolation in Toronto during one of the coldest winters in recent memory, the band drank too much, did too many drugs, and fought over things they shouldn't have. As would always be the underlying problem in Black Sabbath, no one was communicating, especially over the important issues. The members didn't talk about the things that needed to be worked out, causing more of a division, especially between Iommi and Osbourne. As the recording progressed on the album, the band tried to change things up a bit as they did with TECHNICAL ECSTASY, experiment with different sounds like jazz and punk, much to Osbourne's dismay.

"It was clear they had enough of my insane behavior." – Ozzy Osbourne

Black Sabbath was trying to do something special for their 10th anniversary with the new album but was struggling to keep focus. There were combative and defining moments with Osbourne where he would flat out refuse to sing songs unless lyrics were rewritten, much to the anger of Butler, who was still writing most of the band's words. In fact, the song *Breakout* became an instrumental track when Ozzy refused to sing on it. In a sarcastic celebration of their decade together, they decided to call the album NEVER SAY DIE! as a joke because the band members knew Black Sabbath couldn't and wouldn't continue the way that it was.

"People didn't realize that it was sort of tongue-in-cheek, the 'Never Say Die' thing. Because we knew that was it; we just knew it was never going to happen again." – Geezer Butler

Working with the band was Rainbow keyboardist Don Airey, who had just come off the road in support of the very successful DOWN TO EARTH album. This was their first album without Ronnie James Dio, who was replaced by Graham Bonnet. The last year of the decade would be a busy time for Airey, working with Gary Moore on his first real solo album, BACK ON THE STREETS, and Cozy Powell's debut, OVER THE TOP, as well as building a relationship with Osbourne. Airey would make a huge impact on the sound and style of some of the songs on NEVER SAY DIE!, unintentionally of course.

SEARCHING FOR A REASON

Once again, Hipgnosis would be responsible for the cover of the new album. The company, known for their artsy sleeve jackets for UFO, Pink Floyd, and Led Zeppelin didn't quite hit the mark with fans for TECHNICAL ECSTASY, but did a great job conveying the feel for the title… at least I thought so. NEVER SAY DIE! features two pilots standing next to their plane ready to go on a mission. It looks like any pose of any picture featuring pilots in their flight gear but there is something a bit unsettling about it. The oddity or what makes them look alien or what makes it a true Hipgnosis cover is the odd color hosing going into their masks, making them look almost cat-like. The first cover art that was delivered to the band and rejected was of a group of masked doctors in green scrubs with the lead guy putting on a pair of yellow gloves ready for some serious doctor action. If that cover sounds familiar at all it should be because it was the cover for Rainbow's first album with vocalist Joe Lynn Turner, DIFFICULT TO CURE, from 1981.

I love bold and artistic covers and feel the doctor one would have fit the album as well. A bit of trivia, keyboardist Don Airey played on that Rainbow album, too. Another bit of Rainbow trivia is that DIFFICULT TO CURE featured the major league debut of a future member of Black Sabbath, drummer Bobby Rondinelli.

"I really wasn't happy with the way things were going over the last two albums." – Ozzy Osbourne

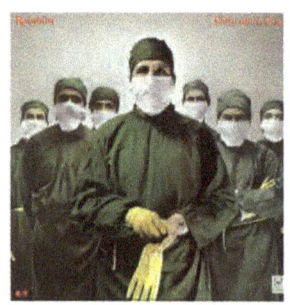 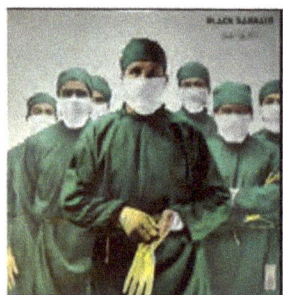

I had a friend in high school create the cover with the Black Sabbath logo and NEVER SAY DIE! script to see how it worked... and it did! This is a more modern photoshop version.

WORLD STILL TURNS

NEVER SAY DIE! was released on September 28, 1978, on Vertigo Records worldwide except North America where it was released by Warner Bros. Records. The album did as one would expect in the UK (where the fanbase was still supporting the brand) going to #12 on the charts but it only went to #69 in the US, the worst showing of a Black Sabbath album ever... and everyone in the music world took notice. In the UK, the single *Never Say Die* reached #21 on the singles chart and earned Black Sabbath an appearance on Top Of The Pops, miming and hamming it up in front of a very eclectic crowd of kids. A second single, *A Hard Road*, went to #40 in the UK, both being the first singles to hit the UK charts since Paranoid back in 1970.

Most of the reviews from critics and fans were concerning the album's inconsistent nature, which I will agree with, but every song has something different to offer and is such a great listen! There are punk, jazz, blues, and even some Beatles textures thrown into the mix making it very experimental for Black Sabbath. Tony Iommi, who produced the album pretty much by himself, said that it was the best they could do given the circumstances. He was becoming quite resentful of the fact that he was doing everything and getting all the blame for the failures.

"Even in my state of oblivion, I knew we were done." – Bill Ward

WHO KNEW WHAT TOMORROW WOULD BRING

The first time I ever heard *Never Say Die* was on Ozzy Osbourne's SPEAK OF THE DEVIL live album. From the first note, I was hooked, and it has remained to this day my favorite Black Sabbath song ever! The track is fast and angry and has an almost punk rock feel to it, complete with no solo in the middle, but lead breaks at the end. Another bit of coolness is the end when in a deep voice, Osbourne sings "never say diiieeee" sounding like Jim Morrison at the end of my favorite Doors song, *Touch Me!* "Stronger than dirt!"

Johnny Blade starts out with some cool Don Airey pipes leading into a crazy roll by Bill Ward. Another amazing song that is more punk than metal with some very visual storytelling going on. The track just motors forward with passion and fire until another awesome Iommi riff shows up that sounds a lot like the riff from Twisted Sister's *We're Not Gonna Take It*... six more years from then.

"Tony came up with that. It's an old rock 'n' roll lick." – Bill Ward

The third amazing song in a row, *Junior's Eyes*, has so much going on within the almost seven minutes of magic. Lyrically and vocally, Ozzy laments the loss of his best friend passing away, a reference to the passing of his father. Within the funky bass and slick drum work, the song isn't a typical Sabbath song, but that is OK because it is that good and works so well.

Knowing what fans Black Sabbath was of the Beatles, *A Hard Road* is a song lyrically and musically a tribute to the RUBBER SOUL/REVOLVER era, trippy with multi-layered backing vocals... something Sabbath didn't do a lot of in the past. Again, not very Sabbath-ish, but a great track is a great track, making side one brilliant!!!

"Me and Tony weren't speaking to each other at all." – Ozzy Osbourne

Side two attacks with *Shock Wave*, a simple and distorted riff until bass and drums jump in and dictate where the song is going. A great jam breaks out as the song winds down to a fade. Complete with "whooo hoooo" backing vocals.

Like the song before, *Air Dance* starts out with a great riff, higher than most Iommi riffs, until it leads into the verses led by Don Airey on the piano and Ozzy singing a little happier and higher than normal. The song goes into a long instrumental moment that turns into a Jazz Sabbath moment that is actually very enjoyable, and I don't like jazz.

Over To You is an interesting song because of the many styles it moves in and out of. Starting with a jazzy moment, then moving into some heavy blues, the song follows the Black Sabbath pattern, just a little more sunny than normal.

Breakout is not a great song at all. It is an instrumental that has a lot of horns and just feels like a waste. Ozzy refused to sing the words Butler wrote but I'm not sure lyrics would have helped.

The 8-Track stereo cartridge for Never Say Die along with the cassette version and the green strip-covered the Japanese version. I can understand why everyone had a problem with the album when it came out, but if you haven't done so... revisit this amazing work!

Sung by Bill Ward, *Swinging The Chain* is another song that really just has no direction and sums up where Black Sabbath was at the time. When the song finally gets going, it sounds very much like Grand Funk Railroad with its masculine vocals. Ward's vocals are great. It is very Motown-influenced, reminding me of the Temptations during their Cloud Nine era.

"Bill wrote Swinging The Chain. I think it was about Hitler." – Geezer Butler

EVIL POWER HANGING OVER YOU

Not communicating, dealing with substance abuse issues, and supporting an album not being received well at all, Black Sabbath hit the road with another Warner Bros. act that was moving in the exact opposite direction in their career, the mighty Van Halen. Supporting their monstrous self-titled debut album, Black Sabbath had with them a band that was helping sell tickets who on many nights were upstaging the headliners. Providing keyboards was soon-to-be-former Rainbow player Don Airey, who would help Black Sabbath fill out their sound, especially on the new songs added to the set, *Never Say Die, Shock Wave*, and *Swinging The Chain*. The last would only be played a few times during the tour.

"To meet Tony when I was so into him was really incredible." – Eddie Van Halen (Van Halen)

  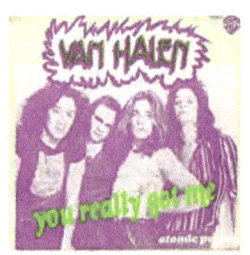

This is what Black Sabbath was competing with in 1978. Van Halen took hard rock and put some pizzazz, flash, and sex appeal into it. But that wasn't all... they had some really solid songs! Pictures courtesy of my pal and VH fanatic, 'Top' Jimmy Smith (Connecticut)

The members of Black Sabbath tried to make the best of the situation as animosity and anger toward each other began to turn into resentment and jealousy for their opening act. How could anyone (especially in 1978) compete with the innovative and explosive Eddie Van Halen and the charismatic, always on, dripping-pure-sex-appeal David Lee Roth. Not to mention the tight and electrifying rhythm section of bassist Michael Anthony and drummer Alex Van Halen. This band was the perfect storm and didn't have a weakness at all! Van Halen's image of fun, sun, and girls also proved to be more appealing than Black Sabbath's mantra of doom and gloom. To illustrate this, while on tour together Van Halen's debut album went to #19 in the US, #34 in the UK, and #18 in Canada, achieving the all-important platinum rating that signified a million albums sold. Van Halen also scored a Top 40 hit single, a cover of the Kinks classic You Really Got Me.

The NEVER SAY DIE! tour went from May of 1978 until December 11, 1978, where it ended in Albuquerque, New Mexico. Following the show, the four members of Black Sabbath all said their goodbyes and returned to their American tax-exile homes for a few months of rest until they would try to get together to work on new songs for a new album. Most people (fans and industry) were wondering if there would be a new album, and, if there was, would anyone care? By now, the broken record of Ozzy's drug and alcohol abuse was becoming more problematic not just on the road but in his personal life, too. With he and Iommi not speaking at all, Butler now began to pull away from the band, and Ward started his own downward spiral. It was begining to look like Black Sabbath had an expiration date.

To celebrate the tour, the band would release a home video called NEVER SAY DIE (no exclamation point). With more people owning VCRs, this was a growing market the band needed to tap into for revenue. The quality is pretty good, especially for pre-hi-def times, and has some great camera angles, but mostly on the left and right of the stage. Recorded at the famed Hammersmith Odeon in London in June 1978, the video contains ten songs and is a great, but sad, documentary of where the band was at the time, like The Beatles' LET IT BE. The video would be released many times, including as the 1984 video now called BLACK SABBATH LIVE! FEATURING OZZY OSBOURNE, which was looking to capitalize on Ozzy's solo popularity. It worked because I bought it... twice!

END THE CHAPTER? NEVER...SAY DIE!

I think NEVER SAY DIE! (and TECHNICAL ECSTASY) suffer from misperceptions and the resulting backlash at the time more than the songs on the album. Black Sabbath was in a seriously bad place but somehow were able to put together a solid album that is my favorite of the Ozzy Osbourne era! The songs are solid and the styles are pretty varied, but I will admit the downfall is the production because it comes out rather flat. Overall, I think it is a great album that was influenced by the punk rock movement and the situations going on within the band. There was a reason that punk rockers went after the more pretentious acts like YES but remained respectful (as much as they could be) for Black Sabbath by never really mentioning them in their anti-rock rants. A lot was going on within the band while recording it, and the tensions make it that much better and angrier. But again, judge this album on its own, not compared to the classic Black Sabbath albums. NEVER SAY DIE! ranks very high on my list, coming in at #5 out of 19 and I give it a solid 8 out of 10, but I know I'm in the minority. As I knew would be the case, the Black Sabbath family on Facebook doesn't agree with me at all, putting it at #12 out of 19. A shame, too, because it is a great album that just needs to be listened to with an open mind.

ALL THAT GLITTERS IS QUARTZ
GEOFF NICHOLLS

With the city of Birmingham becoming a major player in the hard rock world, a local band called Brandy Legs would change their name to the more palatable Quartz and be signed by Don Arden to his label, Jet Records, in 1976. Quartz supported Black Sabbath as well as fellow Brummies Judas Priest before settling in to record their debut album. Produced by Tony Iommi and released in 1977, QUARTZ is a solid 70's rock release that features some backing vocals by Ozzy Osbourne, but it was the multi-instrumentalist Geoff Nicholls (born February 29, 1944) that would make a big impact on Iommi. In the late 1960s and early '70s, Nicholls played in a succession of bands before finding some success with the very poppy/psychedelic singles makers, and kind of weird... World Of Oz.

"He reminded me of myself, how he liked to get things done and work hard at it." – Tony Iommi

A very talented band with a lot to offer, Quartz, unfortunately, got caught between 70's rock and the New Wave Of British Heavy Metal, and could never find the right balance for success. Following major tours with UFO, Iron Maiden, Gillan, Rush, and Saxon, Nicholls would leave Quartz to work with Tony Iommi on his post-Black Sabbath project following the demise of band after NEVER SAY DIE!.

The Tony Iommi produced QUARTZ (1977) would introduce the Sabbath guitarist to multi-instrumentalist Geoff Nicholls. A poster proclaiming Whitesnake to be READY AND WILLING and one of my 10 favorite albums ever, SLIDE IT IN, both featuring Neil Murray.

READY AND WILLING - NEIL MURRAY

One of the most respected bassists in the UK in the mid-1970s was Neil Murray (born August 27, 1950). Murray got his first big break when he toured with Cozy Powell's Hammer in 1974, a group that featured keyboardist Don Airey and guitarist Bernie Marsden. The relationships within this band would define Murray's path for his entire career. He would join Airey in the band Colosseum II in 1976. In 1977, Murray would join Marsden in former Deep Purple vocalist David Coverdale's new project, Whitesnake. Murray would play on the band's first seven studio albums, including 1984's masterpiece SLIDE IT IN and 1987's WHITESNAKE, an album that sold over 16 million copies worldwide.

Neil Murray would also play on Cozy Powell's TILT and Graham Bonnets LINE-UP (with Powell), both released in 1981. Following his unwarranted departure from Whitesnake, Murray would play with the band Vow Wow, the aborted attempt at an all-star metal band, Gogmagog, and Phenomena, before Cozy Powell would recommend the bassist for the open spot in Black Sabbath in 1989.

THILLA IN PHILLA - ROB DeLUCA
(SPREAD EAGLE/UFO/Sebastian Bach)

Sitting in the Philadelphia Spectrum on August 29, 1978, was a young Rob DeLuca enjoying Black Sabbath and being blown away by Van Halen. Pictured is Rob on stage with UFO; with me and my Power Chords Podcast partner, Brian LeTendre, following an amazing show with Sebastian Bach in Stafford Springs, CT, at the Palace Theatre. When Rob isn't keeping classic rock alive, he is the bassist for Spread Eagle, a band which formed in the '80s and returned in 2019 with SUBWAY TO THE STARS.

www.spreadeagle.us

The New Testament
Black Sabbath

The Book of Sabbath
Chapter 3

ReBirth 1:3

Lo, I say unto you, children who read the holy words,
remember the pit where giants were birthed
and know the power will always be there.

With one cast aside,
another born on the coast who rode the four rainbows
will slay the dragons that guard the shadow mountains.

But be warned...
the great deceiver will step in and retrace the circle!

HEAVEN AND HELL (Vertigo/Warner Bros. Records)
Released on April 25, 1980
Produced by Martin Birch
Ronnie James Dio (vocals), Tony Iommi (guitar), Geezer Butler (bass), and Bill Ward (drums)
Additional musicians - Geoff Nicholls (keyboards)
All songs written by Butler, Dio, Iommi, and Ward

NEON KNIGHTS
CHILDREN OF THE SEA
LADY EVIL
HEAVEN AND HILL

WISHING WELL
DIE YOUNG
WALK AWAY
LONELY IS THE WORLD

"We were destined to destroy each other. The band was toxic, very toxic." – Bill Ward

WE LOST THE RISING SUN

In 1979-1980, Heavy Metal music was starting to see a resurgence in popularity! In the UK, the New Wave Of British Heavy Metal featuring young and hungry bands influenced by the Original Big Four were leading the charge. These included Iron Maiden, Saxon, and Def Leppard, despite the latter not wanting to be associated with the movement. This upswing in popularity was also giving new life to some in the old guard like Judas Priest, Whitesnake, Scorpions, and UFO. Unfortunately, Black Sabbath wasn't in any shape to capitalize on the NWOBHM and they were sinking fast. Having finished a successful tour for an unsuccessful album, NEVER SAY DIE!, Sabbath had to compete night after night with Van Halen in the opening slot. They came off the road broken, confused, and without any direction. As the band began sessions for a new album, Ozzy Osbourne was becoming increasingly disillusioned with the band's direction, not showing up when needed, and refusing to participate in writing and rehearsing. It wasn't just Osbourne that was overindulging in drink and drugs. The rest of the band was also a mess, but Ozzy was becoming more of a problem than the rest. It was decided that Osbourne would have to be fired and to do the dirty deed would be drummer Bill Ward, Ozzy's best friend in the band. Following his firing on April 27, 1979, Osbourne ended up in a Los Angeles hotel, snorting, smoking, and drinking away the pretty hefty financial buyout he received from the band.

"Something had to give, and I suppose it was me." – Ozzy Osbourne

When it came to the search for a new singer, one of the people the band reached out to was Graham Bonnet, who had just left Rainbow following an incredibly successful album and tour with DOWN TO EARTH. Not wanting to join another pre-made band and feeling he wasn't Black Sabbath material, Bonnet politely said no and began working on his solo album, 1981's LINE-UP, a star-studded release that featured the single, *Mind Games*.

"I wanted to do something different on my own and not to be in another band as another singer in a revolving door, so I turned it down." – Graham Bonnet (Rainbow)

Without a singer and a plan, Tony Iommi was introduced by Sharon Arden to another former Rainbow vocalist, Ronnie James Dio. Dio performed on their first four albums before personality clashes with Blackmore over the direction of the music, how he treated people, and the constant line-up changes (10 different members just on his four Rainbow albums with more coming... and going) took their toll on the singer who just walked away from it all. Iommi spoke to Dio about the possibility of him joining Black Sabbath or creating a new band together. Following a relaxed jam/writing session with Dio and the band, it was decided Sabbath would continue and Ronnie James Dio would be their new voice. In that first meeting, Iommi played Dio *Children Of The Sea*, a tune that was being worked on with Osbourne before his firing. Within a short time, the lyrics and melodies were completed and another song, *Lady Evil*, was close to being completed. As the band began to get to work, Don Arden was still trying to convince Osbourne to return, thinking it made the most sense... financially. He would tell anyone who listened that a Black Sabbath without Ozzy Osbourne was never going to work and he wasn't a fan of Dio. Arden would sign Osbourne to a solo deal with his label, Jet Records, and still manage Sabbath, having the best of both worlds... for now. Black Sabbath would leave Arden and sign with Sandy Pearlman, an American manager who was riding success guiding the career of Blue Oyster Cult.

"Ozzy was a great showman, but when Dio came in, it was a different attitude, a different voice, and a different musical approach." – Tony Iommi

In September of 1979, Geezer Butler would leave the band to take care of personal issues and get himself right, causing the songwriting to shift to just Dio and Iommi. While working on songs, Dio would play bass (the instrument he started out playing) until his former Elf and Rainbow bassist Craig Gruber came in to help with the recording of the new songs being put together. Gruber would leave but later claim he co-wrote most of the songs being recorded and that it was also his playing fans heard on the new album, not Butler. In his place would be Geoff Nicholls from the band Quartz, who was helping on guitar, but would switch to bass when it was needed.

Meanwhile, Butler, who was going through a divorce, heard the music the band was making, saw how excited Iommi was, and wanted back in. At Criteria Recording Studios (home of the Bee Gees) in Miami and Studio Ferber in France, Butler would re-record the bass parts already laid down by Gruber and add his own style. Producing the album would be Martin Birch, who knew how to get the best out of talented bands. Before working with Sabbath, Birch worked with Deep Purple, Whitesnake, and produced all four of Dio's Rainbow albums. He came highly recommended by their new singer. Iommi was more than happy to pass the production chair to someone else, having produced or co-produced every Black Sabbath album since VOL 4.

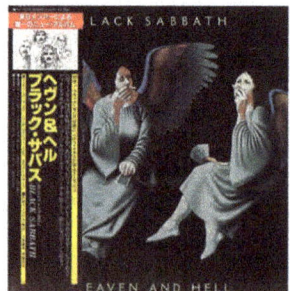

Until I started doing research for this book, I didn't know the HEAVEN AND HELL cover was based on an old photograph from 1928 called Smoking Angels. As the story goes, these women were dressed as angels for a pageant when they needed a smoke break.

While the band was working on their new album, AC/DC vocalist Bon Scott died on February 19, 1980, from "death by misadventure," leaving AC/DC's promising future in doubt. AC/DC found themselves in the same place as Sabbath, needing a new vocalist for their first album of the 1980s. Both bands had to replace a major part of their band's sound, and most visual member, while navigating the unfamiliar musical currents of the new decade. Many in the music scene wondered if Black Sabbath's former vocalist would end up the same way as his friend, Bon Scott, dying alone from substance abuse. Also struggling with substance abuse was drummer Bill Ward, who liked the music the band was creating and got on very well with Dio. However, he missed Ozzy and felt this line-up was not Black Sabbath. Despite his feelings and condition, Ward would press on and do some amazing work on the new album. As the recording sessions finished in January, Birch and the band were all quite excited about the music that they had created as well as about their future together, a future no one would thought would ever see.

"This is an album where they had a lot to prove." – Ronnie James Dio

AND IF IT BREAKS, YOU RUN

With high expectations for the new Sabbath line-up, the cover art had to be as perfect as the music inside. Considering the band's struggles to have great album visuals in the past, this put the pressure on them to find something that was just right and someone who could represent visually what the band was doing audibly. Inspired by a 1929 photograph of women dressed as angels and smoking at a pageant, artist Lynn Curlee painted his version of the photograph, angels representing Heaven, the cigarettes and the cards represented vices, or Hell. Many, like myself, thought the cover was created for the album because it fits so perfectly, but this wasn't the case. It just fit so well. Warner Bros. execs knew they needed a big splash and kept going back to the artwork of Blue Oyster Cult's breakthrough album, AGENTS OF FORTUNE, also painted by Curlee. Interesting to note, that cover also featured playing cards, so there is a theme. The cover for HEAVEN AND HELL is so iconic and fits the mood and style of the new Black Sabbath. The smoking angels were also perfect for posters and concert shirts. The back cover would be a very stylish drawing of the band, including a well-groomed Bill Ward by artist Harry Carmean.

IT GOES ON AND ON AND ON

HEAVEN AND HELL was released on April 25, 1980, and instantly re-established Black Sabbath as a major act and proved to many there was life after Ozzy Osbourne. The album was released by Vertigo worldwide except in the US and Canada (Warner Bros.) where it hit the charts hard and became the band's highest charter in the US and UK since 1975's SABOTAGE. Reaching #28 in the US, #9 in the UK and #23 in Canada, Black Sabbath would be given platinum awards in the US and gold in the UK. The album would have two singles chart in the UK, *Neon Knights* (#22) and *Die Young* (#41) with both songs having live videos recorded for promotion.

"Sabbath was a band that was floundering and, with my inclusion in it, we pulled ourselves up by our bootstraps, cared about each other, and knew that we could do it again." – Ronnie James Dio

WITH AN AWFUL SHOT

Quite possibly the greatest intro song for an album since Aerosmith's *Back In The Saddle* (from ROCKS), *Neon Knights* just comes right out and attacks you. The heavy riffs of Iommi, rockin' drums from Ward, and thumping bass get you ready for a vocal explosion... and a new era of Black Sabbath has begun! Next to Never Say Die, my favorite Black Sabbath song ever!

Rock Radio in America (or at least in New England where I was listening) began to play *Children Of The Sea*. With an acoustic beginning, heavy middle, and fantasy-based lyrics, I was hooked! The song evokes so much imagery with the words and the time changes, not to mention the amazing voice that goes from soft to almost evil very quickly.

Lady Evil has a funky feel to it with sexy bass playing from Butler and funky percussion from Ward. A total fan favorite and a nice song to fit between two classics. The solo is so un-Tony Iommi yet pure Iommi at the same time

"Ozzy would sing with the riff. I don't want to sound like I'm knocking Ozzy, but Ronnie's approach opened up a new way for me to think ..." – Tony Iommi

The epic *Heaven And Hell* would become the anthem for Dio era. With the driving bass and heavy riffs, this song would be the line-up's Black Sabbath, being eerie, soul-stealing, and challenging. Lyrically, Dio straddles the line between Rainbow's fantasy and Black Sabbath's darker side with brillliance and ease.

Incredibly melodic, *Wishing Well* is, for me, the surprise track on the album. The song is possibly the most Rainbow-sounding on the album, with a nice bridge leading into the chorus and some deep lyrics. And how about the second part of the solo (that changes tone a bit) which has a hint of acoustic guitar and bass underneath it? Another very Rainbow-sounding track.

Die Young was the second song released as a single and I could never understand why. The track is good and a solid rock song with a lot of great moments (the swirling keyboards at the intro) as well as thoughtful lyrics, but I never heard it as a song that had mass appeal and rate major airplay.

Having an almost RUSH feel musically, *Walk Away* is another departure for Black Sabbath. It moves in and out of different textures and is a song that seems to have been written to be heard in the big arena. The bass work and the drums again create a great foundation for the vocals and guitar.

Lonely Is the World is possibly the weakest song on the album but it isn't a bad song at all. It just suffers from everything that came before it being so good. Great lyrics and brilliant performances that sound more like Whitesnake or Gary Moore than Black Sabbath. But again, a good song.

IT'S THE ONLY ROAD I KNOW

Support for HEAVEN AND HELL would begin with shows in early April in Germany and Austria before shifting to the UK and then three months in the US, concluding with a stop in Japan. With the US in a recession and weathering a gas shortage, many tours were not making any money and seeing poor ticket sales, so it was suggested by their new manager to do a co-headlining tour of the US with Blue Oyster Cult. Blue Oyster Cult had just released their seventh album, CULTOSAURUS ERECTUS, and was looking to make a big splash on the road.

"The first projects are usually the most stunning because you have a collection of ideas that are dramatically different from each other." – Ronnie James Dio

There would be issues between the two bands on who would close each show as well as Sabbath feeling Pearlman was always looking out for his other band more. Despite the issues behind the scenes, The Black & Blue Tour would be a huge success and bring both bands into the largest arenas in the United States. Sabbath, who was the bigger band of the two, felt BOC was just benefiting from their success and treating them like the opening act. For Black Sabbath, issues became a bit closer to home with Bill Ward slipping deeper into substance abuse and trying to work through the grief of losing his parents. Following a show at the Met Center in Minnesota on August 19, 1980, Ward would just pack up and leave without warning, forcing Sabbath to cancel the next night's show in Colorado. With a few weeks away from their next show (in Honolulu, Hawaii) a call was made to Cozy Powell (who had just left Rainbow) who declined the offer. After listening to tapes, the band brought in Vinny Appice, younger brother of a drumming legend, Carmine Appice. Despite his tiny drum kit that got lost on the drum riser, Appice impressed his new band as well as the audience and diehard fans. Performing behind the stage, Geoff Nicholls would play keyboards and add needed texture to some of the songs, especially the newer ones.

The average setlist would feature 5 new songs; *Neon Knights, Lady Evil, Heaven And Hell, Die Young,* and *Children Of The Sea.* Also included in the 12-song set were staples like *Paranoid, Black Sabbath,* and *Iron*

Man, while shows would open with *War Pigs*.

Many long-time Sabbath fans had a tough time warming up to Ronnie James Dio and his voice. This may be a shock now, considering the legendary status RJD has, but at this stage in his career his legacy was just being forged. A lot of fans didn't know that he was in Rainbow before joining Black Sabbath. He didn't prance around the stage like Ozzy did and he did struggle a bit with the Ozzy-era material. Dio's Sign Of The Horns now replacing Ozzy's peace signs. His voice was so different, more a singer's voice that didn't always translate well on the classics. Ozzy's style had almost ten years of history with fans.

"I blamed everybody and everything for my problems and I just fell apart." – Bill Ward

CRAZY ...BUT THAT'S HOW IT GOES

As Black Sabbath picked themselves up and moved forward, former vocalist Ozzy Osbourne was written off by anyone and everyone. Despite his efforts to reunite Ozzy and Black Sabbath, this was no longer an option and Don Arden signed him to a deal with his label, Jet Records, the home of hitmakers like the magical Electric Light Orchestra. Arden sent his daughter Sharon to help get Ozzy clean enough to put a band together, record an album, and eventually get on the road. Arden wanted the new project to be called Son Of Sabbath and even envisioned Ozzy's new project touring with Black Sabbath. He also tried to pair Ozzy with superstar guitarist Gary Moore, but Moore said no to the invite, thinking Ozzy had nothing to offer. Moore would end up working with Greg Lake (who had just left Emerson Lake & Palmer) on two brilliant albums and two tours before focusing on a solo career that saw him become a guitar hero and then a blues master.

 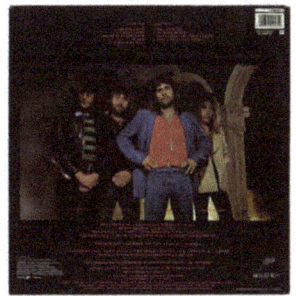 

Ozzy Osbourne put together an incredible band and a brilliant debut album which showed everyone that Ozzy was back! The middle picture is the original (UK) pressing back jacket that shows a bearded Osbourne and a band (other than Randy Rhodes) that looks old. The last picture is of the late Lee Kerslake and Brent Hoag flashing the horns and chatting about all things Uriah Heep and Ozzy in 2019!

"Working with Randy was like night and day compared to working with Black Sabbath." – Ozzy Osbourne

Putting a band together, Ozzy began working with former Rainbow bassist Bob Daisley, former Uriah Heep drummer Lee Kerslake, and a young American guitarist named Randy Rhodes, who had spent the past few years with the struggling L.A. based band, Quiet Riot. Rhodes was hand-delivered to Ozzy by bassist Dana Strum, who would find success in the mid-1980s with the Vinny Vincent Invasion and Slaughter. Following a shift to the UK, the band started writing songs for the first album by the band Blizzard Of Ozz. But, as the sessions began to progress, the band was to become an Ozzy Osbourne solo album. A little bent out of shape, the musicians entered the studio with Chris Tsangarides as producer. The relationship soured when Ozzy was not happy with the production. The production credits would be given to Osbourne, Kerslake, Daisley, and

Rhodes, but behind the scenes Max Norman came in to finish the album. Norman did an amazing job capturing their raw energy, although his work went uncredited. The result was BLIZZARD OF OZZ, a pure rock masterpiece that was a shock to many that it even got made, let alone how good it was. Also appearing on the album was another former Rainbow member, keyboardist Don Airey.

Released September 20, 1980, the album hit US Radio by surprise with the catchy *Crazy Train*, the epic *Mr. Crawley*, the pure rocker *I Don't Know*, and the beautiful *Goodbye To Romance*, the first song Ozzy and his guitarist wrote together. The album is driven by some great songs but what really caught the eyes (and ears) of many was the lighting fast leads and neo-classical guitar play of Rhodes. The guitarist was only 23 at the time and would not only become the musical partner for Osbourne but his best friend and much-needed confidant. The front cover of the album (on the floor holding a cross in the air) would become an iconic picture and added to the Satan Worshipper tag Ozzy received as a member of Black Sabbath... and would now work to his advantage. The back cover on the UK album features a posed shot of the band, looking very old school (Ozzy is even featured with a beard) and not so menacing. The US back cover and subsequent releases would feature a concert picture that seemed more appropriate.

"On the first album we never played together, so it was everything at once." – Randy Rhodes

BLIZZARD OF OZZ would be certified platinum in the US and go gold in the UK. Chart-wise it would go to #21 in the US, #7 in the UK and #8 in Canada, establishing Osbourne as not just a credible solo act, but a major player in the hard rock world. For those counting, and many were, the album ended up being more successful than Black Sabbath's HEAVEN AND HELL. It wouldn't be out of order to say that sales were certainly helped by Osbourne's unpredictable behavior like biting off the head of a dove at a record label meeting and urinating everywhere other than where you are supposed to. Dissension in the ranks would begin with Daisley and Kerslake feeling they were lied to about the band being a band and not a solo vehicle for Osbourne. No matter their feelings, Osbourne and his band hit the road. The Blizzard Of Ozz tour would start in September without keyboardist Don Airey, who was back with Rainbow recording DIFFICULT TO CURE. His spot would be filled by Lindsay Bridgewater for the first leg of the tour, starting in September 1980, and finish in early November. The tour would cover the UK with the second leg bringing Ozzy Osbourne to the US for the first time as a solo artist. Following the UK dates, the band would enter the studio to record tracks for the next album with Max Norman.

In the meantime, to appease the growing UK fans and American record collectors, a live mini-album, MR. CRAWLEY LIVE EP was released in late 1980 by Jet Records. The 12-inch single and picture disc featured three live songs; *Mr. Crawley, Suicide Solution* (both live), and the unreleased, and quite good, *You Said It All*. The live songs were recorded on October 2, 1980, in Southampton, UK, and are an amazing audio snapshot of Ozzy and his band early on in their careers when momentum was pushing the band. The album's biggest bonus is hearing Randy Rhodes live on stage, ripping solos and leads like the star he was becoming.

LIVE, BUT NOT BY CHOICE

Meanwhile, another live Black Sabbath album was released without any input or permission from the band. NEMS released LIVE AT LAST in July 1980. Produced and put together by Black Sabbath's former manager, Patrick Meehan, the album isn't bad and the listening quality isn't horrible, but it isn't as polished and clean as audiences were accustomed to. What it represents is the original line-up on stage in 1973, warts and all, and displays the lack of control Black Sabbath had on their career during the Meehan era. The front and back cover are horrible (the moon?), look like they were done very cheaply, and contain many errors in the text, including forgetting to put Embryo on the sleeve and misspelling singer Ozzy Osbourne's first name, calling him 'Ossie'. Was this on purpose? Maybe. Shockingly, LIVE AT LAST would get to #5 on the UK charts before it was forced to be pulled out of shops due to an embargo by Black Sabbath. The interest was heightened by the success of HEAVEN AND HELL and the anticipation of BLIZZARD OF OZZ.

Another Patrick Meehan cash grab. The songs recorded here were to originally be part of a live release in 1976, but Warner Bros. and Vertigo didn't think the quality matched up well with Deep Purple's MADE IN JAPAN.

BLACK SABBATH VS. OZZY OSBOURNE
ROUND ONE

Following the success of both HEAVEN AND HELL and BLIZZARD OF OZZ, both parties played fairly nice in the media, focusing on their own careers and current goings-on rather than looking too much at each other. They would both take shots but nothing too scandalous or inflammatory. Ozzy would publicly wonder why his former band still played *Iron Man* and *Paranoid* since those songs were identified with Ozzy! "Do they not have confidence in their own material?" he would ask! In the Black Sabbath camp, Ronnie James Dio would say he was too busy to pay attention to what Ozzy was doing. Cordial relations between the two camps would NOT last and things would get heated and ugly... real ugly... real fast.

To put an exclamation mark on this amazing year, I asked my Facebook family which album do they like better, HEAVEN AND HELL or BLIZZARD OF OZZ? Thank you to Black Sabbath Legion Of Fans, Black Sabbath Family, Power Chords Podcast, Melodic Mafia, and my own Facebook group of friends. This was not easy! Both albums were amazing beginnings for both Ozzy and Sabbath and a few people, including my friend, House Of Lords/Dokken drummer B.J. Zampa, said there was no way to pick just one of them with B.J. Even being angry that I asked. The fans who replied to the poll gave the edge to HEAVEN AND HELL with 57% of the vote.

FINAL THOUGHTS
TRAVELING THROUGH HEAVEN AND HELL

HEAVEN AND HELL is *the* best Black Sabbath album and on the list of my 20 favorite albums of all time. Wow... where do you go from there? Looking at where the band was at the time, the only way they could have succeeded was by bringing in Ronnie James Dio! Would HEAVEN AND HELL have been as good if Brian Johnson (who joined AC/DC following the death of Bon Scott) was the singer? There is a certain magic and chemistry that Ronnie James Dio brought to any project, but the combination of Tony Iommi's riffs and Dio's lyrics created something incredibly special. This is also a great time to see that my thinking and the Black Sabbath faithful's hive mind all come together, with all of voting HEAVEN AND HELL our favorite Black Sabbath album, ever!

Back when the album was being recorded, many said this project should have been released under a different name, but if it was, how many of us would have bought it or even known it existed? It's hard to imagine Ronnie James Dio not being a huge name in the industry. But, in 1980, with his Rainbow albums selling very modestly and Black Sabbath's reputation in decline Heaven and Hell was a revelation, and we're all very blessed that it came to pass.

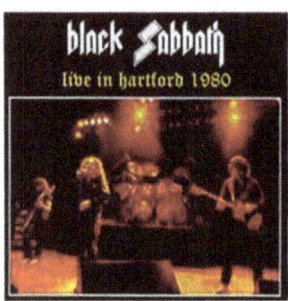  

Since I was only 12 years old this was as close as I was going to get to a concert for a few years, collecting bootlegs, something that made me the cool kid.

ALL NIGHT LONG (SORT OF)
GRAHAM BONNET (RAINBOW/MSG)

One of my favorite voices, ever, belongs to Graham Bonnet! I became a fan the first time I heard Since You Been Gone and with every move he made. From Rainbow to the Michael Schenker Group to Alcatrazz to Impellitteri to the Graham Bonnet Band... I have been a fan of all of it. I finally got a chance to see him live in Pawning, New York, at Daryl's House on January 17, 2018, and he... and his entire band was amazing! I had the thrill of meeting Graham and interviewing him and all I can say... total class act! One wonders, or at least I wonder... what would Black Sabbath sound like if Bonnet joined the band in 1980?

 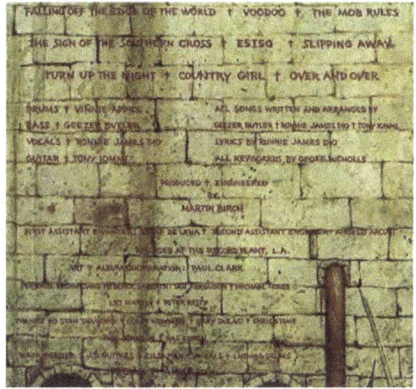

MOB RULES (Vertigo/Warner Bros. Records)
Released on November 4, 1981
Produced by Martin Birch
Ronnie James Dio (vocals), Tony Iommi (guitar), Geezer Butler (bass), and Vinny Appice (drums)
Additional musicians - Geoff Nicholls (keyboards)
All songs written by Butler, Dio, and Iommi

TURN UP THE NIGHT
VOODOO
THE SIGN OF THE SOUTHERN CROSS
E5150
THE MOB RULES

COUNTRY GIRL
SLIPPING AWAY
FALLING OFF THE EDGE OF THE WORLD
OVER AND OVER

"MOB RULES was a confusing album for us." – Tony Iommi

A STORY THAT CAN'T BE REAL

Before recording their next album, Black Sabbath was asked to contribute a song to the high-profile animated movie, HEAVY METAL. The film, based on the illustrated sci-fi comic magazine, was broken down into anthology-style segments featuring well-known actors lending their voices with some of the biggest music artists of the day like Blue Oyster Cult, Sammy Hagar, Journey, Stevie Nicks, and Cheap Trick providing the music. The film was rated R and was full of sexual situations and violence. The Mob Rules scene features an invading alien army overtaking a city. Here, both music and imagery fit together perfectly.

HEAVY METAL didn't do well at the box office and reviews were more on the negative side, but for this 13-year-old, the mashing of music, comic books, and hot cartoon girls (boobs!) were too much not to love and remains a favorite film of mine. Interesting to note, the soundtrack version of the song was recorded at Tittenhust Park in London, the house-turned-studio that was currently owned by former Beatles drummer Ringo Starr. The previous owner, John Lennon, recorded many of his '70's albums, videos (like Imagine), as well as so many home movies there. Black Sabbath was in the house recording the track just days after John Lennon was murdered in New York City, something that made Vinny Appice very uncomfortable.

"We were all going through problems at that time, most of it related to drugs." – Tony Iommi

Black Sabbath, again with Martin Birch, commenced recording the follow-up to HEAVEN AND HELL. Before joining Sabbath back in the studio, Birch produced the second album for the up-and-coming Kings of Heavy Metal, Iron Maiden, titled KILLERS (EMI/Harvest/Capitol Records). The album was a huge success for this determined and hungry band, going to #12 in the UK and #78 in the US. It gave Birch a new perspective on the current hard rock/heavy metal scene. He would make the new Black Sabbath album more aggressive and in-your-face to bring the energy of a young band to his veteran rockers. To try to save money, the band bought their own studio but could never quite get the sound right and so ended up selling it, wasting time and (of course) money that they hoped to save.

Black Sabbath would end up at the famed Record Plant in Los Angeles, CA, to record the album with their new drummer, Vinny Appice. Due to the success of the last album, Warner Bros. Records would extend the band's record contract as a sign of faith in the new line-up, which, as expected, made the band very happy and gave them a lot of confidence. That was the good news. The bad news (at least for the band) was the record label secretly gave Ronnie James Dio a solo contract, as well, causing understandable concerns and dissension within the ranks as to why the label was doing this. In addition, songwriting for the record became a bit problematic for the band. Since Butler wasn't around when the last album was being written, he was no longer needed as Black Sabbath's chief lyricist due to Dio's amazing skills at writing words and melodies. On top of all that were Iommi's, Butler's, and, to a much lesser extent, Dio's, increasing drug dependency, which led to a lack of communication, straight thinking, and paranoia. A change in the balance of power away from the two original members was happening.

"We approached the writing very much differently than the first one. Geezer had gone so we wrote in a very controlled environment in a living room." – Ronnie James Dio

Despite the issues that were starting within the ranks, Black Sabbath moved ahead and recorded MOB RULES, an album that was a slight step down from HEAVEN AND HELL, but how can you recapture lightning in a bottle? There was a slight change in the overall sound. Some of the songs were quite heavy and others were very melodic, especially for Black Sabbath. The drum sound was a bit thicker and fuller with Appice, but being a huge fan of the band and original drummer Bill Ward, he was able to keep the overall feel close to the expected sound.

The Mob Rules scene from HEAVY METAL, the iconic poster that was on my wall for years, and the Japanese release of MOB RULES.

CALL ME THE DEVIL, ITS TRUE

Again, Black Sabbath was able to pick the perfect piece of art for the cover that would capture the title and the music inside. Originally a piece called Dream1: Crucifiers from 1971, the art was done by famed science fiction/fantasy painter Greg Hildebrandt. Since 1959, Greg and his twin brother, Tim (collectively and professionally known as the Brothers Hildebrandt) did some amazing work in advertising, magazines, and comic books, but it was the 1977 "Style B" poster they did for the then recently released film, STAR WARS, that pushed their careers to the next level. Looking for controversy, people thought they could see the words "KILL OZZY" on the ground spelled in sticks and blood underneath the hooded characters. As expected, fans jumped on this as Sabbath's retaliation for the stage antics of Ozzy. In 2019, at the Terrificon comic book convention at Connecticut's Mohegan Sun Hotel & Casino, I had the chance to ask Greg about the cover art controversy and he said, "people will see what they want to see". I then spent the next 20 minutes gushing about how he and his late brother's Star Wars art/poster was what made me a lifelong obsessed Star Wars fan, complete with tears and voice cracking. After five minutes of that, Greg wanted to go back to talking about Black Sabbath and the MOB RULES cover.

"There was a little controversy about some stains on the floor in the picture. According to some people it spelled out 'Ozzy'!" – Tony Iommi

Also, on the back cover, new drummer Vinny Appice is spelled 'Vinnie' with an 'I-E', an error that would, unfortunately, live forever in the media..

BUT ITS GONE TOO FAR

Black Sabbath's tenth studio album, MOB RULES, was released on November 4, 1981, on Vertigo Records worldwide except in North America where it was released by Warner Bros. Records. The album received mixed reviews, some calling it "more of the same" and others saying it was much too different from HEAVEN AND HELL, proving most critics don't know what they are talking about and that you can't please everyone. There was a certain shift in the band's sound and lyrics (courtesy of Dio) and most everyone was completely supportive, but the band was now trying to complete for sales with much younger and flashier bands and MTV. MOB RULES would do solid numbers on the charts, going to #29 in the US, one less spot than the previous album, #12 in the UK, and would go Gold everywhere but North America. It would be a bit of a let-down for not going Platinum like HEAVEN AND HELL did. Rock radio would play the title track, *Turn Up The Night*, and *Voodoo*, but nothing on the much-needed MTV.

"I could be 15 years old for the rest of my life." – Ronnie James Dio

This was the first Black Sabbath album I bought brand-new off the shelf (Record Express in the Enfield Mall in CT) and was absolutely captivated by Dio's voice, the guitar tones of Iommi, the great cover, the thundering drums of Appice, and the non-stop assault of Butler's bass! Although I already had bought (and loved) HEAVEN AND HELL and WE SOLD OUR SOUL FOR ROCK 'N' ROLL, I still consider MOB RULES to be my first Sabbath record and one never forgets their first. I do remember all my sister's friends talking about this album and I now started to understand what it was like to like the music the cool older kids were listening to.

"With MOB RULES we hired a studio, turned up as loud as possible, and smashed through it. So, it made for a different kind of an attitude". – Ronnie James Dio

IF YOU LISTEN TO FOOLS...

It's the new guy (drummer Vinny Appice) that starts the festivities with a four-count and then...*Turn Up The Night*. A great song to kick off the album, this one is the prototypical Dio song with melodic verses and arena-ready chorus. Featuring some great guitar tones by Tony Iommi, this is an upbeat way to kick off an album that is going to get evil fast.

A song I never was really into when I was younger but have since come to love is *Voodoo*. The feel and pace are like old-school Black Sabbath in that it doesn't use volume or crushing chords to get the point across. Despite being riff-heavy, the song is driven by Geezer Butler's thunder and Appice's beat. Dio's voice on this one sounds so open, live, and free, like he is singing from a mountaintop.

"Of all the drummers I've played with, Bill is number one, Vinny is number two." – Geezer Butler

A song I liked better as a kid than I do now is *The Sign Of The Southern Cross*. This was to be the epic Heaven And Hell of MOB RULES, but to me it is just kinda plodding and really goes nowhere cool for almost the eight minutes. The donga-donga-donga keyboards during the verse are still really cool, and I do love how it fades into the verses. It certainly plays like a song that was built for the stage. Big sound.

E5150 is an instrumental/intro track that is eerie and creepy and still scares the hell out of me. The title spells out the word evil; the letter 'E', 5 in Roman Numeral is 'V', 1 in Roman is 'I' and 50 is the letter 'L'. Butler and Iommi play sound tricks with their instruments, complete with synthesized voices and create an amazing introduction to...

The Mob Rules. Possibly the evilest-sounding song ever written and recorded, the song is a call to arms or a sign of the end, depending on how you are feeling at the time. The heavy drumming of Appice provides the added punch created by the amazing Iommi riff, leading into the demon-inspired silo. RJD's vocals here are angry and full of fire, not his normal in-control operatic smoothness. Easily my 3rd favorite Black Sabbath song... short, sweet and leaves you in a pile of dust!

Beginning side two is *Country Girl*, the weakest track on the album. It always seemed weird to have a Black Sabbath song start out with "falling in love", but here we are. Despite the lyrics getting dark as Sabbath lyrics do, it just seems like a forced song. It never was a favorite of mine despite the Rainbow feel it has.

The only problem with *Slipping Away* is that it wasn't a radio hit. The song has a great riff, a terrific melody, and almost has backing vocals. What it also has is a drum solo AND a bass solo, plus a lightning-fast guitar solo in the middle! How can you go wrong? You can't.

"It was a departure for Sabbath and became just one of those natural progressions that should happen as much as possible." – Tony Iommi

Another epic song, *Falling Of The Edge Of The World* has always been a forgotten song, but it deserves so much better. For many, it got lost in the shuffle, but it is slow in the beginning, building to a heavy, almost UFO-like *Rock Bottom* riff, and, once it gets going, you can feel every plucked string and drumbeat! The most underrated song on the album.

The album concludes with a slow and deliberately emotional song, *Over And Over*. Much like *Paranoid* many years before, the track is from the perspective of someone who is in a state of reflection and not seeing life in a bright light. Lyrically, Dio is painting a picture of emotional turmoil as Iommi helps the story along with some weepy and soul-pulling solos. Behind the sadness are the satisfying drums of Appice.

"You can't please everybody. What are you supposed to do?" – Tony Iommi

NOTHING COULD MAKE ME STAY

Black Sabbath would hit the road to support the album from the the time of its release in November of 1981 and conclude in August of 1982. The typical setlist would include *Country Girl, Turn Up The Night, Voodoo, Falling Of The Edge Of The World, Sign Of The Southern Cross*, and *The Mob Rules*. The songs from the previous line-up were limited to four or five, putting the focus more on the current Dio era. Many of the shows would be recorded for a proposed live album that would see release the following year. Supporting the band would be Ten years After's legendary guitarist, Alvin Lee, and a serious bit of Southern Rock with Doc Holliday, The Outlaws, Molly Hatchet, and Johnny Van Zant. On the Canadian dates, hometown rockers Wrabit and speed metal pioneers Exciter would be alternating as openers.

While on the road, cracks began to show in the band's relationships with each other to the point that there was a division, with the original members against the new guys. Clashes in the way things were done began to alienate the members to the point that they started not speaking or even hanging out. Iommi and Butler (both not ones for conflict) resented Dio's leadership and outspoken nature, felt he was talking over their band, and projecting credit for the band's recent success on himself. Plus, having two New Yorkers of Italian descent gave Dio and Appice natural chemistry and camaraderie that threatened the two Brits. With a solo contract in hand, Dio began to think about life outside of the Sabbath box, one where he could do things on his terms. By the time Black Sabbath got off the road and started planning their long-awaited live album, the personal issues were now becoming unfixable.

"Tony and Geezer had no problems with me. It was just Ronnie." – Vinny Appice

The front and back for DIARY OF A MADMAN and the inner sleeve confused me, picturing Rudy Sarzo and Tommy Aldridge as part of the band, although magazine articles I read before release said the players on the album were the same as on BLIZZARD OF OZZ.

BUT THEY DONT REALLY UNDERSTAND

 Following a triumphant first tour, Ozzy Osbourne returned to the studio in February of 1981 with his band and producer Max Norman to record the follow-up to his successful (and quite amazing) debut album. Not caving into any pressures of trying to top BLIZZARD OF OZZ, Osbourne, Randy Rhodes (guitar), Lee Kerslake (drums), Bob Daisley (bass) and Johnny Cook (keyboards, uncredited) wrote and recorded eight solid and somewhat superior songs that would make up DIARY OF A MADMAN (Jet Records). The music on this album shows so much growth, especially the guitar playing of Rhodes, who was creating a whole genre of music with his playing. It was heavy, flashy, and speedy when it needed to be, and classic the rest of the time. Songs like *Over The Mountain, You Can't Kill Rock And Roll, Flying High Again*, and the amazingly brilliant title track would receive massive radio airplay and push this album to unexpected heights when it was released. But, because BLIZZARD OF OZZ was still on the charts and selling well, the decision was made to hold the album back until November 7, 1981, just days after MOB RULES was released.

 With the album completed and ready to go, Osbourne and his new manager Sharon Arden suddenly fired Bob Daisley and Lee Kerslake, replacing them with Rhodes's former Quiet Riot partner, bassist Rudy Sarzo, and former Black Oak Arkansas drummer, Tommy Aldridge. Replacing the steady playing of Daisley with the youthful flash and good looks of Sarzo would be a win for the fans, but it would be a huge, huge loss for Ozzy because of his songwriting skills. Despite the credits he received for the songs, most of the material on the first two albums was driven by Daisley and Rhodes. The new line-up, plus Don Airey, would hit the road for a North American tour beginning in late April and ending in mid-September. Quite a few of the concerts were recorded for radio broadcasts for shows like the King Biscuit Flower Hour, giving Osbourne an even bigger audience and bringing Mr. Osbourne into the mainstream and people's homes.

 DIARY OF A MADMAN would go to #16 in the US, #14 in the UK, and #16 in Canada. The cover for the album featured a fully made-up Ozzy (in his old Sabbath stage wear) coming at you and also features his son Lewis snickering behind his crazy dad. The inner jacket would feature a picture of Ozzy's new, younger, and hipper-looking band, the band that didn't play on the album, except for Osbourne and Rhodes.

 Controversy and Ozzy Osbourne became synonymous at this time as there were more arrests for urinating where he shouldn't and so many drug and alcohol-fueled acts of craziness. This would make Ozzy a household name and make this 13-year-old buy this album and Ozzy's first because I was into the hype but fell in love with the music. Ozzy and his band would hit the road for the rest of 1981 and most of 1982 where Osbourne would tour with the amazing UFO, bite the head off a live bat, and tragically lose a partner in a horrific accident.

"I sell more records and concert tickets than them, just ask them." – Ozzy Osbourne

BLACK SABBATH VS. OZZY OSBOURNE
ROUND TWO

At this point, all bets were off, especially for Ozzy Osbourne, who, as his star began to shine brighter, would go on a major attack on Ronnie James Dio and the entire Black Sabbath organization every chance he got. Looking at the sales of both albums in 1981, MOB RULES and DIARY OF A MADMAN, both were incredible releases and certainly added to their respective legacies, but as far as sales and charts, Ozzy would come out on top, and he let the world know about it every chance he got. Ozzy's amazing second solo album would chart 13 places better in the US, but 4 less in the UK, where the Black Sabbath name was more respected than Ozzy, who in the UK was looked at as a bit of a joke.

Probably the biggest attack from Ozzy was the addition of a little person into his stage show. During the song *Goodbye To Romance*, a dwarf named John Edward Allen would be hung, and, all these years later, I'm still not exactly sure why. The how and why is not that important here but the small victim in the noose was given the name Ronnie The Dwarf, a more-than-obvious slight to Ronnie James Dio's lack of height and Ozzy's insecurities about someone fronting the band he was fired from, despite his own success.

"He couldn't carry a tune if you put a radio in a suitcase and handed it to him." – Ronnie James Dio

Again, I went to my Facebook family to see which album they like better, MOB RULES or DIARY OF A MADMAN? Thank you again to Black Sabbath Legion Of Fans, Black Sabbath Family, Power Chords Podcast, Melodic Mafia, and my own Facebook group of friends, because, wow... this was a hard one to pick for me! Both albums offer so much, but for me, my choice is DIARY OF A MADMAN, although not by very much! The album was a brand-new sound to me. It was a mix of traditional '70's rock and flashy '80's metal with a bit of classical music thrown in for good measure that just resonated with my ears, heart, and brain. The fans who replied to this poll gave a huge margin of victory to DIARY OF A MADMAN with 68% of the vote. Not that we didn't like MOB RULES. We just enjoyed DAIRY a bit more.

YOU'RE ALL FOOLS

As far as MOB RULES, it is an amazing album that may be a slight step down from HEAVEN AND HELL, but song for song it is still so good. Considering the brilliant and near-perfect album they had to follow up, I think Black Sabbath made a heavier and darker album thanks to the heavy drumming of Vinny Appice. Musically, some great moments really challenge the perception of Black Sabbath, but it just falls short in some places. I still give the album a solid 7 out of 10 as a rating and place it just out of my Top 10 by putting it at #11 out of 19 studio albums. The Black Sabbath Facebook army spoke quite loudly and ranked it a bit higher than I did, placing it at # 6 out of 19.

FIRST ALPHABETICALLY BUT STILL THE LAST IN LINE
VINNY APPICE

Drummer Vinny Appice certainly left his mark on Black Sabbath, DIO, Heaven & Hell and now continues the legacy with Last In Line. Last In Line was formed in 2012 by former DIO members Appice, Jimmy Bain, and Vivian Campbell as a way to celebrate the music they helped create with Ronnie James Dio. Joined on vocals by the amazing Andrew Freeman, Last In Line has released two albums and is one of the best bands you will ever see live! Pictures above (in order) are Vinny under the red lights at The Chance Theatre in Poughkeepsie, New York, and next is Vinny at the MGM Springfield's Summer Concert Series. Not only is Vinny amazing behind the kit, but he is also a great guy who still owes me an interview. Don't make me call you, sir!

www.vinnyappice.com

LIVE EVIL (Vertigo/Warner Bros. Records)
Released on December 1982
Produced by Tony Iommi and Geezer Butler
Ronnie James Dio (vocals), Tony Iommi (guitar), Geezer Butler (bass), and Vinny Appice (drums)
Additional musicians - Geoff Nicholls (keyboards)
All songs written by Butler, Dio and Iommi except where noted

E5150 / NEON KNIGHTS (Butler, Dio, Iommi, and Ward)
N.I.B. (Butler, Iommi, Osbourne, and Ward)
CHILDREN OF THE SEA (Butler, Dio, Iommi, and Ward)
VOODOO
BLACK SABBATH (Butler, Iommi, Osbourne, and Ward)
WAR PIGS (Butler, Iommi, Osbourne, and Ward)
IRON MAN (Butler, Iommi, Osbourne, and Ward)
THE MOB RULES
HEAVEN AND HELL (Butler, Dio, Iommi, and Ward)
THE SIGN OF THE SOUTHERN CROSS/HEAVEN AND HELL (CONTINUED)
PARANOID (Butler, Iommi, Osbourne, and Ward)
CHILDREN OF THE GRAVE (Butler, Iommi, Osbourne, and Ward)
FLUFF (Butler, Iommi, Osbourne, and Ward)

Then think of a rainbow...

Following another successful world tour, the members of Black Sabbath took some time off to catch their collective breath and have time away from each other before working on a new studio album. Unfortunately, the band was committed to releasing a live album toward the end of the year with the long and very monotonous task of listening to hours of tapes was now looming. Publicly, no one was aware of the trouble within the band. Relationships were incredibly strained during the MOB RULES tour and probably could have been smoothed over a bit with some time apart, no drugs, and honest communication, but this was not to be the case.

With a ton of tape to get through, Butler and Iommi (who were having cocaine issues and not thinking quite rationally) would mix the album during the day, with Dio and Appice staying out of the process completely. But, according to studio engineer Lee De Carlo (who was also drinking and drugging and maybe not the most credible source), Dio and Appice were sneaking into the studio at night and playing with the mixes, pushing up the vocals and drums, and altering the sound already worked on during the day. Hearing this news only made Butler and Iommi angry, and, instead of talking about it with Dio, they just let the bad feelings fester to unhealthy levels before deciding that Dio needed to leave the band. Appice was given a choice to stay or go and he chose to exit with Dio.

For Dio (and now Appice), there would be anger and frustration, but the two would just walk away and began recruiting musicians for their new project. For Iommi and Butler, their almost knee-jerk reactions created a whole world of problems, not just trying to put together the live album, but what do they do now? They just lost the voice and words that helped save the band in a time when their first former lead singer was surpassing them in everything... and now, losing two singers in three years was not good optics.

But I can see right through it all

The cover of LIVE EVIL is 100% solid gold and follows the pattern of EXIT... STAGE LEFT, the 1982 live album from RUSH. On that one, RUSH used images from previous albums on the cover, waiting to go on stage. Here, in front of a dark sky full of lighting, you have a military-style beach landing, but instead of soldiers on the beachfront (well, there is one soldier), you have characters and physical manifestations of Black Sabbath song titles that appear on the sleeve. In the middle stands the proud Neon Knight surrounded by a War Pig, an Iron Man, Heaven and Hell (visualized by a devil and an angel), kids surfing in a coffin, and on and on. A totally brilliant cover concept that really brought together the dual history (Ozzy and Dio) of the band in one amazing visual!

The art for the cover was done by sculptor/illustrator Stan Watts, whose only previous album art was for THE BEST OF THE DOOBIES, VOLUME 2, from the Doobie Brothers the year before. In the coming year, Watts would illustrate a number-one album, the iconic and hugely successful US debut from Quiet Riot, METAL HEALTH, an album that has Black Sabbath roots, connected by soon-to-be-former bassist Rudy Sarzo.

"I had a real low-tech approach to my work back then." - Stan Watts

I think about closing the door

LIVE EVIL would be released on Vertigo except in North America where it was released by Warner Bros. Records as usual. There was much excitement for this album, especially from me, since I was still too young to go to a concert (according to my parents) and loved a good live album, especially one with great sound and a lot of pictures. I would turn off all the lights in my room, except for a red bulb in a nightlight, put on my headphones, and pretend I was at the concert! LIVE EVIL wouldn't do gangbusters, but it did good, although not great, on the charts, #37 in the US and #13 in the UK. By the time of the album's release, it was already announced that Ronnie James Dio and Vinny Appice were no longer with Black Sabbath and this left my listening experience a bit unfulfilling. It was also weird to read interviews with Butler and Iommi referring to Dio as a former member, yet trying to make us excited about the new live album featuring the now-former guys.

As a childish parting shot by Iommi and Butler, the photo collage on the inside of the gatefold featured two not-so-flattering pictures of Dio and only one of Appice, which was really tiny. The final nail in the coffin was listing Appice as a special guest below Geoff Nicholls (in the smallest of fonts) and referring to the now-departed singer as Ronnie Dio. Back in 1982, even I thought this was a bit mean and very childish, and I was incredibly immature and childish.

"A piece of s@#t! Not the vocals, though, just everything else." – Ronnie James Dio

Too many flames

This double-disc originally had a very interesting sound quality to it, although a bit flat. You know the album is live, but you can barely hear the audience even you know they are there. Recorded on the MOB RULES tour in Seattle, WA., and Texas (Dallas and San Antonio), this captured Black Sabbath at their best. Live, the band is firing on all cylinders as they burn through incredible renditions of *Children Of The Sea, The Mob Rules, Heaven And Hell,* and *Children Of The Grave*. On the classic songs like *N.I.B., Black Sabbath,* and *War Pigs*, Appice's drums bring a whole new heaviness to the songs, but Dio's voice is not quite equipped to pull off these songs. This is not saying that Dio isn't great, because he is one of the greatest vocalists who ever lived, but only Ozzy can pull off Ozzy songs, much like Mr. Osbourne could never do *Neon Nights* with any conviction.

Like Aerosmith's classic LIVE! BOOTLEG from 1978, LIVE EVIL contains audio pops, guitar feedback, and the bum note here and there, making it as much a concert experience as you could possibly get on vinyl. The album was released at a discounted price, too, costing around $9 at the time, a few bucks less than the average double album and for 15-year-old Mattie, a no-brainer. A funny thing I remember about this album was finally being able to understand the awesome lyrics of *Neon Knights*... because it was "time again to save us from the jackals of the streets"! Also, this was where I all discovered drummer Vinny Appice, pronounced his name "AP-PIH-SEE" and not "A-PIECE" like his brother Carmine. Funny, when Vinny and I chatted in 2019, I didn't ask him why.

"Ronnie wanted to do his own stuff and we wanted to keep it going as it was." – Geezer Butler

To take Black Sabbath head-on in the live album wars, and to get out of his contract with Jet records, this was SPEAK OF THE DEVIL.

The family feud, double live style

The battle for live album (or world) supremacy took another surprising turn when Ozzy Osbourne released a live album within months of Black Sabbath's LIVE EVIL. This was an obviously calculated move for several reasons. On the business side, the release of a double live album was a cheap way to get out of his contract with Jet Records, needing to release two more studio albums or one double live one, and move out from under Don Arden's control. Second, there was the vengeful thought of disrupting Black Sabbath's plans and forcing the two sides to duel it out publicly and on the charts, where Osbourne was at his best.

But, before we get to the live album, we must start with the US tour to support DIARY OF A MADMAN and highlight a few incidents that happened along the way. The tour began in December of 1981, but on January 20 in Des Moines, Iowa, Ozzy bit the head off of a then-live bat thrown up on stage, thinking it was a toy. On February 19, Ozzy was arrested in Texas for urinating on the Texas landmark, The Alamo. With all the calamity that followed the tour and Ozzy living up to the moniker of "madman," it only fueled the excitement, fever, and frenzy of Ozzy and his band coming to your town.

Unfortunately, an unthinkable tragedy struck on March 19, 1982, when Randy Rhodes and two others were killed in a tragic plane crash in Leesburg, Florida. When I spoke to UFO drummer Andy Parker in 2017 about the crash, his most vivid memory about the incident was the confusion of who died, what exactly happened, and what was really going on. Add to the fact that there were no cell phones back then and no one knew how to get a hold of anyone since you didn't even know where anyone was (no GPS). Within a few days, all the sad and tragic facts would become the horrible reality Ozzy now had to live in. The next six shows were canceled, including a March 30 stop in Hartford, CT. I tried to convince my parents it was a UFO show, not mentioning Ozzy at all, but no go, literally! To get through the next few weeks of shows a call went out to Michael Schenker, whom Rhodes was a big fan of, but that was not going to happen because the German guitarist asked for too many perks.

"Why are you (Schenker) stipulating your demands at this point? Just get me through the next show and we will talk about it. Y'know what? Go f@#$ yourself!" – Ozzy Osbourne

Originally hired to help was Rudy Sarzo's brother, Robert (from the band Hurricane), but for the next seven concerts, it would be up-and-coming Irish guitar god Bernie Torme stepping in. Formerly from the band Gillan, Torme was hired by Don Arden without consulting Ozzy and not even knowing if he was going to be a good fit. Torme had two challenges in having to learn the entire set and to win over a still-hurting fanbase, who loved Randy. Ozzy always spoke highly of the guitarist for being so professional and helpful in a time of deep need. Finishing the rest of the tour dates would be Brad Gillis from the band, Ranger, who would play with Ozzy for the next four months temporarily.

Gillis, bassist Rudy Sarzo, drummer Tommy Aldridge, and keyboardist Don Airey were at the Ritz nightclub in New York City on September 26 and 27 to record an entire set of Black Sabbath songs. Despite having two solid albums of material to choose from, Ozzy decided to really put the screws to his former band. Produced by Max Norman, SPEAK OF THE DEVIL (TALK OF THE DEVIL in the UK) was released on November 27, 1982, to a ravenous crowd looking for anything Ozzy to put in their collection. Featuring Ozzy and a mouthful of bat guts (or red jello), the double album is an amazing listen that I struggled to like because my loyalty was to Black Sabbath and I didn't want to like this album. The records are so exciting to listen to and just jump out of the speakers, especially my number-one Sabbath song, *Never Say Die*. Featuring all my (and everyone's) favorite Black Sabbath songs like *Children Of The Grave, Sabbath Bloody Sabbath*, and a ripping version of *Paranoid*, Ozzy became more of a favorite with the all-important younger demographic. On the charts, #14 in the US, #21 in the UK, and #10 in Canada... very impressive, especially for an album that was a bit of an afterthought.

"They wait 15 years to do a live album and they do it the same time I do mine?" – Ozzy Osbourne

Following the last dates on the tour, the two shows that made up the SPEAK OF THE DEVIL album, bassist Rudy Sarzo left. Missing his friend Randy Rhodes and becoming tired of the daily calamity Ozzy brought on and off the stage, the bassist left to rejoin his previous band Quiet Riot, who were recording their first major-label release, METAL HEALTH. Coming in to fill the bass position was former UFO bassist (and legendary drinker) Pete Way, who had just left UFO following their tour with Ozzy. The band finished 1982 with seven UK shows (with Lindsay Bridgewater on keyboards). But, with Osbourne and Way becoming drinking and drugging partners, this line-up wouldn't last long. Following the final show of the UK tour in Liverpool, England, Brad Gillis would return to his previous band, Ranger, who was just starting to record their debut album. Due to another band with the same name, Ranger would be forced to change their name to Night Ranger and the rest is history, as they became an album-selling, video, and hit-single machine in the 1980s. Way would leave to team up with ex-Motorhead guitarist "Fast" Eddie Clark to form the band Fastway (get it? Fast and Way?). Way would be forced to leave before the band recorded their debut album (contractual obligations to Chrysalis Records) and form the band Waysted!

"In my experience, Ozzy was very open, pleasant, and funny, but dangerous, too. You never knew quite what he was going to do next or who he might upset. It wasn't as if he went out of his way to annoy anyone, but he liked to have fun at other people's expense. Every day in Ozzy's company was an adventure, and I was always numb enough to be able to handle whatever it was that might happen." – Pete Way

Sabbath vs. Ozzy - round three

In the battle of the live albums, I must admit that SPEAK OF THE DEVIL is far superior to LIVE EVIL as far as listenability. One of the big reasons is the screaming guitar playing of Brad Gillis and the heavy rhythm section of Rudy Sarzo and Tommy Aldridge that gives the '70's classics a modern feel, making the songs fit right in with the current flashy rock/metal of the day. Because he had a younger band and fanbase, Osbourne was able to tap into what the kids were listening to, really taking classic Sabbath and making it sound very modern. Black Sabbath was caught in the '70's way of doing a live album with long jams, that, for me, could have been replaced with at least three or four more songs. Also, Ozzy and Ronnie are vocally universes apart. With Dio, Black Sabbath had the best vocalist possibly ever who could tell a story with his voice and words. Ozzy was pure show with a limited vocal range, but what he did within his limits is astounding. Also, where Ronnie James Dio would speak to the audience almost like he was having a conversation with them, Ozzy would yell at them, swear at them, and tell them what to do. Two distinct styles served each well.

Many were surprised that Black Sabbath kept all their comments professional and not combative toward Ozzy, but it seemed to be the band's nature to avoid conflict. Of course, Ozzy did the exact opposite and would unload venom to anyone who would listen and get it out to the public. Any chance he got, he put down his former bandmates, insulting and hurtful at every turn. Many thought the cordial behavior from Iommi and Butler toward Ozzy was in the hope of bringing him back to Black Sabbath since they didn't have a vocalist. Who knows. Regardless, for Iommi and Butler, these were desperate times.

As far as sales, SPEAK OF THE DEVIL outsold LIVE EVIL by a million copies worldwide and charted 13 spots higher in the US but eight less in the UK, again showing that the UK fans thought less of Ozzy than Black Sabbath. Fans and friends on the Black Sabbath Book Project Page voted SPEAK OF THE DEVIL the favorite of the two, capturing 72 % of the vote, and I agree.

"They'll just have to just buy two great live albums." – Tony Iommi

In conclusion (cue Fluff)

What a difference a year makes, especially in this tale. Black Sabbath went from strength to massive weakness when they said goodbye to Ronnie James Dio. When recently they had been able to compete on a level playing field with anyone, they now found themselves in the same position as they did in 1979, maybe a bit lower. Ronnie James Dio gave the band instant credibility in a time when they needed it and now they would be forced to watch him build up his solo career along with Ozzy. Another massive weight around the neck of Black Sabbath was that they needed to find a vocalist who could make a big splash and give the band instant credibility again. There weren't a lot of those guys around at that time, especially those who could fit into the Black Sabbath mold.

The band also needed a new drummer, and, despite who they brought in, no matter how talented or explosive they were, Geezer and Tony would be working with half the original line-up, something KISS was being criticized heavily for at this time despite the caliber of players they were playing with.

For Ozzy Osbourne, he was unfortunately forced into a crossroads in his young solo career. Despite massive success and growth, he was now off the road and forced to deal with a life without Randy Rhodes, the guitarist who did more to resurrect his career than anyone else, including Ozzy himself. With the release of SPEAK OF THE DEVIL, Ozzy was no longer with Jet Records. He also needed to put together a new band and find someone who could help write songs, since Ozzy wasn't a songwriter. Despite his elevated status, Ozzy wasn't in the best shape to end 1983

Lived to tell the tale
Neil Carter (UFO/Gary Moore)

In 1980, Neil Carter joined UFO, replacing Paul Raymond as the band's keyboardist/rhythm guitarist. Before joining UFO, Neil was a member of Wild Horses with future DIO bassist Jimmy Bain. In 1982, UFO was on tour with Ozzy Osbourne when Randy Rhodes tragically died in a plane crash in Florida. While working with Gary Moore, Neil played with so many others who feature prominently in the Black Sabbath story, including Bob Daisley, Neil Murray, Craig Gruber, Glenn Hughes, Laurence Cottle, and Cozy Powell.

www.ufo-music.info

The New Testament
BLACK SABBATH

The Book of Sabbath
Chapter 4

Crawl 1:4

With the land living in fear of eternal fire and damnation,
the four giants who were now two
stood on the mountain,
watching the madman and the one from the rainbows
claim their treasures of platinum and gold.
With the land barren, many joined forces to feed the masses and
tried to make the circle complete again.
Thus, the giants who have been cloaked in black
would bring in giants of purple
and continue their almighty quest...

BORN AGAIN (Vertigo/Warner Bros. Records)
Released on August 7, 1983
Produced by Black Sabbath and Robin Black
Ian Gillan (vocals), Tony Iommi (guitar), Geezer Butler (bass), and Bill Ward (drums)
Additional musicians - Geoff Nicholls (keyboards)
All songs written by Butler, Iommi, Gillan and Ward except where noted

TRASHED
STONEHENGE
DISTURBING THE PRIEST
THE DARK
ZERO THE HERO

DIGITAL BITCH
BORN AGAIN
HOT LINE (Butler, Iommi and Gillan)
KEEP IT WARM (Butler, Iommi and Gillan)

"When we had finished the album, we took it to the record company and they said, 'Well, here's the contract. It is going to go out as a Black Sabbath album." – Geezer Butler

It Really Was A Meeting

Somehow convincing themselves that they did the right thing in letting Ronnie James Dio go, Tony Iommi and Geezer Butler now had the difficult task of replacing a drummer and vocalist... AGAIN! Considering the heights that the Dio-led Sabbath attained, whoever came in would have to possess an amazing voice, be able to command the stage, and let Iommi and Butler take the lead. Approached was David Coverdale, who, in 1983, was beginning to sour on the idea of keeping Whitesnake together. The singer was convinced to keep it going by Geffen Records. The label had just made a major investment in the band, which was beginning to put together the music for their next album, SLIDE IT IN. If Coverdale said yes to Sabbath's offer, it was hoped he would bring in Whitesnake's drummer, the powerful Cozy Powell, to help round out the line-up. Imagine that?

Also under consideration was Nicky Moore from Samson and then-rocker Michael Bolton. At this point in his career, Bolton was a New Haven, CT-born singer starting a solo career following the break-up of his band, Blackjack, and hadn't discovered the appeal and riches of adult contemporary music. Check him out. He did kinda rock! A solid choice that wasn't to be was John Sloaman, who spent 1979 to 1981 as the voice of Uriah Heep, but Sloaman was a bit too clean-looking for Black Sabbath. Their words, not mine.

Knowing they needed to make a big splash with a big name, manager Don Arden had Iommi and Butler meet with former Deep Purple vocalist Ian Gillan. From playing Jesus in the cast recording of JESUS CHRIST SUPERSTAR to his legendary run as the vocalist in Deep Purple, Gillan was a favorite of UK music fans who supported everything he did. The singer had just disbanded his very successful band, Gillan (to the shock, surprise, and anger of his band who didn't see it coming at all) and was resting his damaged vocal cords when he met with Iommi and Butler, soon to be augmented by the return of drummer Bill Ward. Originally planned as a supergroup of sorts, the band caved in to pressure and ended up calling themselves Black Sabbath. They spent May of 1983 at The Manor Studio in Oxfordshire, England recording a collection of songs for their new album, being produced by the band and Robin Black. Black was more of an engineer than a producer, having worked with Sabbath in the past (SABOTAGE and TECHNICAL ECSTASY) and Jethro Tull, The Damned, and Alice Cooper, but as a producer he was untested, and it would show.

"I was having a drink with Tony and Geezer. We got thoroughly pissed one night and my manager called me the next morning and said, "If you're going to make career decisions, don't you think we should talk it through first?" I said, "What are you talking about?" He said, "Apparently you agreed to join Black Sabbath last night." I couldn't remember any of it." – Ian Gillan

Black Sabbath got an incredible amount of press and goodwill with the addition of Gillan, who was still very popular in the UK and constantly in the news due to the persistent Deep Purple reunion rumors. Until new music was heard, fans began to speculate what the band would sound like, what the songs would be about, and very importantly, what would Gillan wear? Despite the shared history and career similarities, Gillan never seemed to be the right choice to front Sabbath, but only time would tell. With pranks, massive drinking, car crashes, and writing all about it, Black Sabbath finished recorded their new album, but as the talk about touring to support it began, Bill Ward began drinking again. Realizing he couldn't handle the rigors of going back on the road, he gave his notice and left Black Sabbath...again.

"This is a great package, something I could sell in America." – Don Arden

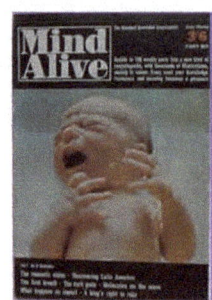  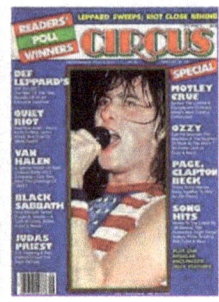

The magazine that artist Steve Joule based the BORN AGAIN cover on. The addition of Ian Gillan gave Black Sabbath a big-name vocalist and larger-than-life personality who was always quotable. In the MTV era, Black Sabbath found themselves in a good position.

The Hungry Look In Your Eye

This could be a chapter all by itself because the cover is so... well... there! First of all, let me just say I love the album sleeve and always have! It is beyond shocking in design and color scheme and does the job perfectly. It brings you in and makes you talk about it. On the record and department store shelves, there was a red devil baby with bright yellow fangs and claws and green eyes on a purple background that just demanded, "Buy Me Now!" and of course, I did. As a teenage Baptist kid, the album's cover caused a few comments from my parents, who said I could buy it as long as it was with my own money and it would not on display for everyone to see. Knowing my albums were all in alphabetical order and by release dates... it was something I could easily agree on.

Based on an image from a British magazine from 1969 called MIND ALIVE, artist/photographer Steve "Krusher" Joule created the Satanic image not expecting it to get used, but Tony Iommi liked the picture and approved it for the cover. In 1982, Joule was the art director of the British magazine, KERRANG!, and before working with Black Sabbath he created visuals for some of my favorite bands like The Sex Pistols, Motorhead, and Uriah Heep. Having designed record sleeves for Ozzy including DIARY OF A MADMAN, SPEAK OF THE DEVIL, and the then-current, BARK AT THE MOON, it seemed to be an obvious ploy by manager Don Arden to pull one over on his daughter and Ozzy. As Joule has recounted, he didn't want to lose the gig with Ozzy, so he submitted several horrible ideas, one being the Devil Baby, that, surprise!, got accepted for the album's cover. The cover for BORN AGAIN has gone on to be considered unjustly one of the worst album covers ever, along with Uriah Heep's ABOMINOG, and I can understand why. I can also see why it is loved by so many people, including me.

"I saw the cover then puked. Then I heard the record and puked." – Ian Gillan

She Looks So Happy

Black Sabbath released their 11th studio album, BORN AGAIN, on August 7, 1983, through Vertigo worldwide except North America (Warner Bros. Records). The world patiently waited to hear what Ian Gillan would bring to the world of Black Sabbath and vice versa, but when we finally heard the finished product, we all knew something was wrong. Dead wrong! For whatever reason, somewhere between the mixing and mastering process, the sound became quite dull and very muted. Vocals, drums, guitar, bass, and keyboards all seem to be mixed at the same level, not giving the music any depth or a chance to live and breathe. As the negative reviews began to see print, the poor sound quality was all anyone really focused on. Well, that and the cover.

The new line-up became big news and saw the band inside magazines like HIT PARADER, CIRCUS, KERRANG, and even the lighter FACES with in-depth coverage. On MTV, the video for Trashed was being played and Ian, Tony, and Geezer were even on with Mark Goodman for interviews. Despite the less-than-stellar reviews and what the fans may have thought, BORN AGAIN did pretty good business in the US, going to #39 and did amazing in the UK, going #4 on the charts. This was their highest UK chart since SABBATH BLOODY SABBATH in 1973 and may have had a lot more to do with the very popular Gillan being the voice on the album.

"I was the worst singer Black Sabbath ever had. It was totally, totally incompatible with any music they'd ever done. I think the fans probably were in a total state of confusion." – Ian Gillan

You'll Be Born Again

As the years have gone on, I feel that time has been less kind to this album than most. Songs I loved when it was first released don't resonate at all with me, and tracks I didn't like, I absolutely love now.

The first single and song on the album is pure Ian Gillan, *Trashed*. The best song on the album, this is a tale about speed, drinking, and the consequences of the action. Lyrically, Gillan does what he best, just tells a story as it happens. The heaviness of Iommi's riff, the thunder of Butler, and the beats of Ward make this the gem of the album.

Not much to say about *Stonehenge*. It's an instrumental track (mostly keyboards) that is moody and just sets up the next song. The song is so much better in its longer (over four minutes) form found on THE MANOR TAPES.

One of those songs I loved as a kid but as an old man not so much is *Disturbing The Priest*. It feels like an attempt to make a Black Sabbath song with Deep Purple's singer. At times, like the chaotic intro, it's pure Black Sabbath. Sounds of hell greet you, but then during the verses and the chorus it is very Gillan/Purple, just with evil lyrics. It does contain the amazing siren scream of Gillan, but musically it begins to sound like Def Leppard, and never gains any traction.

"I watched this incredible transformation of this man (Gillan) that delicately put lyrics together." – Bill Ward

Another instrumental is *The Dark*... a brief introduction to the next song...*Zero The Hero*, which got better for me with age. Beginning with a nice, fat Iommi riff, the band sets the tone and pacing of this mid-tempo song. With big keyboards throughout, this is the most like Black Sabbath we get on the album. It was the only song I could hear Ozzy singing because it has a very '70's lyric to it. The screaming solos and Ward's military drum tempo really keep my interest for over 7 minutes.

"I thought Zero The Hero was a good track and I'm not the only one who likes it." – Tony Iommi

Another pure rocker, *Digital Bitch* is another one that is more Ian Gillan than Black Sabbath. If you didn't know this about Gillan, he can write a lyric very quick and improvises all the time. His lyrics are about women, cars, sex, and more women, and despite the awesome soloing by Iommi, this song is another one that doesn't feel like Sabbath. Not saying it isn't a good song, because it's great. It's just not Sabbath.

The title track *Born Again* is, for lack of a better word, the ballad on this album. It is incredibly bluesy and contains more Gillan screams among the self-reflective vocals. When I first got the album, I thought and hoped the scary title track would reflect the scary cover somehow. Nope! Just a ballad that also includes bongos! Born

Again is about a new life, and very close to something Gillan would record on his own.

"I think Ian is an excellent performer, and often at times I think his lyrics can be brilliant. But I just have a personal difference in what I like to hear in the way of lyrics, and so I felt terribly disconnected." – Bill Ward

    For some reason, I neglected *Hot Line* in 1983, but after giving it a listen in 2020, wow...did I miss a special song. This one was written for the time persiod, with its AC/DC driving rhythm and simplistic drums that fit the song so well. Another un-Sabbath song, the solo is pure Iommi and maybe would have been a better choice for the album's first single. With what radio was playing regarding hard rock in 1983, this fits in perfectly.
    A very Deep Purple-sounding song, *Keep It Warm* isn't a very good song, except the chorus, which isn't complicated at all. This is another song, lyrically, that sounds like Ian Gillan song and not Black Sabbath. It's got a nice solo and heavy percussion from Ward during a cool time change, but ends the album with a "what?" more than a whimper. Confusing. Listen and see.

"I joined Black Sabbath by mistake." – Ian Gillan

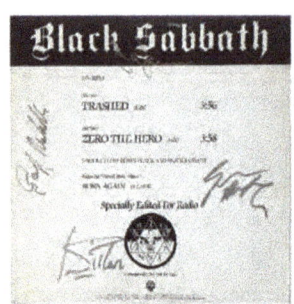

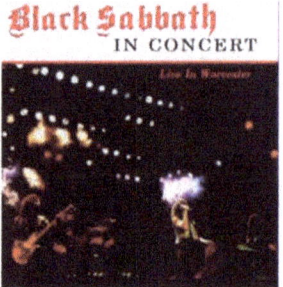

An incredibly rare promo for Trashed/Zero The Hero autographed by Tony Iommi, Geezer Butler, Ian Gillan, and Geoff Nicholls, sent by Patrick Kalmeyer (Netherlands). Two live recordings from the Ian Gillan-led Black Sabbath from Reading '83 and Worcester, MA.

It's Easy And Breezy To You

    Before the band could hit the road, they needed a new drummer, and in stepped Bev Bevan from the Electric Light Orchestra, a fellow Brummie. Following a small tour of the UK, Black Sabbath did a major tour of the US, playing just under 100 shows from August 1983 to March 1984. The tour did solid business and sold out a string of shows that had the hottest band in America opening, Quiet Riot, which was beginning to make a huge jump on the charts. The setlist included a large helping of songs from BORN AGAIN, including *Hot Line, Trashed, Zero The Hero,* and *Disturbing The Priest.* Among the classics only two from the Dio era were performed, *Heaven And Hell* and *Neon Knights*. For Gillan, they would perform his most well-known song from his Deep Purple days, *Smoke On The Water*. This wasn't a popular move with hardened Sabbath fans, but as a huge ELO fan, I wondered what song they could have gotten away with? *Do Ya?*
    I finally got to see Black Sabbath on this tour in New Haven, CT, on November 8, 1983. I was blown away by the volume of the music and how big the stage set was, complete with massive Stonehenge stones that couldn't be used at many arenas due to the size. My parents let me go to the show in New Haven and told me I wasn't allowed to get a shirt with the devil baby on it. Sucks, but If I ever wanted to go to another concert again, I had to listen. I was able to find a baseball jersey style with the LIVE EVIL cover on it, so that was good. A few years ago, I found a devil baby shirt and of course I bought it. Quiet Riot opened the show and

holy cow... they were amazing and such high energy!!! Someone burned a flag hanging on the wall during *Smoke On The Water* and I thought we were all going to die.

In an interview I did with Quiet Riot's Frankie Banali in 2019, I told him how, even as a young kid, I saw the changing of the guard at that show, from the old school rockers to the new kids on the block. He told me how much that tour meant to him personally, playing with his heroes. He said that he could sense the change was in the air, too.

"That tour was so much fun and Black Sabbath were so good to us." – Franke Banali (Quiet Riot)

Following a very successful world tour that ended on March 4, 1984, in Springfield, MA, Ian Gillan would, as expected, leave Black Sabbath and rejoin the Mark II line-up of Deep Purple for a highly anticipated reunion tour. Working through all of the legalities, Gillan would join Richie Blackmore and Roger Glover, who closed shop with Rainbow, Jon Lord, who said goodbye to Whitesnake, and Ian Paice, who bid farewell to Gary Moore. They met up in Stowe, Vermont, to work on their first album together in eleven years, PERFECT STRANGERS. Many say Gillan did this album and tour purely to elevate his profile in the US before a Deep Purple reunion, and that sounds about right.

Following the tour, drummer Bev Bevan would rejoin the Electric Light Orchestra for their last album for a while, 1986's BALANCE OF POWER. In 1987, Bevan would make a short return to Black Sabbath.

The Growing Family

Ozzy Osbourne, who was starting the next phase of his solo career, and Ronnie James Dio, were both in need of guitarists. The search gave them many quality prospects. Also looking for players was Graham Bonnet, putting together a new band and Phil Mogg, who was resurrecting UFO. Among those in the conversations was Yngwie Malmsteen (who would go with Bonnet's Alcatrazz) and Atomik Tommy M (who would join Mogg in UFO). George Lynch (Dokken) would spend a few months on the road prepared to step in as soon as Brad Gillis was finished with live dates. Unfortunately, before Lynch would hit the stage or studio with Ozzy, he would be fired right in front of his replacement, Jake E. Lee. Lee was hired by Dio but would leave, audition for Ozzy, and get the coveted job. Following this horrible time for Lynch, he would return to Dokken and make some of the best music ever until their many break-ups, beginning in 1988. Also now playing with Ozzy was bassist Don Costa, who was a member of Dante Fox (the band that would become Great White) and W.A.S.P. Costa played with a cheese grater, cutting his flesh as he played and becoming a bloody mess... just what Ozzy needed. Before Osbourne's appearance at the US Festival on May 29th, Costa and Ozzy had an altercation about something (the press and participants tell many different stories) with Ozzy head-butting Costa and breaking his nose, resulting in a lawsuit filed and won by Costa. He would be officially fired on the grounds of the US Festival and be replaced by Bob Daisley.

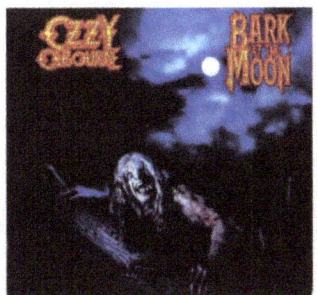 

The highly anticipated third album from Ozzy Osbourne, BARK AT THE MOON, featuring the debut of guitarist Jake E. Lee! Pictured above are the legendary Don Airey (Black Sabbath/Rainbow/MSG/Ozzy Osbourne/Deep Purple) and the equally legendary Brent Hoag!

They Say I Worship The Devil

With all band spots filled, Ozzy and the band went into the studio to record album number three. Released on December 9, 1983, BARK AT THE MOON (Epic/CBS), was another album filled with soon-to-be classic songs but had a more refined sound to it thanks to the production team of Max Norman, Ozzy Osbourne, and Bob Daisley. Daisley was also co-producing.

Knowing his many talents, Osbourne almost had to bring back Daisley to help with not only the bass and production but the songwriting. Jake E. Lee would make his presence felt right away in the recordings with his tones, emotional play, and lightning-fast leads on songs like the title track, *You're No Different*, and *Slow Down*. Despite the heaviness of the album, except for *So Tired*, BARK AT THE MOON was heavily dominated by the keyboards of Don Airey, which was a sign of the times. Drums on the album were played by Tommy Aldridge, who would leave the band before the album's release, being replaced by the legendary Carmine Appice.

"So, I did the first five months of the BARK AT THE MOON tour when I got canned. Sharon, she told me, 'Your name is too big, we want more of a sideman like Tommy Aldridge.'" - Carmine Appice

Songwriting credit for the entire album is given to Ozzy Osbourne alone, something everyone knew couldn't be true. This would be a major issue for Lee, who claimed co-writing credits, along with Daisley, on most, if not all, of the tracks. This was a back-door deal to give Ozzy all the publishing rights, where the real money is made, paying Lee and Daisley lump sum payments for their songwriting.

BARK AT THE MOON would do very well, going to #19 in the US, #24 in the UK, and #23 in Canada. The album would have two singles and videos released, *Bark At The Moon* and *So Tired*. Another successful world tour would ensue with the usual craziness, abetted by opening act Mötley Crüe. Many crazy things would happen and legendary tales have been told. Just read THE DIRT for more. Not surprisingly, Appice would be asked to leave the tour a few months in due to ego clashes with Osbourne and management, replaced by a returning Tommy Aldridge. I could never understand why a major player like Carmine Appice would join Ozzy. I never thought it would last, and I was right! Appice would go on to start the band King Cobra, which would be remembered for everyone in the band being bleached blonde (except for Appice, of course) and a pretty solid debut album, READY TO STRIKE (Capitol Records/ EMI). Following the tour, only Jake E. Lee would be left.

"I can't even fart without someone saying it caused their cat to jump in a fire." – Ozzy Osbourne

Visually a stunning cover for DIO's debut, HOLY DIVER is open for so much interpretation and is the subject of a comic book in 2021.

Maybe It's Just What You Need

With drummer Vinny Appice, Ronnie James Dio set out to create his own band, his own image, and his own destiny! With a record deal in hand, Dio set out to put together the perfect band that would share in his vision and be team players. On bass, Dio looked to his Rainbow past and Jimmy Bain, a solid player who Dio knew quite well and played with him on the majestic RAINBOW RISING. Losing out on Jake E. Lee, Dio came across Irish player Vivian Campbell, who was in the band Sweet Savage. That band was beginning to make a push in the UK. With a little coaxing and promises of bigger and better, Campbell was no longer a sweet savage and now the line-up for DIO was complete!

Put together rather quickly, HOLY DIVER (Warner Bros. in the US, Vertigo in the UK, and Mercury everywhere else), hit metal fans hard, right between the eyes! Dio fans knew what a talent he was, but no one (including me) expected the album to be so good and contain such epic music. *Straight Through The Heart, Holy Diver, Rainbow In The Dark*, and the anthemic *Stand Up And Shout* were loud, melodic, and full of lyrics that made the imagination soar. The performances by the band made this one of the best metal albums ever. Even non-rock radio tracks like Gypsy, and, especially, *Caught In The Middle*, are so well crafted. The cover would feature a controversial picture of a priest being thrown over a rocky cliff into the water in chains by the band's mascot, Murray. Dio would defend the album sleeve perfectly saying, "who is the bad guy, the priest or the devil?" Kinda makes you think, eh? Also, when the band's logo is viewed upside down, you can see (or maybe you can't) the word 'DEVIL' spelled out in the inverted DIO logo. DIO's debut, HOLY DIVER, would go impressively to #56 in the US and #13 in the UK and contain two videos, *Holy Diver* and *Rainbow In The Dark*, that would see mild rotation on MTV and other video channels.

"There were so many good songs – almost all of them are great songs." – Ronnie James Dio

Final Thoughts On "Born, Bark and Diver"

When it comes to who would finish on top in 1983, sales-wise, chart positions and overall good will, BARK AT THE MOON took the title. Despite the high chart showing in the UK for BORN AGAIN, the album never seemed to get any traction and faded as fast as it arrived. The album that has the most sustainability almost 40 years later is DIO's HOLY DIVER. All these years later, it's a go-to album for me whenever I really want to feel something special and magical! It's deep, full of melody, and rocks like nobody's business!

With the verbal/dwarf battles still underway, it was Sabbath manager Don Arden, who was also Ozzy Osbourne's father-in-law now that he was married to Sharon Arden, that made the worst of all comments. According to Ozzy, Arden would joke that the BORN AGAIN devil baby reminded him of his grandchildren. Wow.

In 1983, I really loved BORN AGAIN. Yes, a lot had to do with the super-cool cover, but the music was so heavy, especially Trashed! At the time, I knew something was up with the mix because everything sounded so flat, especially compared to the other music I was listening to at the time. But, in 2004, a remastered version came out, and when I began to listen, wow... I didn't like it like I used to. In fact, the song I never liked (Hot Line) became a song I really liked. Sadly, BORN AGAIN ends up a few spots from the end, #16 out of 19 studio albums and I give it a very weak 4 out of 10 with most of the points going to the cover. BUT, from the votes on the Black Sabbath Facebook groups, the album was rated at #11 out of 19.

  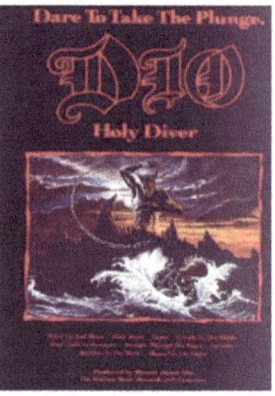

Once upon a time, Black Sabbath had to compare their success (and failures) against one former vocalist - now there were two!

Mr. Not Scary - George Lynch (Dokken/Lynch Mob)

George Lynch (above at the Wolf Den at Mohegan Sun in Uncasville, CT, on March 15, 2018) has an interesting history in the world of Black Sabbath! In 1979, he was runner-up to Randy Rhodes for the job with Ozzy Osbourne and then in 1983 had the job until Jake E. Lee got it. But, despite the setbacks in this story, George Lynch has had an amazing career with Dokken, Lynch Mob, KXM (and a crap-ton of other bands) and is one of the greatest and most expressive guitarists in rock/metal history.

www.georgelynch.com

LIVE AID
JULY 13, 1985

"We took an issue that was nowhere on the political agenda and, through the lingua franca of the planet – which is not English but rock 'n' roll – we were able to address the intellectual absurdity and the moral repulsion of people dying of want in a world of surplus." – Bob Geldof

1984-1985

Before we talk about LIVE AID and the day music tried to change the world (I think it did a great job), let's catch up with Black Sabbath and its expanding family following the BORN AGAIN tour. After the last Black Sabbath show in Springfield, MA, it was announced that Ian Gillan would be leaving Black Sabbath to join the Mark II line-up of Deep Purple for an album and tour cycle that turned out to be quite lucrative. Following sessions in Stowe, Vermont, Deep Purple unleashed the fantastic and amazing PERFECT STRANGERS from Polydor on October 29, 1984. Featuring the best Deep Purple songs ever, *Knocking At Your Back Door, Nobody's Home, Perfect Strangers,* and *Wasted Sunsets*, it is a landmark album and one of their best. If anyone wondered how the world would respond to the return of a classic line-up from a classic band, the answer is very well. The album went to #12 in the US, #5 in the UK, #22 in Canada, and Top 10 in 8 other countries including #1 in Switzerland, Norway, and Sweden. The world tour was a sell-out and a massive success. Well done, lads!

"The rumors of a $2-million-dollar advance for the album were grossly exaggerated." – Ian Gillan

Ozzy Osbourne spent December of 1983 until July of 1984 on the road supporting another hit album, BARK AT THE MOON. Opening shows for Ozzy were L.A.'s latest and greatest, Motley Crue, who Ozzy first saw at the US Festival and loved, not to mention the traveling party they brought with them wherever they went. The band was supporting their latest album, SHOUT AT THE DEVIL (#17 in the US and #23 in Canada), on Elektra Records. It would go multi-platinum and help fuel the band's well-documented, out-of-control lifestyle. Another up-and-coming L.A. band, Ratt (Jake E. Lee's former band) would do a month of shows with Ozzy in April of 1984, just days after the release of their debut album, OUT OF THE CELLAR. The Atlantic Records release would go to #7 in the US and #12 in Canada and make Ratt a darling of MTV, helping to usher in the era of melodic metal.

Following several festivals in the fall/winter of 1984, Ozzy and his band played their final show of the tour in January 1985, Rock In Rio, in Rio de Janeiro, Brazil. The Sunday event featured AC/DC, Scorpions, and Whitesnake, along with Ozzy and several local bands. Following the show, the current band would implode again with Tommy Aldridge walking away and Daisley and Airey rejoining Gary Moore, again leaving Ozzy and Jake E. Lee holding the flag. Interesting to note that following the same show, Cozy Powell would leave Whitesnake, almost ending the band right there. There must have been something in the water. Following the tour, Ozzy would have a few more public and private moments due to drugs and alcohol, and would check into the famed Betty Ford Center to undergo treatment for substance abuse. There must have been a million times during this time when Jake E. Lee thought, "I could have been with Dio and sanity" and George Lynch must have thanked God for Ozzy not picking him.

"It was time for a change. Tommy (Aldridge) and I are still good friends. We just decided to each do different things. He is working in a new band with Rudy Sarzo." – Ozzy Osbourne

DIO (the band) put their heads down to follow a regimented recording/touring schedule that would see them become one of the biggest acts on the Metal scene. On July 2, 1984, DIO released their second album, THE LAST IN LINE (Warner Bros./Vertigo Records), which would go to #23 in the US, #4 in the UK, and #51 in Canada. DIO was now receiving substantial media coverage as well as video play for the title track and Mystery (one of the all-time favorite DIO songs) on MTV. The album cover again features the band's mascot, Murray, overlooking an Egyptian-themed scene with slaves building something for their oppressors. The cover and its themes would feature heavily in the band's stage set, highlighted by the song Egypt (The Chains Are On). The band, consisting of Vivian Campbell (guitar), Jimmy Bain (bass), and Vinny Appice (drums), would be joined by keyboardist Claude Schnell, who while adding a nice flavor to the Dio sound did not excite all DIO fans. Musically, the band was all on the same page, but behind the scenes guitarist Vivian Campbell was becoming quite disgruntled by certain things promised to him.

While DIO was working on their next album, Jimmy Bain, RJD, and Vivian Campbell would put together the metal community's support of famine relief for Africa. With the hard rock world left out of the star-studded USA For Africa, the ambitious project started with a song, *Stars*, and ended with a whose-who of hard rock/heavy metal artists in a freakin' cool video. Featured vocal performances were by RJD, Don Dokken, Eric Bloom (Blue Oyster Cult), Dave Meniketti (Y & T), and so many others along with guitar solos by everyone who was anyone including Yngwie Malmsteen and George Lynch. In total, more than forty rockers helped raise over 1 million dollars for charity. By the time the Hear 'N' Aid single, album, and video were released, it would be January of 1986.

"It's too bad they (Black Sabbath) didn't have time for Hear 'N' Aid." – Ronnie James Dio

In 1985, DIO would return with another strong album, SACRED HEART (Warner Bros./Vertigo Records). Despite being full of amazing songs like *Hungry For Heaven, Rock 'N' Roll Children*, and *Another Lie*, the album, released on August 15, 1985, didn't set the world on fire, but not because of the quality of the music. The scene in 1985 was being dominated by the first wave of hair bands and DIO had a lot of competition for consumer dollars. The cover was classic RJD, featuring a pair of hands holding a crystal ball with a dragon inside. By the time the band hit the road, the relationship between Dio and Campbell was becoming quite toxic and the young guitarist was fired midway through the tour. Brought in was former Giuffria guitarist Craig Goldie, who would finish the tour and begin writing for the new album.

"There was a lot of tension in the studio. No one wanted to be there..." – Vivian Campbell

And now back to our regularly scheduled Black Sabbath! As it appeared to be all gold and platinum for the now three ex-Black Sabbath vocalists, the same couldn't be said for the band they left behind. In 1984, Bill Ward was coaxed back into the band again, giving them a much-needed bit of credibility by having Black Sabbath consist of three out of four original members. The band went through hundreds of tapes and several hopefuls made it to the audition stage with varying levels of success.

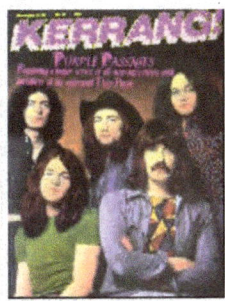

All three former Black Sabbath vocalists moving on to bigger and better things, including the covers of the leading rock magazines.

Sunset Strip fixture Ron Keel came in and recorded several demos with the band. Formerly of Steeler, the band broke up when guitarist Yngwie Malmsteen left to join Graham Bonnet's new band Alcatrazz. While recording demos for the first Keel album with Spenser Proffer, the tapes got in the hands of Iommi and Butler. The band was working with Proffer, who was the hot name in metal music due to the success of Quiet Riot. Iommi and Butler thought Keel would be a great fit for the band and spent time working on new music. Unfortunately, Proffer was looking to turn Sabbath into an '80's metal band complete with outside writers and MTV-friendly music, as he did with Quiet Riot. When that plan fell apart, so did the deal with Ron Keel. Keel (the man) would continue to record with Keel (the band) and the band would release their debut album LAY DOWN THE LAW (Shrapnel Records) later that year. To hear how Ron Keel would have fit with Black Sabbath, listen to him on the Black Sabbath tribute album, EMERALD SABBATH, especially his version of *Die Young*. It rocks pretty hard.

"My time with Tony and Geezer was limited to three days of hanging out in LA getting to know each other and making plans. One thing we all agreed on was that we couldn't let Spencer Proffer turn such an iconic metal institution like Black Sabbath into a commercial '80's hair band, which he was attempting to do by pushing the band to record material that was radio-friendly." – Ron Keel

Another vocal-hopeful that even got a photoshoot was another L.A. based singer, Dave Donato. Vocally and image-wise, Donato had the hair metal vibe going and a great voice, but his pipes were a little less aggressive than desired, closer to Ian Gillan with a bit higher range. During the audition process, a photographer took pictures of the band with Donato, published them in KERRANG magazine, and the world assumed he was the new guy. Well, he wasn't the guy, and would be told so. Audio of Donato singing an early version of *The Shining* exists and you can hear exactly where his voice would have fallen in the range of Black Sabbath vocalists. Following his brief time with Sabbath, Donato would go on to form White Tiger with ex-Kiss guitarist Mark St. John, and the band would release their one and only album in 1986.

"It all seems to be going smoothly. I always had a picture of what the right singer in Sabbath should be, and it was me!" – Dave Donato

Finding nothing but frustration in this process, Bill Ward and Geezer Butler both walked away with Ward proclaiming "this isn't Black Sabbath." Now with only Iommi left, there was no more Black Sabbath and he turned his eyes on putting together a new Black Sabbath or a solo album. To help in the studio, Iommi brought in Lita Ford's drummer Eric Singer (born May 12, 1958) and bassist Gordon Copley to help put new music together and audition possible vocalists. At the time, Ford and Iommi were engaged and Iommi was producing her next solo album, THE BRIDE WORE BLACK, which was never released. The two would break up not long after their engagement, citing Iommi's now out-of-control cocaine use, abuse, and his pilfering of Ford's band.

"Dave Donato seemed to look alright and whatever else, and seemed to be okay, but it was just auditions. We never actually had him in, as a part of the band." – Tony Iommi

Up next was another American, Jeff Fenholt. Like their last singer (Ian Gillan), Fenholt also played Jesus in JESUS CHRIST SUPERSTAR and recorded several demos with the band. He seemed to have the job almost locked down, but an argument with manager Don Arden sealed his fate and he was no longer involved with the project. Fenholt went on to work in an early version of Driver, the supergroup featuring ex-Ozzy members Rudy Sarzo and Tommy Aldridge (more on them a bit later). Fenholt would clean up his life and re-devote his life to his Christian faith, record several Christian albums, and then become a very popular evangelist. Jeff Fenholt's time with Iommi can be heard on the must-have bootleg, STAR OF INDIA, including the most impressive track, *The Eye Of The Storm*, which is very Glenn Hughes-sounding.

"I cut a couple of demos with Jeff Fenholt in LA. Of course, these demos got out and found their way onto a bootleg album. Jeff seemed a nice enough guy. It might have worked with him, even though I wasn't 100 percent convinced that he'd be able to do our older stuff." – Tony Iommi

THE DAY MUSIC CHANGED THE WORLD
IN LONDON AND PHILADELPHIA

Bob Geldof began to plan a mega-concert that would raise money to help save the starving people in Africa. Beginning with the holiday single, *Do They Know It's Christmas*, by Band Aid, the Boomtown Rats vocalist envisioned a day-long concert beamed all over the world that would feature the biggest names in music, past and present. As momentum began to build, the concert was becoming the biggest event of the year. Where once Geldof had a hard time collecting credible acts for the "Global Jukebox," everyone who was anyone was looking to be involved. With simultaneous concerts to be performed in London's Wembley Arena and Philadelphia's JFK Stadium, beamed to the entire world, it would embrace music, raise money, and save lives. It didn't matter the genre, style, color, country of origin, or how old you were, you wanted to be on one of those stages. For me, and almost everyone who saw Live Aid, it was Queen who stole the event. It was also a visual introduction to U2, who I had only just discovered. It was even reported, and would happen, that Led Zeppelin was reforming with drummers Phil Collins and Tony Thompson (Chic) and bassist Paul Martinez. But, the biggest news for this book was the word that Ozzy Osbourne, Tony Iommi, Geezer Butler, and Bill Ward would be reuniting for at least 15 minutes.

"C'mon... clap your f@#$%i' hands!" – Ozzy Osbourne

On this day, July 13, 1985, Black Sabbath didn't exist! Ozzy, fresh out of rehab, hadn't been on a stage in almost 7 months, Ward was working on his sobriety, Butler had put together his own band, and, with the frustration from not finding a singer (and losing Butler), Iommi had put Sabbath to rest and began work on a solo album.

The four former members all met in a rehearsal room, chatted a bit, and caught up, but there were obvious tensions, especially between Osbourne and Iommi. With Ozzy's solo career much bigger than ever, there was no denying who the star and focal point was. Still, the band put their best foot forward even though they did go on stage with an added bit of venom, at least from Ozzy. Before hitting the stage, Ozzy was served papers NOT to appear as part of Black Sabbath, yet another legal battle between father and daughter. Ozzy took it very personally but hit the stage at RFK Stadium with fire and vengeance. The band was introduced by comedian Chevy Chase, whose awkward banter let the fans in attendance knew who, and what, was coming!

"Ladies and gentlemen... Black Sabbath featuring Ozzy Osbourne!" – Chevy Chase

Despite what the members thought of the performance, they were brilliant and really made people remember the power of Black Sabbath! Three songs, no soundcheck, and at 10 in the morning (a very non-rock n roll hour). Everything could have gone wrong...but it didn't. Starting with *Children Of The Grave*, then into *Iron Man*, and finishing with *Paranoid*. This left a worldwide audience quite happy. For me, an hour before Sabbath hit the tube, I was dumped by my girlfriend of over 16 months and couldn't quite enjoy the reunion, or the day, or the next year of my life. At RFK Stadium, Black Sabbath was followed by New York rappers Run-DMC, who were just beginning a nice ride to the top of the charts. Seeing Black Sabbath was a thrill for Darryl McDaniels, who grew up a huge fan!

"We were all drunk when we did Live Aid, but we'd all got drunk separately."- Geezer Butler

A real impressive live debut from the Geezer Butler Band called LIVE AT THE MARQUEE CLUB 1985. The originals on the disc are pretty good and certainly reflective of the '80's metal of the day. This was Geezer's first attempt at putting Black Sabbath behind him for good.

THE BUTLER DID IT

With the world of Black Sabbath in complete disarray, Geezer Butler left the Live Aid stage, never to return to the band. As Tony Iommi worked on his first solo album (that would become SEVENTH STAR), Butler decided to start from scratch and create his own band with the original name The Geezer Butler Band. The band's original line-up featured Butler on bass, keyboardist Gezz Woodroffe on keyboards, Black Sabbath-hopeful Jeff Fenholt on vocals, Gary Ferguson on drums, and Pedro House on guitar. The band would record a rather uninspired three-song demo featuring originals *Lock Myself Away*, *Don't Turn Away*, and *Love Has No Mercy*, but get no interest from any labels. One by one, the line-up would change by the time the band hit the stage at the Marquee Club in London on November 29th, 1985. On that night, Butler would present an impressive band featuring himself, House, drummer John Mee, and the impressive Richie

Callison on vocals. Their sound (as heard on the bootleg LIVE AT THE MARQUEE CLUB 1985) is more in line with the modern metal bands than Black Sabbath. Live, the band had a lot of flash, heaviness, and talent that can be heard on this rather primitive recording, with House sounding like the next guitar hero. With a real focus on original songs like *Patrol* and *Looking Back*, the band certainly had to dip into the Sabbath catalog for encores *War Pigs* and *Iron Man*.

THE KING OF ROCK
DARRYL McDANIELS (RUN DMC)

When I first met Darryl McDaniels in 2017 (the DMC of RUN DMC), I thought all we were going to talk about were the golden days of Run DMC, the way their music broke race and genre barriers, and our mutual love of comic books. What I didn't expect was Darryl to be wearing a Black Sabbath shirt, and, following the interview, we spent the next 20 minutes talking about the stuff you are reading in this book! The last picture features me, Darryl, and the cover artist for this book, Andrew Edge. Before playing Live Aid in 1985, RUN DMC played The Ritz in New York City and their next show in San Francisco, CA, at the Warfield. This was a big show for the group!

www.dmccomics.com

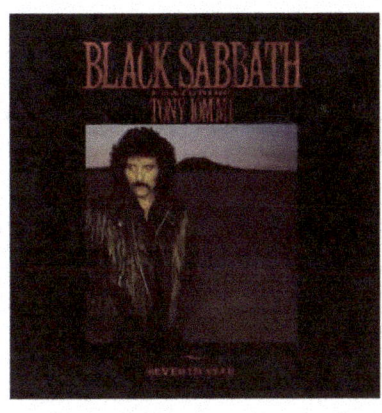 

SEVENTH STAR (Vertigo/Warner Bros. Records)
Released on January 28,1986 (North America) and February 27, 1986 (Europe)
Produced by Jeff Glixman
Glenn Hughes (vocals), Tony Iommi (guitar), Dave Spitz (bass), Geoff Nicholls (keyboards) and Eric Singer (drums)
All songs written by Iommi, Hughes, Nicholls and Glixman

IN FOR THE KILL
NO STRANGER TO LOVE
TURN TO STONE
SPHINX (THE GUARDIAN)
SEVENTH STAR

DANGER ZONE
HEART LIKE A WHEEL
ANGRY HEART
IN MEMORY...

"It seemed to be the band was on its last legs and my heart just went out to Tony." – Bill Ward

LIVING ON THE STREETS

Black Sabbath was no more! Tired of trying to fight to keep the band together and find a vocalist that would fit what the band was about, Tony Iommi decided that his next album would be a solo record, and why not? Geezer Butler and Bill Ward weren't coming back! Ozzy Osbourne, Ronnie James Dio, and even Ian Gillan left Black Sabbath to achieve bigger and better, so why not he? He also noticed that Black Sabbath was even being lapped by former members of Ozzy's solo band like Rudy Sarzo (Quiet Riot) and Brad Gillis (Night Ranger), who were out-selling Sabbath by a lot, a real lot. Now living full-time in California, Iommi was working hard on the material and at the same time destroying his relationship with Lita Ford due to his growing cocaine addiction.

Writing with Geoff Nicholls and producer Jeff Glixman (of Kansas fame), the guitarist's plan was to have several different vocalists perform on the album, including Judas Priest's Rob Halford, Ronnie James Dio, and Glenn Hughes, who had spent his post-Deep Purple career moving from project to project with not a lot of commercial success. Following the break-up of the criminally underrated Hughes/Thrall duo following one killer album in 1982, Hughes went to work with Gary Moore on the RUN FOR COVER album. His near-crippling addiction got the best of him and he was fired from the high-profile project that could have put Hughes back on the map. Due to his issues and unreliability, he was relegated to only a few vocal appearances and was embarrassed by Moore in the UK press, something that really brought the singer closer to rock bottom. In 1985, he was the lone vocalist on the all-star collective Phenomena, who released a fantastic album that to me is the benchmark of Glenn Hughes' non-Deep Purple career.

I got PHENOMENA before Hurricane Gloria hitting Connecticut and made a cassette copy so if we lost power, I'd still have a copy I could listen to. Well, we did lose power for almost a week and this cassette was all I had to listen to... as I recovered from a broken thumb/wrist due to playing football during the hurricane. Nope, no brains at all.

"Do you have any brains inside that head of yours? It's a hurricane out there and you are playing football? And why are you the only one going to the emergency room?" – Stanley Herring

Hughes and Iommi had known each other for years (both being from the Midlands) and both felt comfortable with each other... and the magic was certainly there. Within a few days, Hughes helped write *No Stranger To Love, Seventh Star*, and *Danger Zone*, encouraging Iommi to continue working with him. Unfortunately, Iommi would find out as their association progressed that although Hughes still possessed the "Voice Of Rock," he had the emotional state and reliability of a full-blown addict. As the rest of the album began to quickly fall into place, Iommi, Hughes, and Nicholls were working with drummer Eric Singer and bassist Dave "The Beast" Spitz (born February 22, 1958). Iommi was feeling confident about the songs, amazed at the performance of Hughes and reinvigorated by Singer and Spitz, who brought youthful enthusiasm and excitement to a venerable metal band that needed a jump-start for its heart.

Unfortunately, Iommi's romantic life and engagement were falling apart, due to drug use, abuse, and the fact that Singer had joined up with Tony, leaving her band. Wanting to find a cheaper place to record, Jeff Glixman recommended that Iommi and Hughes travel to Atlanta to finish up the album, and the two agreed.

"Don Arden told me this was going to be a Black Sabbath album and not a Tony Iommi solo record and I thought, f@#$ me!" – Glenn Hughes

THERE'S NO SHELTER FROM THE HEAT

If this was a Tony Iommi solo album called SEVENTH STAR, then the cover art would make complete sense. It featured an amazing picture of Iommi in the desert with the sun just about to go down (or come up) filling the sky with beautiful colors. As a Black Sabbath album, and not knowing the backstory, it appeared to me (and many others) that Iommi was the last man standing who was looking to get all the credit for keeping things going. There were no photos of the band in the album, just lyrics and gothic style art. This upset me because I wanted to see what the band looked like. When we finally got to see the band in advertisements, they looked a bit off. On one side, Iommi and Nicholls (now a full member) looked as you would expect, and on the other Spitz and Singer appeared to be babies, a full decade younger than Tony and Geoff. In the middle was a bearded and slightly larger Glenn Hughes, wearing a buttoned long coat, obviously trying to hide his physical appearance.

"I wanted to get fresh blood and really get cracking!" – Tony Iommi

So now let's discuss the "featuring." I'm still not quite sure why anyone thought "featuring Tony Iommi" was a good marketing idea. This put an unwanted target on the guitarist's back with everyone thinking Iommi was pushing the fact that there was no Geezer and no Bill here, just Tony Iommi, so finally give him all the credit he deserves. Years later, when I heard the whole story about the intended solo album, I wondered if this was a compromise to appease everyone. It's Black Sabbath! It's Tony Iommi! It's both! But it isn't. And it never could be. Future releases of SEVENTH STAR would just go out as Black Sabbath.

"I wasn't singing it as a Black Sabbath record, I was singing it as a Tony record." – Glenn Hughes

SHE WAS NEVER MEANT TO LAST

SEVENTH STAR was released by Warner Bros in North America and Vertigo everywhere else but Japan (Nippon Phonogram. The album would be released in the US a month before it saw a UK release, and, as expected, the album didn't do that well. In the US, the album would be their worst charter (#78) and the same in the UK (#27) which is a shame, because this album is excellent and falls in my Top Three. By the time Black Sabbath hit the road to support, the album was already falling off the charts.

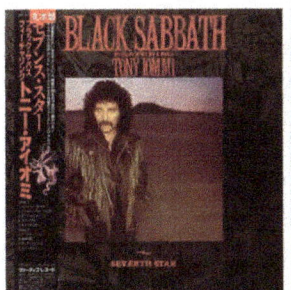 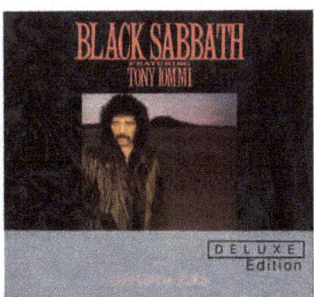 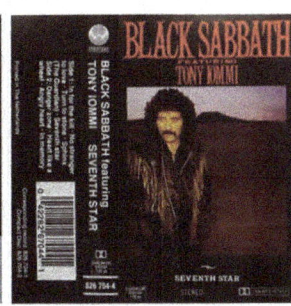

The "featuring Tony Iommi" didn't help the image of the album and fans didn't quite know what to make of the album, CD, or cassette.

Black Sabbath managed to get a video released for the single *No Stranger To Love*. It is a great video for a great song but certainly comes across as a Tony Iommi solo production. Featuring a bit of Glenn Hughes with his bruised face (shadowed out), a little Spitz, a little Singer, no Nicholls, a lot of Denise Crosby (pre-Star Trek: The Next Generation), and a Doberman. Again, nothing to show this as anything other than Iommi being the big fish in the Sabbath pond.

"Not really a big seller. I don't think I even noticed it." – Tony Iommi

I GAVE YOU MY HEART

SEVENTH STAR kicks off with a killer track, *In For The Kill*. Leading the charge is drummer Eric Singer, who has his heavy-hitting prints on every track. Although the spirit of Black Sabbath is present, this song is quite different from what has come before. However, I always thought this was the perfect mix of the Dio and Gillan-era Sabbath sung by the master.

"What started out of a solo project became another Black Sabbath record, although Tony was the only member of Black Sabbath left."- Eric Singer

One of my favorite Black Sabbath songs, *No Stranger To Love* is more a pure blues song than the traditional power ballad. Released as the first single, I always loved the passion and pain in the performance. Here Hughes sings his heart out and gives one of his greatest recorded vocal performances,ever. The video and single version have extra backing vocals provided by Hughes and sound cool, but I'm glad it isn't the album version. It does the song a more soulful lift for .

Another total burner of a song is *Turn To Stone*, a cut that is fully loaded with fire and passion. Here you can feel the Judas Priest influence (especially *Freewheel Burning*) and the straight-ahead bass of Dave Spitz leading the charge. If any song had a chance to cross into mainstream metal, this was it, but it didn't. It has a nice, driving beat with some flashy Iommi leads and again...a lot of Singer.

Sphinx (The Guardian) is a minute and twenty seconds of keyboards that lead into the title track. I would like to say it is a showcase for Geoff Nicholls, but it really is just him holding down a few notes.

Seventh Star is the typical classic Black Sabbath song, very moody and plodding, but with Hughes's voice it makes it less scary and more alive! Every Black Sabbath album needs a *Heaven And Hell* style epic, and on Seventh Star this is it. Possibly my least favorite song on the album, but it still does have its moments. There isn't anything special about this one, and, at times, it just seems to fill space.

"I know everything Geezer ever played. He was the man." – Dave "The Beast" Spitz

Danger Zone starts off with a killer riff and just explodes into melodic metal fury. The song takes another jump with some awesome work from Iommi in the guitar solo as it moves into the bridge, where everything seems to jump a level. This is another one that could have shown Black Sabbath to be as good as anyone else out there. Hughes brings a lot of swagger without sounding forced or fake. Another song that ranks high in my all-time list of Black Sabbath songs for a good reason. It is amazing!

"Sabbath has always been Tony's baby and he's the only one who's kept it going."- Eric Singer

Heart Like A Wheel is a song that I like, but don't love. I feel it just doesn't have the same passion as the others here. It certainly plays into Hughes's vocal style and range, but almost sounds like a song written for strippers to dance to. Maybe it was?

"I thought it would be great to use Glenn on all the songs." – Tony Iommi

Angry Heart is another one of my favorites. It is so up and down, being led by Hughes's amazing vocals and certainly has a Deep Purple feel to it. Finally, Nicholls gets his keyboards into a song and not just as background filler. Iommi's guitar sounds as heavy as on the classics, and this is the perfect mix of Black Sabbath/Deep Purple. Sorry, Ian.

In Memory... is the album's fade-out song. A tender guitar piece with some incredibly dark lyrics just sung over a beautiful melody. Here, you are getting a pure sampling of Hughes's vocals, full of pain, anger, desperation, and sadness. And just like that...the song, the album, and the name Black Sabbath is all over... quite unjustly.

"I lost my voice before the first concert." – Glenn Hughes

DON'T LEAVE ME STANDING HERE

This is where this story has such an ugly ending. It is a wonder Black Sabbath and Glenn Hughes even survived. In the worst shape of his life, spiritually, emotionally, and physically, Glenn Hughes hit the road with Black Sabbath in the US for a massive tour featuring W*A*S*P* and Anthrax in support! The tour started in Michigan on March 18th, and, six shows later in Worcester, MA, Hughes was mercifully fired following the concert and sent back home. It only took a few shows to realize that Hughes's voice, mental state, and inability to perform without his bass would derail the entire tour, so the band had a plan. Bassist Dave Spitz knew a singer who had the vocal chops and attitude to pull off the challenging set and was easy to work with. So, in came New York City native Ray Gillen (born May 12, 1959), who would practice with the band at soundchecks, just waiting to step in.

"I didn't feel comfortable in the Black Sabbath format." – Glenn Hughes

Following a canceled show in Glens Falls, New York, Gillen would hit the stage with the band in New Haven, CT, on March 29, 1986. Not knowing anything that was going on, I was at that show and thought, "Wow, Glenn Hughes looks and sounds amazing." It wasn't until a few days later that I found out the truth. As disappointed as I was, the show was incredible, and Black Sabbath gave a great show with a killer set. Following the insanity of W*A*S*P* and the youthful excitement of Anthrax, Sabbath played everything I wanted to hear at the time, including *The Mob Rules, Children Of The Sea, No Stranger To Love*, and *Neon Knights*.

The SEVENTH STAR tour would continue in the US until May 21, finishing up in Dallas, Texas, before 12 very well-received dates in England. Despite how the tour started, it was certainly ending on a high note, with people really taking notice of the vocal ability and range of Gillen, who could handle the Dio and Ozzy material quite well. Maybe the future was finally looking bright for Black Sabbath?

Looking back at this entire chain of events, I am so thankful that after a few more years of self-destruction, Glenn Hughes was able to clean up and prove that anyone can fix their circumstances if they want to. I am so thankful that after a few more years of self-destruction, Glenn Hughes was able to clean up and prove that anyone can fix their circumstances if they want to. I am also blown away by how Gillen, who was a club singer before this, was able to come in, keep the ship afloat, and help the band save face, because everyone was just waiting for Black Sabbath and the tour to end in ruins.

"I was a mess..."- Glenn Hughes

ALWAYS CREEPING UP ON YOU

While Tony Iommi and Black Sabbath were having trouble getting out of their own way, Ozzy Osbourne seemed to just keep getting stronger and stronger no matter what was thrown in his way. Before anything could happen musically, Ozzy would spend the beginning of the year at the Betty Ford Clinic trying to get better. With Ozzy away, Jake E. Lee and Bob Daisley were cutting demos with drummer Jimmy DeGrasso and working on the material that would be the new Ozzy album, with the working title KILLER OF GIANTS. This time, Lee would refuse to turn over his music unless he was given a contract guaranteeing songwriting credit. With Ozzy now out of rehab and ready to go, he was not happy with the songs put together, and following (another) disagreement over songwriting and due credit, Daisley would be let go. Originally not credited at all, Daisley wouldn't be listed as a songwriter until later pressings of the album. Caught in the constant musical chairs, DeGrasso would also be let go but land on his feet in Y&T, replacing founding member Leonard Haze.

Ozzy Osbourne once again would have another massive hit on his hands with 1986's THE ULTIMATE SIN and hit the road hard! The albums art was done by artist Boris Vallejo, who, among the countless magazine covers, worked with Ted Nugent and Molly Hatchet.

Once again, needing a drummer and bassist, Motley Crue's Tommy Lee found out about Ozzy's drum vacancy while at a party and called his friend, Randy Castillo, who was playing with Lita Ford. Despite having a broken leg sustained in a skiing accident and not able to audition, Ozzy basically took the drummer sight unseen. On bass, Ozzy would select Phil Soussan, who was previously with the band, Wildlife, and following their break-up was working with Jimmy Page in an early version of The Firm. Once Ozzy became interested in Soussan, the bassist had the choice of staying with Page or going with Ozzy, and he chose the Madman! Other than his obvious skills on the bass and solid stage presence, Soussan brought in the song *Shot In The Dark*. Originally credited to Steve and Chris Overland and Soussan, the song had never appeared on any Wildlife albums. By the time Ozzy was done, Overland's credits were gone, and the song was now written by Osbourne and Soussan.

Working with producer Ron Nevison (UFO, The Babys, Led Zeppelin, The Who), Ozzy and the band recorded nine songs for the album now called THE ULTIMATE SIN. Featuring keyboardist Mike Moran, lyrically the songs would be much deeper than previous albums, featuring themes of war and nuclear devastation, but with a commercial feel. Overall, Ozzy wasn't happy with the album. He blamed his dissatisfaction on the production and on Nevison for thinning out the sound. Despite Ozzy's thoughts, THE ULTIMATE SIN (Epic/CBS Associates) released on February 22, 1986, was a hit, led off by the single and video for *Shot In The Dark*. The song was a huge hit, helping to push the album to #6 in the US, #8 in the UK, and #19 in Canada, selling over 2 million copies in the US alone. Ozzy would hit the road for another major tour, and, in the tradition of always having a solid opening act, Metallica was brought along for the ride in support of their latest album, MASTER OF PUPPETS. On the road, Ozzy and Sharon Osbourne were not happy with Jake E. Lee, who was beginning to pull away from everything, and rumors began to circulate that Lee was on his way out. Following the last show of the tour, Lee was fired by Sharon Osbourne on the phone.

"Working with Ron Nevison wasn't enjoyable for me." – Ozzy Osbourne

THE ULTIMATE SIN is an interesting album that is set up and plays like almost every other Ron Nevison production, very controlled and hooks-heavy. There are moments on the album that just explode like the title track, *Shot In The Dark* and *Killer Of Giants*, and then a lot of songs that just seem to be for radio without anything going for therm. This certainly is an album I go in cycles with. Sometimes I love it... other times not so much.

Looking to break in DIO's new guitarist with as little pressure as possible, the band wouldn't release a new album, just this EP.

AND YOU CAN FEEL

Following the firing of Vivian Campbell and bringing in former Rough Cutt/Giuffria guitarist Craig Goldie, DIO finished their roadwork in support of SACRED HEART and began to write material for their next album. In the meantime, the band would issue a live EP, although the running time is longer than most studio albums. The band had hoped to have a double album released to thank the fans and give them something to enjoy as the new album was being put together. Warner Bros. refused to commit to a double-disc but greenlit INTERMISSION, an EP that contained five live songs and one studio track. Featuring the original line-up on stage, the band tears through *Rainbow In The Dark, King of Rock And Roll, Sacred Heart,* and the crowd-pleasing *We Rock*. Also recorded live is the almost 10-minute medley featuring *Rock 'N' Roll Children, Long Live Rock 'N' Roll,* and *Man On The Silver Mountain,* an amazing musical journey through some moments that young DIO fans may have never heard before.

"The unfortunate thing to me is DIO never made a live album and that was an opportunity well missed, not missed by us but missed by the record company." – Ronnie James Dio

To introduce fans to the new DIO featuring Dio, Goldie, bassist Jimmy Bain, drummer Vinny Appice, and keyboardist Claude Schnell, is the mid-tempo studio track, *Time To Burn*. From the first listen I loved this song and thought Goldie did an incredible job stepping in for my then-current favorite guitarist, the departed Vivian Campbell. Lyrically, the song is one of Ronnie James Dio's most inspiring. It's a song of hope in a time of despair and fear. It wasn't a burner of a song but they all don't have to be. INTERMISSION wouldn't do great on the charts, going to #70 in the US, #22 in the UK, and #85 in Canada, but it would keep the band in the hearts and minds of the fans while they began work on their latest and very important album, due out in the next year. A valid criticism of the recording is that Campbell's live guitar work seems to be a bit muted. But to me, it still sounds amazing.

BLACK SABBATH VS. OZZY VS. DIO...AGAIN

With Black Sabbath starting the year with a great album (despite sales) and a lot of promise, it would fall apart on the road in an epic way. But, in the end, the band would catch itself and right the ship. For Ozzy, the year started in rehab, followed by more line-up shuffles, a successful album, and tour, followed by the firing of guitarist Jake E. Lee. As Heavy Metal was at an all-time high with chart, video, and radio dominance, Black Sabbath and Ozzy were sadly unable to capitalize on this as they should have, and there was a lot of competition out there. Despite DIO not releasing a studio album in 1986, we must throw INTERMISSION into the mix. The Hard Rock and Heavy Metal scene was now dominated by younger bands like Motley Crue, Iron Maiden, Poison, Def Leppard, and Bon Jovi, and 1986 would see a major shift in hard rock music. Taking Black Sabbath's dark image and lyrical content and putting it into overdrive with a heavier and faster approach, the success of the New Big Four, Megadeth, Anthrax, Metallica, and Slayer, was becoming a threat to any band who found themseves ten years after their prime.

As far as sales, chart position, and ticket sales go, Ozzy comes out the winner with THE ULTIMATE SIN. It must have been a bitter pill to swallow for Iommi to have two of his singers out-chart SEVENTH STAR, especially with DIO's INTERMISSION being just a live EP. Things were bleak for Black Sabbath, but with Ray Gillen establishing himself as the voice that could connect Sabbath with the younger generation, the future looked a bit brighter...for now. For me, the clear choice for my favorite album of the three is SEVENTH STAR by a lot! Despite people thinking it wasn't a real Black Sabbath album, it had the band's name on the record, so it is a Black Sabbath album, and a damn good one, too. In an online poll, THE ULTIMATE SIN beat out everyone, taking 53% of the votes, with Black Sabbath getting 31% and DIO getting 16%. I still think THE ULTIMATE SIN has some great music and performances on it, but it can't match the feel of Ozzy's first three, and INTERMISSION could have (should have) been a double-disc, but with only six songs there was no fat, only meat!

I still look at SEVENTH STAR as such an amazing listening experience. The band certainly was fired up and in the mood to create some timeless music, but lofty expectations and drugs derailed this from going any further than it did. Nonetheless, I consider this one my #2 Black Sabbath out of 19 and rate it an easy 9.5 out of 10. The Black Sabbath family who I love dearly completely disagrees with me on this one, only putting it at #14 out of 19. C'mon fans, really give this one a chance.

ALL IN THE FAMILY
LAURENCE COTTLE

Young Laurence Cottle (born August 29, 1955) had little choice as to what his vocation would be. Both he and his brother took piano lessons and when their father urged them to take up a second instrument, young Laurence chose the trombone. His father had his sons performing in a traditional jazz band until it was decided they would become a dance band. Ultimately picking up the bass, Cottle began to create quite a buzz for himself and became a very sought-after session bassist in the UK. Following work with Eric Clapton and The Alan Parson's Project. He appeared on Gary Moore's AFTER THE WAR, where he met Cozy Powell. Moore recommended Cottle to Cozy Powell when Black Sabbath needed a bassist for their upcoming album, HEADLESS CROSS.

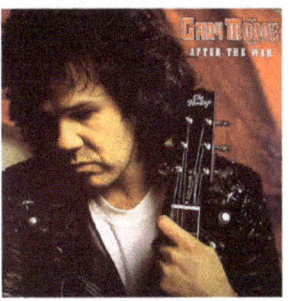 

THE VOICE OF ROCK
GLENN HUGHES

My introduction to Glenn Hughes came sometime in 1980 when my friend Kevin Cianfarani and I decided to listen to some of his older brother's albums. The first one that dropped was Deep Purple's BURN, side one. My mind was blown. Through so many ups and downs in his career and personal life, I have always rooted for the guy. Now, so many years clean and sober, he is at his best and always busy! The dude still has the Voice Of Rock!

www.glennhughes.com

The New Testament
BLACK SABBATH

The Book of Sabbath
Chapter 5

Born again...Again 1:5

With the purple rent asunder from the black,
it was time for the sole giant standing to seek new allies.

From the north would come the snake,
and from the south would come the drum.
Beating the path of resistance
as the village waited for the legend's return...

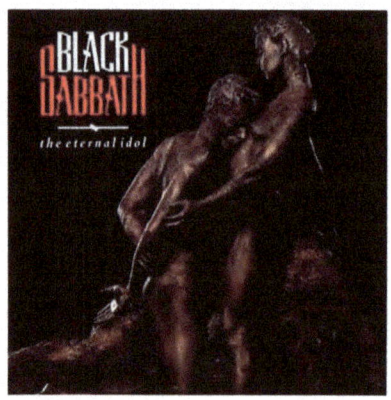 

THE ETERNAL IDOL (Vertigo/Warner Bros. Records)
Released on November 1, 1987
Produced by Jeff Glixman, Vic Coppersmith-Heaven and Chris Tsangarides
Tony Martin (vocals), Tony Iommi (guitar), Bob Daisley (bass), Geoff Nicholls (keyboards) and Eric Singer (drums)
Additional musician Bev Bevan (percussion)
All songs written by Iommi (later credited to Iommi, Daisley and Gillen)

THE SHINING
ANCIENT WARRIOR
HARD LIFE TO LOVE
GLORY RIDE

BORN TO LOSE
NIGHTMARE
SCARLET PIMPERNEL
LOST FOREVER
ETERNAL IDOL

"I always felt like I was going mad because all these things were happening to me." – Tony Iommi

no one said it had to be this way

Black Sabbath, especially Tony Iommi, ended 1986 much better than it started. Following a tour that began in utter shambles due to Glenn Hughes's inability to perform, it was the literal last-minute addition of unknown vocalist Ray Gillen that saved the band's already destroyed reputation. With Gillen now in the band, Black Sabbath had a focal point and something to build on. Not only did he have an unbelievable voice and great stage presence, but he was young and possessed rock-star good looks, something that could help sell the band to a much younger audience. For fans that went to the shows with Gillen (like me), they were treated to a voice that could sing the high and the low, switch from Ozzy to Ronnie to Glenn and even Ian without any effort at all.

Black Sabbath followed the US leg with a short UK tour that was not only well attended, but very well received by those in attendance and surprise…the UK media even gave the band praise. Following the shows with German rockers Zeno opening, the band (all staying in England) began to write material for a new album with studio time set for October in Montserrat again with Jeff Glixman, who created a full and ear-pleasing sound with SEVENTH STAR.

"When Tony's ready to go into the studio, you better have all your homework done." – Ray Gillen

Iommi and Black Sabbath had once and for all separated from manager Don Arden but not really by choice. All the bad treatment of his artists (especially owing royalties to Electric Light Orchestra and Jeff Lynne) and tax evasion finally caught up to Arden, who was looking at a lengthy prison sentence that would have resulted in him spending the rest of his life in jail. But to his financial rescue came his current cash cows, Air Supply and Iommi, who helped settle his massive debts. Needing a scapegoat, it would be Arden's son David who took the fall and served jail time for his dad. Needing representation, for some odd and insane reason even unknown to Tony Iommi himself, he signed on again with Patrick Meehan. The man who destroyed the band and the members of Black Sabbath all those years ago was back in control of the brand and the finances. Things started out great with bills being paid and money in the bank, but, of course, things would go very bad, very fast!

During the early stages of writing, demoing, and recording material, bassist Dave Spitz, according to the band and producer, was distracted by personal matters back in the States and became less interested in the music. He would eventually leave and be replaced by former Rainbow, Ozzy, and Uriah Heep bassist Bob Daisley, who would do his usual by providing solid bass playing, a professional work ethic, and much-needed lyrics. With one setback taken care of, Black Sabbath had a chance to record a song for the third installment of the popular horror movie franchise, Nightmare on Elm Street 3: Dream Warriors. The film went on to be another huge hit for the franchise and ended up featuring Dokken performing their song, *Dream Warriors*, because Meehan asked for way too much money. Another unexpected problem was that producer Glixman left the sessions before they were completed (due to issues with Meehan) and in came Vic Coppersmith-Heaven, fresh from his success with The Jam and The Europeans, featuring a pre-Marillion Steve Hogarth. This was a return to Black Sabbath for Coppersmith-Heaven, having served as an engineer on VOL4 fifteen years earlier.

"Singing the Ozzy and Ronnie songs are fun, but I can't wait to get my own stuff out there." – Ray Gillen

As recording finished in the Bahamas, the band returned to England with optimism running high when suddenly it would all begin to unravel. Following a return to London to finish recording, drummer Eric Singer abruptly left the band, opting to join Gary Moore as he supported his brilliant (and my favorite Gary Moore album) WILD FRONTIER. Singer would get the job on a recommendation from Bob Daisley, who left Sabbath as soon as his recording was completed to re-join Gary Moore. Then the worst possible disaster happened… vocalist Ray Gillen was gone! There are a million stories and reasons why he suddenly quit Black Sabbath, from too much partying, to his inability to write lyrics in the Black Sabbath mold, or the most plausible story, that it was a result of miscommunication, non-payment, and mismanagement that made him leave. Gillen would return to the US and begin working with guitarist John Sykes, fresh from his departure from Whitesnake, in the band Blue Murder with bassist Tony Franklin (The Firm) and drummer Cozy Powell.

"I always met new people and that always led me to do something else, another gig." – Eric Singer

Whatever the reason, Iommi was once again looking for yet another vocalist and trying to smooth over the already disillusioned fanbase as well as the critical, skeptical media. It was just Iommi and Geoff Nicholls left, with an almost completed album and a big question mark about how to move forward. Realizing he couldn't release the album featuring his latest former vocalist, Iommi spoke to his friend, Albert Chapman, who was managing a young Brummie named Tony Martin (born Anthony Harford on April 19, 1957), who he said could do the job. Iommi listened to the singer and his band The Alliance, liked what he heard, and with yet another producer, the legendary Chris Tsangarides, they all went into Battery Studios in London to re-record the vocals and make everything try to fit and sound as natural as possible. So, Martin went in and did a fantastic job in an impossible situation, re-recording all the vocals and keeping his style a bit suppressed to fit the music that was already recorded. Not an easy thing to do since singers have their individual styles, but Martin made the songs his own, and eight days later, his parts were all recorded.

Needing something more behind the drum tracks and unable to call on Eric Singer, Iommi brought back Bev Bevan to add some cymbals and percussion to a few of the songs. Since the end of the BORN AGAIN tour, Bevan rejoined Electric Light Orchestra for their 1986 release BALANCE OF POWER (Epic/Jet Records), an album that ended up being the last release for the band until 2001.

With the album completed, Iommi tried to get Geezer Butler to return to Black Sabbath, explaining what a great singer they had (true), how solid the new album was (yes again), and how to secure the management situation was (umm..... not so much). In the summer of 1987, rehearsals for an upcoming tour began with Iommi, Nicholls, Martin, Bevan, and Butler, but when dates fell through, Butler would leave again and Martin would fly to the US and replace the man he replaced, Ray Gillen, in Blue Murder. You can only imagine what Iommi was thinking and feeling, considering he just recorded an album's vocals twice and now the replacement singer may be gone before the album had even been released. This, of course, wasn't making anyone happy at Vertigo and Warner Bros. Records, who were waiting for an album, the last album of Black Sabbath's contract.

"They were in a difficult time when I joined and it was becoming a joke." - Tony Martin

In the end, Martin would return to Black Sabbath while Blue Murder, now with drummer Carmine Appice, would feature John Sykes as vocalist with the assistance of Geffen guru John Kalodner. To show for his efforts, Martin would receive a writing credit for the song *Valley Of The Kings*, the band's debut single and video. With Martin back, the band was given an opportunity to play the Sun City Super Bowl in South Africa. These six shows would bring a massive payday for the band, but would open up a world of controversy due to the cultural boycott of the resort casino issued by the United Nations for their support of apartheid. All this before the album was even released!

"We'd gone so far down there was only one way left to go." - Tony Iommi

  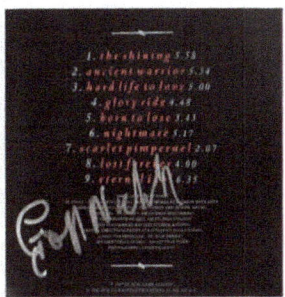

Reviews were good for THE ETERNAL IDOL and the hype machine was in full swing, but unfortunately, no one was bitting...or buying! A real cool item from Patrick Kalmeyer (Netherlands), the back of THE ETERNAL IDOL booklet autographed by keyboardist Geoff Nicholls.

Almost 100 years before the Black Sabbath's The Eternal Idol album, French sculptor Auguste Rodin created a beautiful piece of the same name. Among the hundreds of sculptures created by Rodin, his most famous work is The Thinker, one of the most recognizable pieces of art in all the world. The Eternal Idol features a woman sitting on top of a rock with a lover (or at least a good friend) laying against her and kissing her stomach with his hands behind his back. This statue is very sexy indeed, especially for Black Sabbath, but it does work as an album cover. The problem was, the band couldn't get the rights to use the actual sculpture, so the idea was brought up to recreate the piece with two painted models in the exact pose.

If you are a James Bond fan, then you know the classic scene in the film, GOLDFINGER, where the bad guy (Goldfinger) who was obsessed with gold, covers a woman in gold paint as a message to 007! In the classic film the victim, Jill Masterson, dies because all of her body is covered in gold paint, suffocating her. Unfortunately, that almost happened at the photoshoot to the two models used for the album's cover. However, in the film, it is explained that the cause of death is suffocation due to the skin not being able to breathe, but, in reality, that can't happen. However, the human body will have some adverse reactions like a spike in blood pressure and body temperature if the skin is covered up. Apparently, the two painted models didn't feel too well following the shoot. The back cover is a black no-frills sleeve featuring the songs and credits. The only bit of color, front or back, is another great new logo for the band in light blue and red. Hard to imagine a band like Black Sabbath never really had a set logo...

"We had two people done up in bronze paint! They stood there for bloody hours having their photo taken, to duplicate the idea of the original Rodin statue." - Tony Iommi

live long live now!

Featuring a lot of musicians listed, three producers, three studios, and taking almost five months to record, THE ETERNAL IDOL finally saw its release on November 1, 1987, from Vertigo (UK) and by Warner Bros. Records in North America on December 8, 1987. To say a lot was riding on this album is a massive understatement, considering this was the final release on their current contract, and, at this point, the Black Sabbath

THE ETERNAL IDOL finally saw its release on November 1, 1987, from Vertigo (UK) and by Warner Bros. Records in North America on December 8, 1987. To say a lot was riding on this album is a massive understatement, considering this was the final release on their current contract, and, at this point, the Black Sabbath name was nearly worthless. For Tony Iommi and the band, the worst possible scenario happened. The album stiffed on the charts, almost like it was never released.

If SEVENTH STAR caused concerns, THE ETERNAL IDOL would cause massive panic with the album only going to #168 in the US and #66 in the UK... both the worst charting of any Black Sabbath album ever. A video for *The Shining* was released and despite how cool the band looked, how hot the girls were, and how great the song is, it failed to ignite any interest other than sad curiosity. As soon as the album began to slip from the charts, the label(s) pulled all promotion for the album and sent the message that Black Sabbath was done. Such a shame, because the album is so friggin' good.

"It's horrible to be dropped, but that's the way it goes." - Tony Iommi

there is no end, there's no beginning

A song with a long history of not getting recorded, *The Shining* is an amazing song from start to finish. It has a great intro (very Dio era) that grabs you as the music begins to swell into the riff and then Tony Martin is introduced in a bed of gentle bass and keyboards! As an unknown commodity at the time, I was instantly hooked as he reached some high notes. A great way to start.

Ancient Warrior is a song that took me some time to get into, but I have since come to love it. It starts out with off-beat drumming against the riff and vocals that put you a little off, but once it all comes together, it makes sense. The song has an epic feel to it that I always thought sounded like an Yngwie Malmsteen song with toned-down guitar. Bob Daisley's bass is so subtle but effective and keeps the song flowing.

A pure rocker, *Hard Life To Love*, was the song that could have competed with the hit songs of the day with its driving beat, catchy chorus, and the guitar tones of Iommi. Martin really has a solid performance here despite the song not being written for him, which is the strength of Martin as a vocalist.

"It is difficult for me to evaluate him. I haven't heard anything else that Tony done." – Bob Daisley

Glory Ride is almost perfect! It starts out with the trademark heavy metal sound before jumping into a Rainbow style in the verses and then bringing us to an Iron Maiden-type chorus. The song takes a few twists and turns and gives drummer Eric Singer so many chances to show off.

It is a good song but *Born To Lose* is kind of the throwaway for me on the album. I think what gets me out of liking mode is the "ah-ah-ah haha" Martin does before the verses. The solo is brilliant and flash, even for Iommi, and the band plays fast and tight, but it is just an average song.

Knowing this could have been involved with Freddie Kruger's world, *Nightmare* is an amazing song that just evokes so much imagery...and all of it is bad! The song starts out a bit funky until it takes off into a solid rockin' direction! Despite the new vocals added by Martin, you can hear Ray Gillen's sinister laugh still in the track.

"They sent me a script and I spoke to the producer a few times. I was all set to do it, but then Meehan asked for too much money and they backed out." – Tony Iommi

It's an instrumental, it's interesting, it has some cool guitar tones, and that is *Scarlet Pimpernel* in a nutshell.

With the heaviness and guitar tones of *Trashed*, Black Sabbath kicks it up a lot for *Lost Forever*, a song that has a lot going on, especially the driving riffs and soloing. Here (and on the rest of the album), Eric Singer proves once again what an amazing and talented player he is, especially moving from cymbal to cymbal. He puts a lot of wicked fills in, giving the song another dimension of cool.

The title track, *Eternal Idol*, is a long and epic song that is scary and a throwback musically to old-school Black Sabbath. The beginning is pounding and very forceful until it enters a much smoother side. The song isn't super-special but Martin's vocals are, proving he is more than a replacement. He is the new voice of Black Sabbath.

the soldiers of fortune will ride

If recording the album became a tale of misadventure, so did planning a tour to support it. If having a stiff of an album really hurt the band, so would the rest of 1987! Piecing together a band, Black Sabbath committed to a show on July 18 that would feature the return of Geezer Butler, something Iommi desperately needed. On drums, the hope was Bill Ward would return, but when that didn't happen, Bev Bevan was back along with Tony Martin (vocals) and Geoff Nicholls (keyboards). When that show fell through, a show in Greece was scheduled for July 21, with Butler was gone and joining Ozzy Osbourne's band (replacing Bob Daisley) in time for the NO REST FOR THE WICKED world tour. But, out of nowhere, Dave Spitz would return. Confused already?

In one of the most controversial moves in the band's history, Patrick Meehan booked the band six shows at the Sun City Super Bowl in South Africa with a massive financial guarantee for them. The problem was the cultural boycott set forth by the United Nations years before was in place in protest of the South African policy of apartheid, the racial segregation of the black population that had been going on in South Africa since 1948. In 1985, Artists Against Apartheid, a project created by Little Steven (Bruce Springsteen's E Street Band) brought together some of the best and most politically active acts of the day like Run DMC, Bono (U2), Eddie Kendricks & David Ruffin (The Temptations), Bob Dylan, Peter Garett (Midnight Oil), Michael Monroe (Hanoi Rocks) and Joey Ramone (The Ramones) to warn artists "Not To Play Sun City!"

Well, Black Sabbath didn't listen, accepted the gigs, and then all hell broke loose! First Bevan refused to go and left the band, being replaced by Terry Chimes of The Clash, and, more recently, Hanoi Rocks. When the band returned from the shows, the press either destroyed the band for playing or just didn't care, thinking they were not relevant and targeted Queen instead for doing the same thing. In November, THE ETERNAL IDOL tour would start properly in Germany with Jo Burt (Virginia Wolf) on bass and play 13 dates with none in the US and only one in the UK, on May 29, 1988, a charity show that saw the band play only three songs.

"Bev Bevan wouldn't go, and it didn't matter what management said to him." – Tony Martin

I could have been a dreamer

With all the turmoil in the world of Black Sabbath, former vocalist Ronnie James Dio's issues were nothing in comparison. Following the firing of guitarist Vivian Campbell and the introduction of Craig Goldie, DIO went to work in March of 1987 on an important album, DREAM EVIL. With their last album, SACRED HEART, not performing to the expected standards, there was pressure on DIO to deliver a solid and electrifying album. On July 21, 1987, DREAM EVIL would be released by Vertigo and Warner Bros. Records, and would fall very short in the US (#43) but would do solid business in the UK (#8). The album would feature slower-paced songs like *I Could Have Been A Dreamer, Sunset Superman*, and *All The Fools Sailed Away,* and despite how good the album is and how fantastic Goldie's playing is, there was a noticeable lack of flash.

Much excitement and curiosity was surrounding the release of DREAM EVIL, based on the addition of Craig Goldie.

Reviews would be mostly negative for the album, citing a major shift in the band's sound. Following the tour, Ronnie James Dio would announce the mutual and amicable split between the band and Craig Goldie. Fans began to get excited when, around this time, Vivian Campbell walked away from Whitesnake following the band's most successful tour to date. Even Dio was a bit intrigued by the possibility of a return, but the talk would be short-lived when the guitarist joined the band Riverdogs before joining the mega-popular Def Leppard in 1992, replacing the late Steve Clark. It would be three years before DIO would release their next album with a line-up that would feature Ronnie James Dio and an all-new band.

we shot the dice...

Two years after the release of the first Phenomena album, Tom and Mel Galley put together another stellar line-up heavy on the vocals. Brought back were Glenn Hughes, who would join John Wetton (ASIA), Max Bacon (GTR), and a young vocalist making his recording debut, former Black Sabbath vocalist, Ray Gillen! With each vocalist taking lead on different songs, the album would have a well-designed flow and help tell a story...of what I'm not sure. Telling KERRANG magazine how much he enjoyed working with his (and my) heroes, Glenn Hughes and John Wetton, Gillen's performances are phenomenal (pun intended) and make the listener at the time so sad and frustrated at what Black Sabbath could become with Ray Gillen at center stage.

PHENOMENA II: DREAM RUNNER (Arista/RCA Records) was released sometime in the early summer of 1987 and also features drummer Michael Sturgis, guitarist Scott Gorham (Thin Lizzy), and bassist Neil Murray, fresh from his time with Whitesnake. Gillen would be the lead vocalist on four songs including the album's first track, *Stop!* The album would have a surprise hit single in South America, *Did It All For Love*, featuring Wetton on vocals.

Following the completion of the album, Gillen would return to the United States and work for a brief time work with John Sykes's Blue Murder with bassist Tony Franklin (The Firm) and drummer Cozy Powell. Gillen would leave that project and go to work with his former Black Sabbath drummer Eric Singer, bassist Greg Chaisson, and former Ozzy guitarist Jake E. Lee on a new project signed to Atlantic Records, known as Badlands.

"We never sat down and said we wanted to be real British sounding." – Ray Gillen

the land of ozzy and geezer!

As 1987 drew to a close, Ozzy Osbourne was coming to the end of his search for the coveted guitar spot in his band. The final list was down to two incredible players, Connecticut-based guitarist Jimi Bell (who was recommended by Kramer guitars), and a clean-cut pretty boy from New Jersey named Jeffrey Wielandt, who would change his name to Zakk Wylde and ultimately get the gig. In a weird twist of fate for Bell, he would receive a call from Geezer Butler, who was looking for a flashy and skilled player to build a new version of the Geezer Butler Band and Jimi Bell was his man. Bell flew to the UK and started working with Butler, drummer Gary Ferguson, and vocalist Carl Sentence to write songs for demos to pass around to labels. The band recorded two videos to help promote themselves (*Heat In The Street* and *Computer God*) that had a very traditional British rock sound sounding much like UFO and the Michael Schenker Group. The band signed with MCA Records but, unfortunately, the label executive who signed the band was fired by the record label for allegedly misusing money, and the project died. Videos are available on YouTube for the above two songs and show where the music, look, and style was headed for the Geezer Butler Band. Butler would abandon the idea of his own band and join his former vocalist (and his new guitarist) in Ozzy Osbourne's band. A move I'm sure sent Tony Iommi reeling...

taking a shot in the dark
phil soussan

I became a fan of bassist Phil Soussan a few years before he joined Ozzy Osbourne in 1986. As a reader of KERRANG! magazine, I was always exposed to the newest bands. In 1983, Phil was a member of the band Wildlife, who were getting a lot of press because of their drummer Simon Kirke (Bad Company fame) and because they were signed to Led Zeppelin's Swan Song Records. Wildlife didn't make it (a bummer, too), but for Soussan it was the beginning of a steady climb that would see him work with Jimmy Page, Ozzy Osbourne, and Vince Neil. In 2016, he joined Vinny Appice, Vivian Campbell, and Andrew Freeman in the band Last In Line. The above pix are from Last In Line's stellar performances at The Chance in Poughkeepsie, New York, and The MGM in Springfield, MA.

www.philsoussan.com

HEADLESS CROSS (I.R.S. Records)
Released on April 24, 1989
Produced by Tony Iommi and Cozy Powell
Tony Martin (vocals), Tony Iommi (guitar), Geoff Nicholls (keyboards) and Cozy Powell (drums)
Additional musicians Laurence Cottle (bass) and Brian May (guitar solo on *When Death Calls*)
All songs written by Martin, Iommi and Powell unless otherwise noted

THE GATES OF HELL (Martin, Iommi, Nicholls and Powell)
HEADLESS CROSS
DEVIL & DAUGHTER
WHEN DEATH CALLS (Martin, Iommi, Nicholls, May, Cottle and Powell)

KILL IN THE SPIRIT WORLD
CALL OF THE WILD
BLACK MOON (Gillen, Martin, Iommi and Nichols)
NIGHTWING
CLOAK AND DAGGER (Bonus Track)

The Seal Is Broken

Before Tony Iommi could think about putting together songs for the new Black Sabbath album, he had a few important things to take care of. Again, he needed a bassist and drummer, a new record label, and before finding the first two he needed solid management representation. Finding band members was the easy part, the management situation fell right into his lap, and the record label problem looked tense at first but ultimately sorted itself out. This situation is not where a legend should find himself but here he was, all alone. If Black Sabbath was going to survive, Iommi had to fight for it. Oh yeah, he was also given a very large tax bill that the British Government wanted paid in full yesterday.

Following the debacle with Patrick Meehan AGAIN, Iommi needed to find someone who he could trust to do the right thing and have the best interest of Black Sabbath be a priority. To help sort out the tax issues, Iommi reached out to Phil Blanfield (who was still managing Ian Gillan) and he suggested Ernest Chapman possibly manage him and the band. Already managing Jeff Beck, the meeting went well but the relationship was started at his word and was exactly what Iommi needed, reassuring him that he would take commission only when things were sorted out and asked, "What do you need?" This refreshing and much-needed treatment by a manager meant so much to Iommi after years of the opposite. Entering the picture was a Chapman associate, Ralph Baker, who would to this day represent Iommi. Despite having accountants paying for things and handling the money (like accountants do), Iommi had no recourse and was on the hook to pay his tax bill. Iommi had his income frozen during the investigation, but once it was all over Chapman worked out a deal to get his royalties sorted out and paid.

Needing to rebuild the rhythm section from scratch, the first person Iommi reached out to was Geezer Butler, who was not about to rejoin the band with no record deal in place. Butler had already committed to Ozzy Osbourne's band for Ozzy's NO REST FOR THE WICKED tour. Needing some credibility as well as an amazing player, Tony had one drummer in mind, the legendary Cozy Powell. Powell had several opportunities to join Black Sabbath over the years but now seemed to be the best opportunity, with Iommi looking for a partner, not just a drummer. Powell was someone who would do interviews, co-write, and co-produce with Iommi, not just be a hired hand. Since leaving Rainbow in 1979, Powell had jumped from project to project, which usually ended badly due to personality clashes. One look at the big personalities or alpha males like Richie Blackmore, Michael Schenker, and David Coverdale tell a story that it may not have been all Powell's fault. This was his chance to work with a legendary band and a player (Iommi) who would not interfere with his very outgoing personality, and just let Cozy just be Cozy.

"The egos with members of bands has always been a stumbling block." – Cozy Powell

As far as the record label (or lack of) was concerned, Tony Iommi had met with several labels and it was frustrating not being able to deal from a position of strength. It was Miles Copeland, one of the founders and owners of I.R.S. (International Record Syndicate) Records, an indie label formed in 1979, that was instrumental in the punk and post-punk rock world, signing bands like The Alarm, R.E.M., and The Go-Go's, and seeing many of their rosters achieve massive successes, especially R.E.M. The label was also known for helping break The Police with their first single, *Fall Out*. In case you didn't know, Miles Copeland was the brother of the Police's drummer Stewart Copeland and also was the band's manager. Obviously, Black Sabbath certainly didn't fit the mold of the typical I.R.S. acts, but Copeland wanted Tony Iommi to focus on making the best Black Sabbath album he possibly could and let the label worry about getting them in the shops and selling it.

With almost everything now in place, the band began to write new material for what could have been their most important album since HEAVEN AND HELL. The pressure was obviously on for the boys to write music that celebrated the name and legacy of Black Sabbath, but also could compete with the more down-to-earth bands dominating the charts at the time like Iron Maiden and Guns N' Roses. Music was changing, with faster and heavier bands like Megadeth, Anthrax, Testament, and Slayer releasing groundbreaking records and capturing the hearts, and money, of metal fans. Black Sabbath was now competing with the bands and a movement they helped create. Behind the scenes, Iommi was still looking for a big splash by bringing Ronnie James Dio back, but Powell convinced him to stay with Martin. Maybe Iommi was still a bit resentful at Martin's leaving last year to work with John Sykes, and maybe Powell pushed for Martin simply to keep Dio out since the two weren't exactly on good terms.

Writing for the album, as always, began with the legendary tapes of riffs compiled by Iommi. Iommi gave Martin the autonomy to write lyrics for the music he and Powell (and sometimes Nicholls) were coming up with. Martin explained that his way of writing lyrics was telling stories. From the death of an entire town (*Headless Cross*) to a white owl's hunting patterns (*Nightwing*), Martin took on the subject matter with skill and passion, and considering this was his first big project, he did quite well. With the songs together, it was time for the band to get into the studio, but Black Sabbath still needed a bassist. With the door slammed shut and bolted closed on Geezer Butler, Cozy Powell suggested a session player who had worked with Eric Clapton, named Laurence Cottle. Despite Cottle being known for his jazz style, he helped to write his bass parts and even received a songwriting credit, but never would or even wanted to be a member of the band. Cottle would make only one appearance with the band in the video for *Headless Cross*.

The album was recorded over four months, starting in late August and finishing up in November of 1988. The album was produced by Tony Iommi along with Cozy Powell, who, together, created an album that sounded modern and classic at the same time, not an easy thing to do. A bit of star power was also brought in, Queen guitarist Brian May, who was a longtime friend of Iommi. Not only would May co-write the song *When Death Calls*, but he would also play the solo on the track, something the band always frowned upon. But this was the new Black Sabbath and chances had to be taken!

With the album now completed, Powell suggested NO COMPROMISE for the album's title, but the album would be called HEADLESS CROSS! As the final touches were being put together for the album's release, Cozy Powell reached out to his friend Neil Murray, whose band Vow Wow had just broken up, about playing bass. Murray accepted the offer to join the band and hit the road for what they hoped would be a triumphant return to glory.

"Certainly, one was aware that Sabbath wasn't as big as they had been before." – Neil Murray

  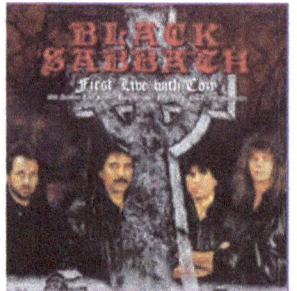

A few recordings from the HEADLESS CROSS tour. Despite bad promotions for he shows in the US, the band never sounded better.

On A Night Such As This

While Black Sabbath went a bit artsy for the cover of THE ETERNAL IDOL, the band almost went back to basics for the cover of HEADLESS CROSS. Here, we have a black cover with a cloud-covered moon in the top left corner and a large stone cross rising out of a foggy field or graveyard. On the top right above the cross was the band's stylized name in blue and purple, and the album's title was on the left near the base of the cross. The simplistic illustration was done by artist Kevin Wimlett and I can tell you from experience (like it happened yesterday) that this cover popped on the record store wall display and called to me. I walked into Strawberry's Records on Queen Street in Southington, CT, and there it was, jumping out from the red carpeting and pristine white record bins and racks. The back cover of the album featured the same cross, with the head now broken and laying on the white ground. Get it? Headless Cross? The song listing is on he top left and in the bottom right corner is the I.R.S. logo with the wording "I.R.S. METAL." Was this promising a new subdivision from I.R.S. featuring awesome metal bands? I also remember being really excited seeing the famous all-white I.R.S. label with the G-Man logo and thinking it was so cool to have a band like Black Sabbath on the label that was more known for alternative or college rock.

Many Spirits Are Lost Forever

With a lot of press, as much as greeted the Ian Gillan-led BORN AGAIN release, Tony Iommi and Cozy Powell hit the media rodeo full force before the release of HEADLESS CROSS. The duo was everywhere selling the new album, the new line-up, and the new era of Black Sabbath. Both Iommi and Powell acknowledged that things weren't exactly where they wanted them to be, and hoped that the new album would remind people what Black Sabbath was all about. Would it work?

HEADLESS CROSS was released internationally by I.R.S. records on April 24, 1989, and both I.R.S and Black Sabbath flooded the U.K. collectors' market with singles, picture discs, and limited-edition items. The album received more good press than bad, calling it the best album since HEAVEN AND HELL, and, for the first time in a long time, praised the current line-up as opposed to constant and unjust comparisons to the Ozzy or Dio eras.

Unfortunately, all the band's efforts, the positive press, and even getting solid MTV airplay with the *Headless Cross* video, yielded unspectacular album sales all over the world. In the UK, the album went to #31 on the charts, 35 spots better than THE ETERNAL IDOL. In the ultra-important US market, the album only went to #115, 53 spots better than the previous album, but that isn't what the band wanted or the album deserved. So what happened? The music was solid and exciting and the band was getting the word out there, but the fans just weren't biting. One problem the band noticed when doing record shop appearances in the States was that there were no copies of the album in the stores... no promotion... not a single poster up.

"What the f#$@s going on? There's no advertising and no albums in the shops!" – Cozy Powell

Despite yet another Spinal Tap moment (remember Artie Fufkin from Polymer Records?) becoming the band's reality, Tony Iommi would praise I.R.S. promotion in Europe for working the album and getting it to an appreciative fanbase, helping save the album from complete death.

Misguided Mortals, You'll Burn With Me

HEADLESS CROSS starts out much like the old days with an instrumental introduction called *The Gates Of Hell!* A bit over a minute long, the song was obviously created for the dry ice, stage lights, and then, BAM...

Headless Cross is an incredible introduction to the new line-up with thunderous drums by Cozy Powell. The song tears it up with a great riff from Tony Iommi. The vocals by Tony Martin are a mix of Ozzy's style with Dio's tones and range. The song is moody and really keeps you on edge.

The next track's name was changed in order not to be confused with Ozzy's *Devil's Daughter. Devil And Daughter* is another great song that just puts its head down and charges forward. Heavy drums and a driving spirit are all led by Martin's wailing vocals, where time after time he achieves amazing range. Great keyboards by Geoff Nicholls keep the mood flowing amidst the chaos.

A fan favorite, *When Death Calls*, was a song that I never liked, but the more I listen to it, the more I love it. The song is moody and is the longest on the album at just under seven minutes. The track is so good because it has very distinctive parts to it. The heaviness is my least favorite part. It's midway through the song where it becomes something else, with dancing guitars and a great solo by Iommi's friend, Queen's Brian May.

"I left him in the studio for an hour and came back. He just improvised." – Tony Iommi on Brian May's playing on *When Death Calls*

The next two songs are easily in my Top Ten of all Sabbath songs. *Kill In The Spirit World* is driven by Lawrence Cottle's driving bass line, which lets Powell fill the hell out of it. Iommi has some incredible moments with tasty riffs and a ripping lead that culminates in a held Martin note that leads into more thrashing drums! What's not to love?

Next, another brilliant one-two punch with *Call Of The Wild!* Many Sabbath fans shy away from this one because they feel it is the band trying to formulate a radio hit. I say, "Who Cares?" Again, thumping bass leads soaring vocals, inspired drums, and guitar magic with a sprinkle of keyboards from Geoff Nicholls. Listen to Martin's range and you will understand how he is the perfect choice as a vocalist. How about the "herroooo" chorus? Brilliant!

"He (Lawrence Cottle) did a great job and that was it." – Tony Iommi

A song left over from the Ray Gillen sessions, *Black Moon* was co-written by Gillen but re-worked by Martin. Originally released as a B-side for The Eternal Idol, the song has a real funky vibe that certainly could have been a radio hit in 1989 if given the chance. The song has a nice hook, lazy drums, and a solid bassline, that, if marketed right, should have had a better life than being relegated to side two.

Nightwing is a slower song that closes the album in an epic way. Cottle's bass sounds much like Tony Franklin (The Firm/Blue Murder) and gives the cut a different feel. Once the band joins in, it almost sounds a bit like Blue Murder. The song features so many different time changes, going from heavy to fast and back again, all being held together by Nicholls's subtle keyboards. Powell's drumming is loud and has an echo that creates a bigger sound. Wow...just wow! To be honest, a song I wasn't as fond of when the album was released.

The bonus track, *Cloak And Dagger*, is a bit of a filler for me, and, when you listen to it as the last song on the album, makes it end flat, unlike *Nightwing's* beautiful fade. The song is a heavy blues tune that sounds like it was written for strippers to dance, too. Not needed. It was cool having two songs on the same album which bear the names of comic book characters, Nightwing (DC) and Cloak and Dagger (Marvel).

All Eyes Are On You

For Black Sabbath's HEADLESS CROSS tour, it would be a best of times/worst of times story. Starting on the East Coast of America in May, Black Sabbath had dates scheduled that would take the band through the US (with one date in Toronto, Ontario, Canada) and end in July, but the worst thing that could possibly happen did. The band managed to play only 13 shows (with Kingdom Come and Silent Rage) before the tour would end up being canceled. According to Tony Iommi, there was a serious lack of promotion, which resulted in horrible ticket sales. It sounded to me like a huge excuse to keep face until I did research for this book. I didn't even know the band played in my hometown of Springfield, MA, on June 8, 1989, so now I tend to believe Mr. Iommi. If I had known the band was playing 10 minutes from my house (with easy parking) I would have been there! In total, over 25 dates were canceled, and the band came home with their tails between their legs. It wasn't that the band was booked into massive halls, either. This was a huge downgrade in venues for the Black Sabbath. Adding insult to injury, Ozzy Osbourne (with Geezer Butler) was playing the bigger arenas in town and not having any problem selling them out.

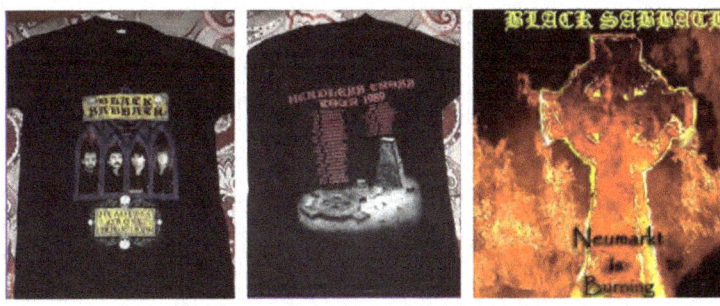

Thank you to Lothar Ha (Germany) for not only buying but keeping this awesome shirt for all these years. This was from the band's show in Neumarkt, Germany, on September 23, 1989. Also, the cover of a not-too-bad-sounding bootleg recording of that very concert!

Now for the good news. Black Sabbath would play shows in the UK starting in September which featured several special moments for the band and the fans in attendance. First, On September 10 in London, the band was joined on stage by Queen's Brian May, and on September 11, 1989, former Black Sabbath vocalist Ian Gillan joined the band on stage in Bristol. One wonders if the thought of a reunion with Gillan crossed Iommi's mind, considering that Gillan had recently been fired by Deep Purple on the insistence of Richie Blackmore.

There would be a successful run through Sweden, Denmark, Germany, Austria, Hungary, and Italy, with some well-attended and positively reviewed shows for the band, something they needed badly. Black Sabbath would end this part of the tour in October 1989 in Japan and see a show in Mexico canceled due to religious protesting and pressures. For Black Sabbath, you never want to lose a gig, but having it canceled for religious reasons is always a good feather in the cap. But Black Sabbath would be one of the first bands to tour Russia when premier Mikhail Gorbachev's policy of Glasnost opened the country and helped bring an end to Communism a few years later. The band took up a residency of sorts in November at the Olympic Hall in Moscow that would see the band (with Girlschool in support) play ten shows followed by ten more in Leningrad at the SKK Hall. Black Sabbath was taking full advantage of the new freedom (immortalized in *Winds Of Change* from Scorpions) in the soon-to-be-former Soviet Union, and, like many Western bands like ASIA, found new and quite excitable audiences to play to.

Sing Me Your Sweet, Sweet Song

Wanting to get away from the doom and gloom of Black Sabbath and the insanity of Ozzy Osbourne, vocalist Ray Gillen and guitarist Jake E. Lee wanted to create a band where the music would come first. On drums would be former Sabbath and Gary Moore drummer, Eric Singer, and bassist Greg Chaisson, who Lee met on an Ozzy audition a few years before, would form Badlands. Signing with Atlantic Records, the band released their highly praised self-titled debut in June of 1989, featuring the video and single, *Dreams In The Dark*. Despite the positive press and the quality of music created, the album didn't sell well, only going to #57 in the US and #39 in the UK.

Before recording their second album, VOODOO HIGHWAY, Eric Singer would quit and join Paul Stanley's solo band, and, following the death of Eric Carr, would join KISS where he remains to this day. Gillen and Lee started to not see eye to eye on anything and this came to a violent head when the singer read a KERRANG! article from the stage featuring Lee's negative comments about Gillen. Lee would fire the singer and replace him with John West, but Atlantic Records didn't see a future with the band, and Badlands would be dropped, which caused them to break up. Unfortunately, the Ray Gillen story has a tragic ending. Plans to bring Phenomena to the stage in Europe with Gillen on vocals were being discussed but would never happen because sadly, on December 1, 1993, Ray Gillen would die from AIDS in New York at the way-too-young age of 34. One of the best voices in rock was now gone, way before his time.

I Remember They Warned Me

I always loved HEADLESS CROSS and thought when it first was released in 1989 it was one of Black Sabbath's best albums. As I listened to it again as prep for this writing, I was blown away by how amazing the album still sounds and how it not only hasn't aged a bit, but only gotten better. Sure, there are moments when you can hear the band trying to create something that would get them airplay, but you can't blame them for trying to reclaim a spotlight they were in for so long.

"I'm confident in what I'm doing." – Tony Martin

Black Sabbath was all alone in 1989, with Ozzy releasing his last album, the hit NO REST FOR THE WICKED the previous year, and DIO on a bit of a break as they sorted out their line-up issues following the DREAM EVIL tour. Despite not being in direct competition against HEADLESS CROSS, it's not hard to see how both former singers consistently outsold, out- charted, and out-toured Black Sabbath. In fact, Ian Gillan's 1988 release with Deep Purple, the live and somewhat shaky (but good) NOBODY'S PERFECT (Mercury/Polydor Records) sold better. But what a difference a year made, especially for Ian Gillan, now an ex-member of Deep Purple...again.

If you have never listened to HEADLESS CROSS because you gave up on Black Sabbath by this time, that is understandable. But this is a great time to give it a chance, much like the entire Tony Martin catalog, except one of them! For me, HEADLESS CROSS gets an incredibly high ranking, #8 out of 19 studio albums, and a solid rating of 8 out of 10! In a surprise for me, the Black Sabbath collective have also rated this song incredibly high, #9 out of 19, making it their highest-ranked Tony Martin-led Black Sabbath album. If you have never listened to it, why not now?

The highly touted and much praised Badlands featuring former Black Sabbath members Ray Gillen and Eric Singer, plus former Ozzy guitarist Jake E. Lee. Despite a solid debut the band would implode due to egos, drugs, lack of communication and expectations

Smoke On The Water
GEOFFREY DOWNES (ASIA/YES/THE BUGGLES)

Geoffrey Downes made music history in 1981 when MTV chose The Buggles hit Video Killed The Radio Star (a hit released in 1979) as the first video the network ever played. From the Buggles, he joined YES for their best album, 1979's DRAMA, and in 1982 was the final piece of the puzzle that would be the supergroup, ASIA. Downes would begin to work as a producer, with GTR (featuring Steve Howe and Steve Hackett) and in 1989, Downes would co-produce the Rock Aid Armenia version of Smoke On The Water featuring Tony Iommi (Black Sabbath), Brian May & Roger Taylor (Queen), Ian Gillan & Richie Blackmore (Deep Purple) and countless others. Currently, Downes splits his time between ASIA, YES, and anything else that can keep him busy. One of the best...

www.originalasia.com

TYR (I.R.S. Records)
Released on August 20,1990
Produced by Tony Iommi and Cozy Powell
Tony Martin (vocals), Tony Iommi (guitar), Neil Murray (bass), Geoff Nicholls (keyboards) and Cozy Powell (drums)
All songs written by Martin, Iommi Murray, Nicholls and Powell

ANNO MUNDI
THE LAW MAKER
JERUSALEM
THE SABBATH STONES
THE BATTLE OF TYR
ODIN'S COURT
VALHALLA
FEELS GOOD TO ME
HEAVEN IN BLACK

"My favorite album is TYR." – Tony Martin

A SOUL MUST BE SAVED

For the first time in quite a long time, Tony Iommi was able to focus on the music and just the music. With a record deal in place, solid management, and a stable Black Sabbath line-up for the first time since... well, a long time, it was time for the guitarist to focus on rebuilding the Black Sabbath brand, especially in North America. For the most part, this chapter is going to be pretty uneventful and just be focused on music. In a nutshell, the band comes off the road from one tour and records an album, then goes back on the road. But let's try to flush it out a bit more, shall we?

Following the many ups and downs of the previous years, Black Sabbath optimistically headed into Woodcray Studios in early 1990 to begin work on a new album. With two albums now under his belt, vocalist Tony Martin was feeling more comfortable in his role with the band, not feeling he had to tiptoe around Tony Iommi, Cozy Powell, Geoff Nicholls, and now, Neil Murray, anymore. Martin got a bit of criticism for his lyrics on the last album for them being over the top, and, at times, a bit corny with the death and Satan angles. Martin thought that writing lyrics for Black Sabbath meant they had to be a certain way, but now he was looking at other things to write about. Me? I had no problem with his lyrics at all.

Since joining the band, Martin had gone from just a voice (THE ETERNAL IDOL), to a contributor with limits (HEADLESS CROSS) to now, an earned spot as an equal, or as equal as he could be. Feeling more a part of the band, Martin was able to get away lyrically from what he (and others) thought the content should be and write from the heart, or at least subjects other than death, plagues, and darkness. Some of the new album's songs would take on a theme of Norse mythology without being a concept album in the traditional sense. There would be four songs with that connection. Martin would also write about ecology, TV evangelists (an easy target in 1990), and lost love.

"I'm proud of my work with Black Sabbath." – Tony Martin

Again, Black Sabbath began to get away from their more known traditional sound much as they did in the mid-1970s. The difference from then to now was (then) Black Sabbath was an established and massively popular band when they experimented with their sounds on VOL 4 and SABBATH BLOODY SABBATH. If the experiment failed, sales would be affected a bit, but concert tickets would still sell, and their popularity would not wain. Now, the band was looking to still regain its credibility, sustain a stable line-up, and build on the past few years' failures. For Martin, he was also bringing in more harmonies and choruses that were more natural for him as a vocalist and writer considering his musical background was much more melodic. Not that any change was snuck in, because if Tony Iommi and Cozy Powell didn't want it, it wouldn't be there.

"It's not possible to get Tony Iommi to do something he's not happy with." – Neil Murray

According to Martin, most of the writing and creating came in the studio and the results were quite positive. He felt more part of the family when Powell began bouncing ideas off him and encouraging him regarding his work. Much of the ease and chemistry had to do with the fact that this was the line-up that toured together, and, other than Murray, all appeared on HEADLESS CROSS. Interesting to note, only Murray had any issues or complaints about the recording process or at least the mixing and finished product. He felt that his bass was buried in the mix, and it's a valid point. Geezer would have never been buried, so why should Murray?

When it came to a title for the album, THE SATANIC VERSES was considered, inspired by the title of the novel by Salmon Rushdie. Due to the fatwa placed on Rushdie because of the "blasphemous" writings in the eyes of the Muslim world, the band thought it probably wasn't a good idea. It may have made for great press, but not at the expense of band members being killed. Another title the band toyed with was THE SABBATH STONES, a choice that would have been very cool and also fit expectations for a Sabbath album title. Ultimately, the title would come from an instrumental track on the album called *The Battle Of Tyr*, snd the album title would be TYR.

"It's pronounced 'teer' and it rhymes with 'beer', that shouldn't be hard to forget." – Tony Martin

With the new album finished, Iommi had understandable reservations about I.R.S Records and how they were going to push this one. Considering the failures and marketing misses during the release of HEADLESS CROSS, especially in the US, Iommi wanted to know TYR wouldn't meet a similar fate. He laid much of the blame on label president Miles Copeland and his lack of understanding of how to market a heavy rock album and a legendary band. Iommi felt that despite the support the label showed, it wouldn't be enough to put the band back on top, or at least near the top.

"I'm fortunate to have a large range." – Tony Martin

TO SEEK THE SOULS OF SINNERS

For TYR, the cover art would be based on Norse mythology with a dark-framed photo of a (I assume) fiord in Norway. Around this cold photo is a bit of a colorful frame in green and purple made up of twisted branches and in each of the corners, we have dragons. The band's logo would be in orange and yellow, fill the top of the cover would jump from the darkness, as does the stylized title in red on the bottom spelling T-Y-R.

For me, this was my first non-vinyl release from Black Sabbath, and everything looked so small, compressed, and unimpressive. No longer could I just study the artwork like I could on an album and read the lyric sheets. I had to look at a small booklet. The back listed the song titles and credits within grey and olive drab colors. Inside the booklet were art, credits, and, of course, lyrics. The center spread would feature a brief history lesson on Tyr and what it is. Interesting to note that, inside, Geoff Nicholls's name appears in a smaller font, the perception of his diminished role and standing within the band.

The art and graphics for TYR were created by the design house, Satori, who in the past created the artwork for Def Leppard's PYROMANIA and HYSTERIA, as well as such non-rockers as Thompson Twins, Dead Or Alive, and the sleeve for one of Phil Lynott's last singles, the beautiful King's Call.

DOES IT NOT SEEM STRANGE TO YOU?

The 15th Black Sabbath studio album, TYR, would see a worldwide release on August 20, 1990, via I.R.S. Records. I remember picking this one up the next day (my 22nd birthday) along with Stryper's AGAINST THE LAW, and had mixed feelings about both albums at the time, mostly negative. First, I was confused that these releases were CD only, and yes, I could listen to them driving home, but I wanted my 12 by 12 packages to look at! I.R.S. did a much better job getting the word out by having magazine and in-store advertisements announcing its release. It's how I knew about its release. Unfortunately, in the US, TYR would be the first Black Sabbath album not to chart, ever! This came as a huge shock to me and an I assume an even bigger shock for the band. It would go to #24 in the UK and do solid sales in Germany, Finland, Switzerland, and Austria, apparently the band's new territories.

1990 would be a huge year of change in music, especially hard rock and Heavy Metal, where established bands like Judas Priest (PAINKILLER), Iron Maiden (NO PRAYER FOR THE DYING), AC/DC (THE RAZOR'S EDGE), and Scorpions (CRAZY WORLD) were fighting the new, younger, and prettier bands like Winger, Firehouse, and Warrant for chart space, video play on MTV, and the all-important consumer dollars.

TYR would have a video released for the song, *Feels Good To Me*. The video featured the band (introduced in the shadows) playing in an empty theatre (no jokes, please), with scenes of a hot motorcycle girl meeting and frolicking with a shirtless and shoeless rock dude. The video fits perfectly with the, dare I say it, power ballads of the day in its softness in style. Diehard Black Sabbath fans complained about the song as an obvious attempt at airplay and calling the band sell-outs. This fan loved seeing another Black Sabbath video on MTV. The band looked amazing, and, as I always will say, a great song is a great song!

The lack of sales in the US obviously upset Tony Iommi and kept Black Sabbath from touring the States because there was no demand for Black Sabbath anymore, at least with this line-up on a North American stage. This was no reflection of the album's quality and more about the changing tastes of fans.

CAN YOU SEE ME?

Another amazing song to introduce an album! *Anno Mundi* has a very clean guitar sound to it from Tony Iommi, sounding a bit like *Children Of The Sea* in its tone and build-up. Chanting voices give us a bit of a jolt until Tony Martin comes in with a lot of range and a nice depth to his voice. Not a lot of people knew this song was about saving the environment. I just knew it was an amazing song that really showcases the power of this line-up. Heavy drums from Cozy Powell (as expected) really make this song something special.

Unfortunately, *The Law Maker* brings the mood down right away. The song is fast and ferocious, but seems to be this way just for the sake of being fast and ferocious. Technically, this is the first of the mythology-based songs, separated from the others.

Such a great song, *Jerusalem* is. The verses are very melodic and showcase Martin's vocal range, style, and control. However, this is one where you really miss Neil Murray's bass in the mix. This track has a lot of great moments but the chorus isn't one of them. It's this part that really loses me.

The most Dio-era sounding song on the album, *The Sabbath Stones* is a plodding, heavy riff-driven track that really makes the song special. But, at times, it really struggles to find its direction. Iommi's playing is very clean and the perfect complement to the vocals.

"I like those heavy riff-type things, and The Sabbath Stones is particularly heavy." – Tony Iommi

And now, we take a journey to the days of Vikings for the instrumental, *The Battle Of Tyr*. Here Nicholls and Iommi bring us along on a journey...that I know nothing about. Musically, though, very cool.

Thie next one sets up the story (I guess). *Odin's Court* is a wind-filled campfire song that, for me, does nothing but just move the story ahead (I guess). It is certainly mysterious, and the band really gives us a lot to listen to, unless you are looking for drums, cuz there isn't any.

The payoff of the musical TYR trilogy is *Valhalla*. Here we get the full band and, again, a very Dio-sounding track. It is epic and has a lot of cool parts, especially the chorus and the double-tracking Martin vocals in the middle section. Overall, the three-song, mini-concept album-within-an-album is cool and different for Black Sabbath. I'm just glad the band decided not to do a full album of Viking music.

I hate that *Feels Good To Me* gets so much flak from fans. I have spent a lifetime defending it but I shouldn't have to. It is so unjust because it is an amazing song that Martin really brings home with a beautiful vocal performance and Iommi's gentle playing. Nicholls's keyboards add a soothing bridge between verses and chorus, with Powell really making you feel every drum and cymbal smash.

The album finishes with an amazing song, *Heaven In Black!* There is nothing flashy or unique about it. It is just a great jamming song with a simplistic approach. Tony plays a riff, Cozy hits the drums, and Neil and Geoff add some color for Martin's vocal. That's it in a nutshell.

WORLD TURNS SLOWLY

This would end up being the shortest "world" tour Black Sabbath ever conducted! Hitting the road to support TYR, Black Sabbath would start September of 1990 in the UK, playing 10 shows (with throwback rockers Circus Of Power) before the last six dates would be canceled due to poor ticket sales. Black Sabbath, especially Tony Iommi, would be forced to confront the fact that maybe their time had passed. They would spend October and November playing for the fans who came to see them in Germany, Norway, Sweden, and Italy.

Early shows saw several new songs added like *Anno Mundi, The Sabbath Stones,* and *Feels Good To Me,* before almost all the new material would be wiped from the set, save *Anno Mundi*. One of the big highlights on the tour happened on September 8 at London's famed Hammersmith Odeon where the band was joined by Queen guitarist Brian May AND.... former bassist Geezer Butler! It was the first time Iommi and Butler shared a stage together since 1985's Live Aid event when he played *Iron Man* and *Children Of The Grave* with his former band. More than just a two-song jam, this felt like it could be the beginning of opening a dialogue about the possibility of working together again.

Things were bad and both Tony Iommi and manager Ralph Baker knew something had to change! They could blame I.R.S Records all they wanted, but as the world was in the midst of a global recession and war in the Middle East, fans were forced to be more choosy on what they purchased, and a Tony Martin-led Black Sabbath wasn't what the world wanted!

Many fans were a bit confused by the humor for the original cover for Bill Ward's ALONG THE WAY (pictured above)... but I loved it

MANY OPEN DOORS

Surprising, the first Black Sabbath-related release in 1990 would be the first solo album ever from former drummer Bill Ward and his new project, Ward One, called ALONG THE WAY, from Chameleon and Capitol Records. I remember not expecting much from this release. After all, Ward was the drummer and yes, he had a great voice, but even Ringo Starr or Peter Criss couldn't quite carry a full album on their own. Wow...was I so wrong on that assumption. With an incredible guest list including Ozzy Osbourne, Zakk Wylde, Jack Bruce (Cream), Bob Daisley (everyone), Lanny Cordola (Giuffria), and Eric Singer (KISS)... this album is a fun listen.

More Fish (former Marillion vocalist) than Black Sabbath, the album's twelve tracks all have a different sound than a Sabbath fan would expect. Ward's voice is very strong and filled with emotion. From progressive rock to classic rock, songs like *Light Up The Candles* (with Jack Bruce on vocals) and *Shooting Gallery* are ones that I tend to listen to quite often. If you've never heard this album, seek it out right now and hear another side of Bill Ward. You won't be disappointed, I promise.

The no frills art for the JUST SAY OZZY live EP.

C'MON...LET ME SEE YOUR HANDS!

With no new music to put out, Ozzy Osbourne released a very no-frills, low-budget live EP called JUST SAY OZZY on March 17, 1990, on Epic/CBS Records. Recorded in November of 1989 at the Brixton Academy in London, this six-song collection features Ozzy and his band very stripped down and sounding pleasing on the ears. However, there are stories that the album was re-recorded and mixed in the studio, but whatever the truth is, I don't care. The album sounds great with Ozzy's band, guitarist Zakk Wylde, drummer Randy Castillo, keyboardist John Sinclair, and bassist... Geezer Butler. Butler had joined Ozzy following the release of NO REST FOR THE WICKED and certainly adds a new level of sound to the songs in the collection, especially *Sweet Leaf* and *Shot In The Dark*.

Despite being an EP, a format not that popular with American record buyers, JUST SAY OZZY would prove to be another hit for Osbourne, who could do no wrong, hitting #58 on the charts and going gold. Following the tour, including a stop at the Moscow Music Peace Festival with Scorpions, Motley Crue, and Bon Jovi, Butler would leave the band and a possible reunion with Black Sabbath.

NO JOKES FROM THE JESTER!

As DIO prepared for work on their follow-up to DREAM EVIL, the priority was a flashy guitarist who could help bring the band into the new decade. Chosen was 17-year-old Rowen Robertson, who had that needed flash and could play in any style required, something much needed as the music scene was beginning to change. As work began, the band began to fall apart with Vinny Appice, Jimmy Bain, and Claude Schnell all leaving (or being fired) at different stages of recording. By the time the new album, LOCK UP THE WOLVES (Verigo/Reprise Records), was released on May 15, 1990, DIO now featured bassist Teddy Cook, keyboardist Jens Johansson (ex-Yngwie Malmsteen), and former AC/DC drummer Simon Wright. The album wouldn't chart well, going to #61 in the US and #28 in the UK, with sales in the US being less than 50,000 copies. Again, not a reflection of the quality of music but an indicator of the coming storm from Seattle.

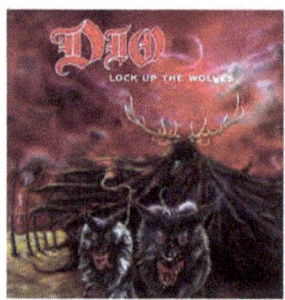 

A very good album that came out at an interesting time for metal music and Ronnie James Dio. With grunge beginning to take over, many wondered where not only DIO, but all the bands we knew and loved would fit in.

LOCK UP THE WOLVES is interesting, but a solid album that, to me, had a more classic Rainbow style rather than a DIO feel, and I love that about the disc. Lyrically, the subject matter was less about fantasy and dealt more with the darker side of the human condition. While on tour, Dio noticed the band playing to fewer and fewer people, understanding that the music of the '70s and '80s was now out, being replaced by a more stripped down and angrier sound, much like the song and video from the album, *Wild One*. A chance meeting between Dio and Geezer Butler in Minneapolis, MN, would result in the bassist joining DIO on stage for several songs, including *Neon Nights*, and opening the doors of communication between the two that have been closed for some time.

FAMILY FEUD - SWINGS AND MISSES

Things were not good in the house that Sabbath built for everyone not named Ozzy. Black Sabbath was struggling to attract an audience with their new line-up(s) and would see their tour fall apart, with TYR doing nothing on the charts. DIO was seeing the same issues on the charts and the road with audiences becoming smaller and smaller and sales a fraction of what they used to be. Both TYR and LOCK UP THE WOLVES offered the fans nothing they wanted to hear. For me, DIO's music became less enjoyable from this album on. I'm not saying it wasn't good, because it certainly was up to his usual high standards, but lyrically it just wasn't resonating with me anymore. I always loved the fight-the-world', slay-any-real-or-proverbial-dragon, and the general believe-in-yourself messages in his music, but now he just seemed angry, like he just gave up. For Ozzy, he always seemed to be having nothing but a good time, sometimes too much of a good time. And, once again, he outsells everyone in the family, even with a live EP!

I wasn't a huge fan of TYR when it first came out, but I certainly liked it. Now all these years later, I love it! Forget the semi-concept album thing and the album is full of great songs with fantastic performances. I put TYR at #14 out of 19 studio albums. TYR is a great album and the last of the ones I consider brilliant because #15 to 19 is where the quality drops right off! The Black Sabbath family of crazies place the album at #16 out of 19, with very little good to talk about.

ANYTIME THAT YOU CALL
JOHN PAYNE (ASIA/DUKES OF THE ORIENT)

Before joining ASIA in 1991, John Payne was picked to participate in Bev Bevan's post-Black Sabbath project, Electric Light Orchestra Part Two. Following rehearsals and behind-the-scenes fighting over the name, Payne accepted the invitation to join keyboardist Geoff Downes in a new version of ASIA following the departure of John Wetton. With ASIA, Payne recorded six stellar albums before the original ASIA got back together and ended his time in the band. Currently, Payne tours regularly as ASIA Featuring John Payne and records with his band, Dukes Of The Orient. Payne was also a friend of Ronnie James Dio and would perform at his memorial service.

The New Testament
Black Sabbath

The Book of Sabbath
Chapter 6

Concede 1:6

With doubt comes the return of the mob,
and a return to the rainbow.
With the giants together once again,
the world was theirs for the taking,
but once again the unity would be broken
by words spoken and unspoken.
Putting the puzzle pieces in place
would set the angel's wings afire
and the beat change
at the behest of the one with the gold.

DEHUMANIZER (I.R.S./Reprise Records)
Released on June 30, 1992
Produced by Reinhold Mack
Ronnie James Dio (vocals), Tony Iommi (guitar), Geezer Butler (bass) and Vinny Appice (drums)
Additional musician Geoff Nicholls (keyboards)
All songs written by Butler, Dio and Iommi

COMPUTER GOD
AFTER ALL
TV CRIMES
LETTERS FROM THE EARTH
MASTER OF INSANITY
TIME MACHINE
SINS OF THE FATHER
TOO LATE
I
BURIED ALIVE

TIME MACHINE (Wayne's World version)

"We wanted to capture what we are live. That's really what I think we did." – Ronnie James Dio

A WONDERFUL DAY FOR A KILLING

At this point, all the talk of a Black Sabbath reunion strictly revolved around Ozzy Osbourne being the vocalist, so word of Ronnie James Dio returning came as a shock to many. Behind the scenes, Iommi's manager, Ralph Baker, was reaching out to Gloria Butler (Geezer's wife and manager) and Wendy Dio, about the possibility of reuniting the trio. Once Iommi and Dio communicated with one another and cleared the air of any (many) unpleasantries between the two, the plan began to move forward at a rapid-fire pace. No one member was coming in with any real power over the others since all their careers had stagnated over the last few years, and so no one really made any demands. The only problem was that there already was a band called Black Sabbath that had four members with two of them, Tony Martin and Neil Murray, no longer needed. The plan for Iommi was to use drummer Cozy Powell, but Iommi wasn't aware of how deep the personal issues between Dio and Powell were. Everyone knew how big this reunion could be, especially for the Black Sabbath brand, so everyone went into this project wanting it to work.

"We went to the states to do some rehearsals for a couple of months and it didn't particularly gel. The chemistry just wasn't right." – Cozy Powell

The current line-up of Black Sabbath had already begun to write and rehearse new material, looking to start work on an album in late 1991. Obviously, the record labels and concert promoters worldwide were becoming excited about the return of Ronnie James Dio and were behind the reunion...not the current band. Everyone knew the Martin-led line-up would result in more of the same: low charting albums and minimal touring due to a lack of interest by fans and promoters. Iommi also knew this could be a huge shot of much-needed cash and publicity for the Black Sabbath brand, even if this didn't work out beyond one album.

For Neil Murray it was easy. He would always comment on how the band was Geezer's and seemed to always be expecting Butler to return someday. In fact, Butler had all but returned and planned on working with Iommi and Powell in Black Sabbath, but not a Martin-led version. For Tony Martin, it was a bit more difficult. He'd finally cemented his place in the band and was helping them make some excellent albums despite the sales and chart numbers. He would hear the news as he was heading out the door to go to rehearsals.

"Literally on the way out the door the phone rang, and it was my manager. He said, you better sit down."
– Tony Martin

Tony Martin would be able to cash in (a bit) on him being a former vocalist of Black Sabbath. He secured a modest record deal with Polydor Records and began to work on his first solo album. Playing all the instruments on the demos, Martin had a solid bit of material to work with since he had been writing for the next Sabbath album. But with Dio back in the fold, all was not good, aqnd was, in fact, almost toxic. As Iommi and Butler would find out during the first set of rehearsals, the issues with Dio and Powell were deep, unresolved, and were setting up to derail the entire project. Conversations with Iommi and Powell led the drummer to believe this was just a one-off to re-establish the band and was willing to go along with this situation, no matter how uncomfortable it may be. In one really tense moment, Dio packed his bags and returned to America, forcing Iommi to reach out to Martin to bring him back in to continue work. Already well into work on his solo album, Martin returned much to the anger of his label and co-producer. Then in an unfortunate accident, a horse that Cozy Powell was riding had a heart attack and fell on the drummer, breaking his hip, laying him up for six months. With the drummer now out of the picture, Dio came back and Martin was unfairly out again. For the drummer spot, Dio suggested his current (and former AC/DC) player, Simon Wright, but the consensus was to bring back Vinny Appice, for consistency and to be able to market this as a reunion of the MOB RULES / LIVE EVIL line-up. Appice was in California working on his new project, WWIII, with former Dio bassist Jimmy Bain, singer Mandy Lion, and a heavy riffing guitarist named Tracy G., when he got the call. With the chance to pick up where he left off in 1983, Appice jumped at the chance.

With the line-up now set and everyone seemingly on the same page, rehearsals, writing, and recording would commence. Years later, tracks surfaced featuring Powell in the line-up (*The Night Life* and *Bad Blood*) as well as full sessions, giving the listener a glimpse into "what if?" Powell remained.

The cassette inlay for DEHUMANIZER and the all-important press kit photo making it all official! This is what the fans (like me) wanted!

In putting together songs, especially the lyrics, the band decided (well, Butler and Iommi) to stay away from the typical Dio lyrics about rainbows, dragons, and fantasy. Instead, they told the singer to write about what is going on in the world today, much like the now-popular grunge bands were doing successfully. Reluctantly agreeing, Dio did his best to step out of his comfort zone and did the best he could within the parameters he was given. To get the sound right, Dio suggested German producer Reinhold Mack put this new album together. Well known in the industry as Mack, bands like Electric Light Orchestra, Queen, Billy Squier, and Extreme would have some of their biggest successes with Mack at the helm. Black Sabbath would travel to Wales (Rockfield Studios) in the Fall of 1991 and begin working on this line-up's first studio album together in over a decade. One of the songs for the new album that didn't feature DIO's lyrics was the song *Master Of Insanity*, a song brought in by Butler from his ill-fated Geezer Butler Band project. The song was written by Butler and guitarist Jimi Bell, who received no credit or payment for the song but would publicly be given credit for his contribution.

"There was a lot of pressure because everybody was expecting so much from us." – Tony Iommi

Like the band did for MOB RULES, they would first record a song for a film, but this one a comedy, WAYNE'S WORLD. The film, based on a comedy skit appearing on Saturday Night Live, did much better at the box office than HEAVY METAL back in the day, so the track wouldn't be lost in a film no one saw. But the song wouldn't be featured in the film, just the soundtrack. WAYNE'S WORLD was a number-one hit at the box office and grossed almost $122 million. The soundtrack to the film (featuring an all-star line-up of talent) was driven by Queen's *Bohemian Rhapsody* and sold over two million copies, going to #1 on the US charts.

The recording of the album, now called DEHUMANIZER, took a little longer than expected, with the band stepping away from their desire to make a raw-sounding record. There ended up being issues with Mack's styles and the band's expectations not quite lining up. Iommi later say how his friend Brian May, who worked with Mack, didn't have a positive experience and asked Iommi, "Are you sure you're going to use him?"

DEMENTED SOUNDS OF LAUGHTER

Black Sabbath decided to go full-on comic book sci-fi for the cover to DEHUMANIZER and for me, it has mixed results. Featured is a futuristic and robotic take on the Grim Reaper complete with a scythe and mechanized body underneath the traditional robe of death. In his clutches is a young victim that appears to be assimilated (like the Cyberman or Borg) from human to machine. At least that is what I interpret the cover as. It could just be a robot-on-robot crime, but considering the title I'd go with assimilation. Either way...BAD NEWS for the dude!

I'm not exactly sure what I have an issue with when it comes to the cover because I love the art and the story it tells. I always felt a bit uncomfortable with the odd angle. Not being able to see feet or floor makes me look at it as a badly cropped photograph. I do love the old-school cathedral with high-tech inside, and the logo and title are awesome, but the angle is just off for me. With music, specifically metal, relying heavily on mascots (like Eddie and Vic Rattlehead) and cool imaginative imagery, I think this could have been something special. Artistically, the illustration by Wil Rees is great and fits into the mood of the music and continues a theme and style first started with DIO's VHS collection TIME MACHINE (1990) and LOCK UP THE WOLVES (1990).

STAY OUT OF THE SHADOWS

Before the album's worldwide release on June 30, 1992, the press machine was in full force for Black Sabbath. It was huge news in 1992 that the Dio-led Black Sabbath was back and looking to save Heavy Metal and Hard Rock from disappearing in a sea of flannel, much like they helped do in 1980 with AC/DC. The world already heard *Time Machine* on the Wayne's World soundtrack and fans were excited. I was excited. Really excited. A lot was riding on DEHUMANIZER to be the monster everyone hoped...maybe too much expectation.

Against all odds, DEHUMANIZER hit the charts and hit them hard, bringing the band back on the charts in the US (#44), the UK (#28), and Canada (#36). Critics praised the heaviness and many old school fans came back out of curiosity. What they heard was not the band from 1980 – 1982, but a heavier, louder, and more approachable Black Sabbath. But, for many, something was missing. Despite the bit of a disappointment in the sales, the album was the best-charting in the US since SEVENTH STAR, but in the UK the album didn't chart higher than TYR did in 1990.

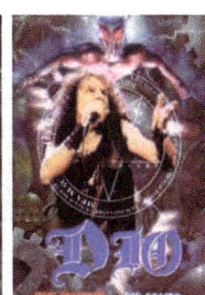

Illustrator Wil Reese came into the DEHUMANIZER project already having worked with DIO on the TIME MACHINE collection.

A video for *TV Crimes* was shot and seen on MTV and other video outlets quite a bit (among the Weezer, Pearl Jam, and Nirvana stuff), showing a more down-to-earth Black Sabbath just performing and looking like just another band, something much needed to survive.

"The communication problem came up. Is anyone gonna talks about this?" – Ronnie James Dio

GET YOUR MONEY ON THE LINE

I remember hearing the heavy drums of Vinny Appice starting it all off and getting really excited, but once *Computer God* got going, I was taken back by the sheer heaviness of the song. I was shocked that Ronnie James Dio wasn't singing above the song. Bass and guitar seemed to be playing the same notes, taking away any real depth. I always thought the song was a bit boring until about halfway when it changes tempo.

"It is so unfortunate that people hate so much." – Ronnie James Dio

Once After All (The Dead) started I was already feeling like it was more of the same monotone stuff and I was not impressed. I can now listen to this song and hear the beauty of it, the melodies and time changes leading into the choruses, but back then I wanted *Neon Knights* and *Mob Rules*. Tony Iommi pulls out a lot of familiar sounds that gives this one some life and a subtle reminder that this is Black Sabbath.

TV Crimes is as close to the classic Dio line-up as anything else on the album. The track is very riffy and a straight-ahead rocker that really has a lot of serious symbol work from Appice you can feel. The guitar solo is amazing and has all the magic without a lot of effects. Possibly the best song on the album and one I will go back to time and again to listen to.

"Lyrically changed! Melodically changed! Rhythmically changed!" – Ronnie James Dio

Again, I know that *Letters From Earth* is one of the most popular songs on the album, but until it picks up the pace it really does nothing for me. I find it a bit too plodding and kinda boring and it never goes anywhere. Again, very cymbally! Although it does have a *Tempus Fugit* (YES) thing going on which gives it some extra points.

A song that Geezer Butler brought in, *Master Of Insanity*, holds a special place in my heart because of my friendship with the uncredited co-writer, Jimi Bell. Musically, this one has more life than the other songs, featuring some cool riffs, and gives you a greater degree of satisfaction than most of the stuff on the album. I think what really grabs me is the classic Rainbow feel to it (due to Bell's love of Richie Blackmore), with Geoff Nicholls keyboards below everyone really creating a musical bed for the rest of the band to follow.

Although I already heard *Time Machine* on the radio a few times, the song really does it for me. It sounds like it came from MOB RULES and I think that gave me a false expectation of what to expect from the entire album. The song is exactly that, a song, intro, verse, chorus, repeat, solo, chorus, and fade. Every song doesn't have to be epic or make a grand statement. Sometimes we just need a song to be a song.

"You can't hear the bloody thing in the film." – Geezer Butler

Sins Of The Father is as close to Dio singing Ozzy as you can get. The beginning has a real SABBATH BLOODY SABBATH or SABOTAGE feel to it, with the high vocal riding the riff. The problems start for me when the song turns into something else and goes nowhere. When it begins to pick up the pace, with some tasty leads, it gets good. Other than that, not a big fan.

  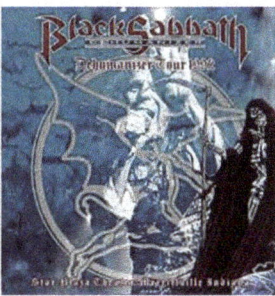

First, the Japanese release of DEHUMANIZER. Next is a three-disc set called REHEARSALS that features the band working through the new songs for the album, and comedy from Cozy Powell, and a song called Bad Blood. Last is a cool recording of a show from the tour.

Not being able to sing about rainbows and fantasy began to really grate on me with this song. *Too Late* is, for me, the least likable song on DEHUMANIZER for the simple fact that it goes nowhere. The acoustic pieces from Iommi with Dio singing are the only good parts of this song.

A song that breaks the mold on the album is *I*. This song would be one of the best Black Sabbath songs ever, but suffers a bit from blending with what came before it. Lyrically, we finally see hear Dio standing up to the masses from the top of a mountain with reaffirming confidence. We are also treated to a lot of great Iommi.

Trying to get through *Buried Alive* became a struggle and still kinda is. Another one that is heavy and pounding but really never goes anywhere. I know this one is another really popular song on the album and certainly reflects Black Sabbath in 1992, but I was still looking for Black Sabbath 1982.

The CD's bonus track, *Time Machine* (Waynes World version) is the song you hear on the soundtrack and the song that was played on the radio months before the release of the album. With Dio returning, this was big news and this song got a lot of play. The intro is more fun, with the keyboards being a bit brighter and the riff toned down a bit. Vocally, Dio doesn't sound so angry and is full of the light and passion we are used to. And man, does Geezer's bass sound so good! Better production than the album version.

"I think apart from the original line-up it's the other one that worked." – Geezer Butler

THE FIRST TO ESCAPE

Black Sabbath started their support of DEHUMANIZER in late June of 1992 in South America, playing nine shows before beginning a very important and visible trek into the United States. Despite the hype, the line-up, and the overall good showing off the album on the charts, metal was in a bit of a slide and not able to fill arenas anymore. Not to mention, a financial recession had hit the US and disposable income was nonexistent. This was why I couldn't afford to see the band in Hartford in September. Even the two biggest bands of the day, Metallica and Guns N' Roses, had to team up to sell tickets, so Black Sabbath had to play to smaller halls and theatres. Opening for the band would be Danzig, Love/Hate (with Jizzy Pearl), Exodus, and Skew Siskin. In the UK, Testament would have the honors of opening the shows.

"When you have to get Guns N' Roses and Metallica on the same tour to sell tickets, it shows everyone that you have to put big packaging together to make a difference." – Ronnie James Dio

Black Sabbath also got a chance to play some major European festivals in 1992. The Monsters Of Rock had something for everyone in Reggio Emilia (Italy), with Sabbath sharing the bill with Warrant, Testament, Pantera, Megadeth, and Iron Maiden. Another Monsters Of Rock festival (this one in Mannheim, Germany) featured some of the heaviest bands out there: Helloween, Slayer, Testament, The Almighty, W.A.S.P., and Iron Maiden. The Iron Maiden appearances would be some of the last shows to feature vocalist Bruce Dickinson until his return in 1999. Added to the setlist were five songs from DEHUMANIZER: *Computer God, Time Machine, After All (I'm Dead), I,* and *TV Crimes. Master Of Insanity* would make an appearance when the band had a longer set to play. As expected, there was a heavy dose of Dio-era music and six Ozzy songs, yet no Tony Martin, Ian Gillan, or Glenn Hughes material.

Word from the band members was that this was not a relaxed or even enjoyable tour as people would have hoped. Many of the bad feelings from the 1980s came back again and began eating away at what the band was trying to accomplish. Iommi couldn't get his much-needed alone time. Dio and Appice would share a dressing room, creating unhealthy divisions, again. There was almost a physical altercation between a very drunk Butler and Dio, with the result being Geezer head-butting a statue. Performances weren't affected at all, with the band pulling out some of the best shows of their career and the audiences appreciating every second of it. Then the real trouble started...

"I really thought getting back together with those guys would be easier." - Ronnie James Dio

As the tour began to wind down, Sharon Osbourne reached out to Black Sabbath to see if they would be interested in helping Ozzy say farewell, thinking this was going to be the last show of his career. Due to a misdiagnosis of multiple sclerosis, the singer thought his career was over and the hope was to have Black Sabbath play two shows with Ozzy in Costa Mesa, CA. Black Sabbath would play a bit of an abbreviated set and then Ozzy and Bill Ward would come out and finish the show(s) playing four songs. Iommi and Butler agreed right away but their current singer, Ronnie James Dio, did not. For Iommi, Butler, and Ward, it was a great way to cap off an amazing and quite interesting run for their friend and former vocalist.

"Yeah, OK... of course, we will be there." – Tony Iommi

No matter how the band tried to sell it to Dio he wasn't biting, understandably, and was insulted that he was even be asked to do this, considering the bad blood between him and Ozzy...and also feeling that this move would be a huge step back for Black Sabbath. No matter how much convincing was done or pressure applied, Dio stood his ground, and, following the last contracted show on November 13, 1992, in Oakland, CA, Ronnie James Dio was gone again.

"I'm not doing that! I'm not supporting that clown!" – Ronnie James Dio

Without a singer again, Black Sabbath now had to figure out who would lead the band for these two shows. The first call went out to surprise, surprise (no surprise) to Tony Martin, who was just finishing up his first solo album. Always the team player, Martin agreed to do the shows, but some visa problems arose, and he couldn't get into the US. Then, saving the day would be fellow Birmingham vocalist, Rob Halford, who had just recently left Judas Priest in May of 1992 and was putting together his own band, Fight. The band flew to Halford's Arizona home and rehearsed a 12-song set featuring some Black Sabbath classics, as well as a few Dio favorites. Halford did the two shows, giving the band a serious vocal kick as only the metal god could.

Following the Black Sabbath set, and then Ozzy's solo show, the original Black Sabbath, Tony Iommi, Geezer Butler, Bill Ward, and Ozzy Osbourne, would return to the stage together and finish the show with *Black Sabbath, Fairies Wear Boots, Iron Man,* and *Paranoid*. 1992 started off for Black Sabbath with one reunion with Ronnie James Dio and ended up with another reunion, an unexpected one altogether, with Ozzy Osbourne.

"You know, I just get goosebumps thinking about it now. It's just very overwhelming, the emotion is very overwhelming." – Rob Halford (Judas Priest/Fight/Halford)

Tony Martin's amazing album BACK WHERE I BELONG and a clip of Tony performing If There Is A Heaven on German TV with a few of his Black Sabbath friends, like drummer Cozy Powell, bassist Neil Murray, and Mario Parga on guitar. Damn... this album is so good!

NINE LIVES FOR THE CAT

Between his on-again/off-again time in Black Sabbath, Tony Martin was able to release an amazing solo debut in 1992 called BACK WHERE I BELONG from Polydor Records. Going back to his more melodic roots, Martin wrote all the songs on the album by himself, except the reworking of Jerusalem, the Black Sabbath song that appeared on TYR. Interesting that the album has an almost Marillion feel to it, possibly due to co-producer Nick Tauber having produced the first three Marillion albums. It dances in and out of styles, yet has a cool vibe to it. I remember hearing this album for the first time around 2000 and being blown away by how mature and full of radio hits it was, if only radio was playing good music. *Angel In The Bed*, the title track, and *If There Is A Heaven* are the stand-out songs on an album featuring a lot of stand-out songs. Sounding more like Foreigner and Bad Company than Black Sabbath, this release validates the talent and misuse of Tony Martin. Featuring Brian May, Neil Murray, Laurence Cottle, Geoff Nicholls, Zak Starkey, and Nigel Glockler, Martin surrounded himself with talented friends and it shows in the music.

As expected, the album didn't do anything because there wasn't much of a push from the label, especially internationally, and Martin found himself caught in the middle of Black Sabbath fans thinking he is too smooth and soft for their band and AOR fans passing because of the expectations of being an ex-Black Sabbath singer. Song for song.... an easy 8 out of 10.

"Ian Gillan asked me once if I had actually been fired and I said, "No." He said, "Neither have I." We should just turn up one day and walk on stage!" – Tony Martin

FINAL THOUGHTS

I will admit here and now that I expected way more from DEHUMANIZER than I was given. I also wrongly expected a Dio-led Black Sabbath to continue where they left off and give me the son of MOB

RULES or the cousin of HEAVEN AND HELL...and I got neither. DEHUMANIZER is a tough album to pin down style-wise because it sounds so much more like the follow-up to LOCK UP THE WOLVES than a Black Sabbath album. The guitar tones Iommi uses are mostly the same from song to song and the riffs he plays are certainly heavier than anything before, but there isn't any personality, or, at least, his personality. I would also come to realize that this reunion wasn't as organic as I had hoped and it shows in the music. I much prefer Tony Martin's solo album to DEHUMANIZER and rate this album as my #17 out of 19 studio albums. The Black Sabbath and Dio fans on Facebook who love this album rank it very high, placing it at #10. But I will say this... I like DEHUMANIZER much better now than I did before, but DEHUMANIZER wasn't the album I wanted, and that is my fault for expecting something they didn't want to make.

The year should have been one of the greatest in the history of the band, but things couldn't have gone any worse for Black Sabbath in 1992. With the return of Ronnie James Dio, Geezer Butler, and Vinny Appice, Tony Iommi had a line-up that would make the world take notice. As big as the return of Dio may have been, it always seemed to be unfairly a runner-up to the big prize, a reunion with Ozzy Osbourne. There isn't anything wrong with that, but the two shows in Costa Mesa not only destroyed the relationship with Dio, it also added another frustrating moment in the Tony Martin saga. Following the shows, Iommi and Butler were hoping that a reunion would happen with Osbourne and Ward, but that wouldn't happen, at least not yet.

From Rage Against The Machine (a band I didn't like) to Audioslave (a band I loved) to his own brand of sugar-free lemonade, Olade, Wilk has led a very successful life inside and outside of the music world and is active in raising money for diabetes awareness.

RAGE AGAINST THE AUDIOSLAVE
BRAD WILK

As Black Sabbath struggled to keep their line-up together in 1992, drummer Brad Wilk (born September 5, 1968) and his band, Rage Against The Machine, released their politically charged self-titled debut album to much fanfare and excitement. Going triple-platinum in the US alone, Wilk would be the backbone for a sound and feeling that resonated with music fans but would run its course in 2000, with vocalist Zack de la Rocha announcing he was leaving, ending the band's career with four albums and nine million albums sold in the US alone.

The remaining members of the band: Tom Morello (guitarist) and Tim Commerford (bass) would join Wilk and Soundgarden frontman Chris Cornell to form the much-celebrated Audioslave. Success came easy for the band with their radio-friendly music and Cornell's smooth voice helping Wilk to catch lighting again until tensions split the band in 2007. Despite his alternative passions, Wilk was influenced by the best of the best: John Bonham, Keith Moon, and Alex Van Halen. In 2012, producer Rick Ruben thought so much of Wilk's playing that he asked him to play on Black Sabbath's reunion album in 2013. A massive honor indeed!

CALLING ON YOU
MICHAEL SWEET (STRYPER)

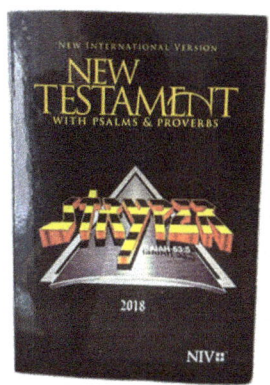

www.stryper.com

"I always loved Black Sabbath even when it wasn't cool for a Christian to like them." Stryper recorded Heaven And Hell for their awesome cover album called THE COVERING in 2011 and then recorded After Forever for their brilliant 2015 release, FALLEN! The last two pictures were taken by Bryan Grenier.

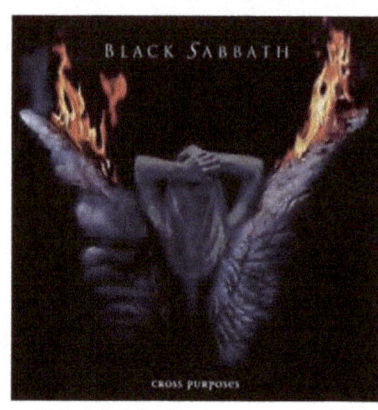

CROSS PURPOSES (I.R.S.Records)
Released on January 31, 1994
Produced by Leif Mases and Black Sabbath
Tony Martin (vocals), Tony Iommi (guitar), Geezer Butler (bass), Geoff Nicholls (keyboards) and Bobby Rondinelli (drums)
All songs written by Butler, Iommi and Martin

I WITNESS
CROSS OF THORNS
PSYCHOPHOBIA
VIRTUAL DEATH
IMMACULATE DECEPTION
DYING FOR LOVE
BACK TO EDEN
THE HAND THAT ROCKS THE CRADLE
CARDINAL SIN
EVIL EYE
WHAT'S THE USE (Japanese Bonus Track)

"When I rejoined Sabbath, I didn't view it as a short-term venture." - Ronnie James Dio

BEHIND YOU, HISTORY

Tony Iommi just couldn't catch a break at all, seeing every decision he made endeing up with one step up and two steps back! In 1990, Iommi led an incredibly talented line-up of Black Sabbath but no one really cared or supported the effort because it wasn't the line-up the fans wanted. When Ozzy found out that his MS diagnosis was wrong, he at first planned on reuniting with Butler, Iommi, and Bill Ward. But, following months of speculation, Ozzy ended up back in the recording studio working on the album that would become NO MORE TEARS. This now left Iommi and Butler with no band and forced them to scramble.

"Of course, after that there were rumors all over the place about the old line-up getting together again. Everyone assumed..." - Tony Iommi

Unknown to many, before and following the Costa Mesa gigs, Iommi was stuck in the United States, unable to go home due to his passport being seized following an unsubstantial claim by his ex-wife (living in California) that he owed back child support, and a lot of it. One step up and two steps back.

For Ronnie James Dio and Vinny Appice, there were hurt feelings but the duo ended up reuniting for another DIO album, the heavy, angry, and very monotone STRANGE HIGHWAYS, in 1993. Along with Jeff Pilson (bass) and new guitarist Tracy G (Grijalva), the album would continue the downward spiral of bad sales and shows playing to less than half full clubs/small theatres. Again, this wasn't a reflection of the music's quality. The music scene was changing drastically and everyone, except a handful of rock/metal bands, was struggling just to survive. One of those who was surviving was Ozzy Osbourne, who, rejuvenated from his misdiagnosis, would hit the road and release the two-disc set LIVE & LOUD, showcasing the best of Ozzy on stage. The set would go platinum and peak on the US charts at #22. To prove Osbourne's staying power and popularity, he would win a Grammy for Best Metal Performance in 1994 for the song *I Don't Want To Change The World* from this collection. As far as Ozzy and Sharon Osbourne were concerned, there would be no reunion with Black Sabbath, ever!

"We didn't have a band anymore!" – Tony Iommi

When Iommi finally got back home his first goal was to put Black Sabbath back together, but this time he wasn't alone. Geezer Butler, having nothing else going on, stuck around to help resurrect the band, but he wasn't happy at all at how things fell apart so badly. For a vocalist, the first inquiry was to Rob Halford. Halford had just put together his own band, Fight, and was ready to release their debut album, so he declined the offer. Next came the thought of trying to bring back Ronnie James Dio, but the call would eventually go to Mr. Reliable, Tony Martin. Black Sabbath wasn't the only band trying to find their way in this unfortunate time in history. Both Judas Priest and Iron Maiden were trying to survive with new singers, Priest with the Rob Halford soundalike Tim "Ripper" Owens and Maiden with the anti-Bruce Dickenson, Blaze Bayley.

"We didn't look for other singers. We simply asked Tony Martin back again." – Tony Iommi

History would sort of repeat itself when it came to the drumming spot with Cozy Powell understandably not wanting to come back to the band. His was an easy decision considering his then-current work with

Brian May. In his place would be the player that replaced him a decade (plus a few years) earlier in Rainbow, Bobby Rondinelli. Between session work, Doro, Quiet Riot, and his own band, Rondinelli, the drummer heard about the vacancy and reached out to Tony Iommi to express his desire and dream to play with Black Sabbath. Iommi was impressed with his impulse to get the gig. He offered it to Rondinelli on the phone, knowing what type of player he was. With the band built up again, Black Sabbath spent a few months finishing up music that was already started with Martin (when Dio left before recording DEHUMANIZER) and moved their operations to Monnow Valley Studios in Wales to begin recording.

Once again, Black Sabbath decided to produce themselves but would use a co-producer, Leif Mases, who the band worked with on the soundtrack (and far superior) version of Time Machine the previous year. Before working with Sabbath, Mases worked as an engineer, mixer, producer, and arranger with Ian Gillan on his amazing and criminally neglected NAKED THUNDER, as well as work with Europe, Jeff Beck, and Jimmy Page. Mases began his career mixing Led Zeppelin's post-break-up album, CODA, in 1983.

Black Sabbath would be in and out of the studio, delivering their seventeenth studio album to I.R.S. Records, who would actually spend some money on TV advertising (on MTV) to help promote the album. Titles thrown around were SOULED OUT and IMMACULATE DECEPTION, but the band settled on the very cool CROSS PURPOSES. Rock-It Comix would release a Black Sabbath comic magazine, written by Geezer Butler before the album's release, and bring the world of Black Sabbath to the comic book shelves.

"I'm a fan of early Silver Age Marvel, especially Stan Lee and Jack Kirby." – Geezer Butler

Say Goodbye to the Rainbow

Going back to the days of upsetting the church or anyone with a spiritual reverence, the cover for CROSS PURPOSES was created to stir the pot...but no one was tasting. It featured the back view of a emale angel, hands on her head in almost a surrender pose with her wings beginning to burn from the top. Her body language indicates that the angel almost seems to have given up and given into her fate. Shocking and quite gripping, the black cover with the grey figure and bright flames really jumps out at you, even in the smaller CD format. The graphic designer was Matt Curtis using a photo by Peter Mountain. Model Melodie Hampson should be applauded for helping to create one of Black Sabbath's best album covers.

There was a thank-you to the Modesto County Jail "for their kind hospitality and making me realize that there's no place like home." Seeing that back in 1994 didn't make much sense, but years later when Iommi wrote of the story in his autobiography, IRON MAN, about his imprisonment before the Ozzy reunion shows the previous year for overdue child support, the thank-you was less funny.

The back cover continues the same theme with the song titles and some credits at the bottom of the jacket and flames rising almost to engulf them. The album, CD, and cassettes also contained lyrics which was a nice bonus for listeners to be able to follow along with what Martin was singing. Overall, CROSS PURPOSES was a solid package, despite you not being able to read the lyrics in the booklet, even back then when my eyes were still good.

There Are No Rules Here

Black Sabbath released CROSS PURPOSES (I.R.S. Records) with much anticipation and expectations on January 31, 1994. Sadly, for the band, it became just more of the same thing, at least as far as recent history. Despite some very positive press and reviews, the album did very little chart-wise or with sales, only going to #122 in the US and #41 in the UK. A video was produced for the song *The Hand That Rocks The Cradle*, but no matter how good the song was or how cool the video looked, no one would see it until years later on YouTube. This is becoming a broken record in the band's story, but people stayed away from another brilliant Tony Martin album for whatever reason.

"For once, I.R.S was getting behind it, they were doing advertisements on MTV." – Tony Iommi

As mentioned above, Rock-It Comix, the magazine arm of the then incredibly hot Malibu Comics, released a Black Sabbath comic as part of their rock comic (but magazine-sized) line that featured other artists like Santana, Metallica, Megadeth, Lita Ford, and the ultra-popular Pantera! Each book contained a comic story, ads for cool merchandise, a discography, interviews with the band, and a lot of cool pictures. Some were better than others, but it was always great to see my favorite bands and artists in the 4-color world.

 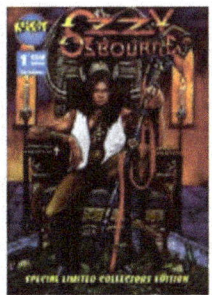  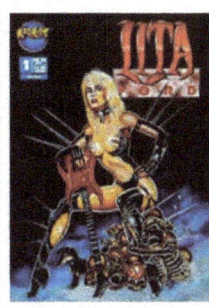

In the late 1980s and early '90s, comic book companies like Revolutionary and Rock-IT Comix began to cross over into the rock world with some success. Above are four of the magazine-sized books from Rock-It Comix that had instant credibility due to a lot of input from the bands they worked with.

PEOPLE ALWAYS TRY TO CHANGE ME

Another burner of an album intro, *I Witness* has an incredible build-up leading it into a lower register and an almost Axl Rose-like vocal provided by Tony Martin. Musically, the addition of Geezer Butler adds another level of awesome missing on the last bunch of albums. Bobby Rondinelli's drums are well recorded and crisp, which really help to push the song.

Moody and dark, *Cross Of Thorns* is a very Dio-inspired track where we hear Martin's amazing vocal range. Obviously, the song, like all of them, is set up by Tony Iommi perfectly, with acoustic moments leading into the heavy. Geoff Nicholls's keyboards provide the perfect backdrop to the band. My favorite song on the album and a pure Sabbath classic.

Unfortunately, the album takes a bit of a step down with *Psychophobia*. The song isn't bad, but it takes a while to set up and become interesting. The verses don't really do much, but the chorus is pretty cool, and leading into the guitar solo does grab you for a bit. When Martin sings for us to "kiss the rainbow goodbye," is that a reference to Ronnie James Dio? Lyrically, Martin is very expressive, paints a great picture, and sadly, doesn't get the credit he deserves as a lyricist.

"I thought he was a really good singer." – Geezer Butler

I get a little lost with the album on *Virtual Death!* Musically, lyrically, and production-wise, it is pure Grunge in the vein of Alice In Chains, a band many Metalheads like, but not me. As a hater of all things grunge, I automatically shut off on this one. But, when you listen to it without prejudice, you can hear so much Sabbath in the grooves that shows Black Sabbath's early 1970's output was so instrumental to forging the Grunge sound.

Picking it back up is *Immaculate Deception*, an amazing title, and a great song. Again, Martin uses his voice in another range and style, really showing how versatile he can be. Once the song really gets going with classic Iommi riffs and Butler's dancing bass, we begin to get something really special and cool. Musically and delivery-wise, this one seems to show Iommi and Butler were formulating musical ideas with Dio's vocal style still in mind.

"Working with Geezer Butler was great." – Tony Martin

Slowing down (but not ballad slow), we get the very bluesy *Dying For Love*. This song is wide open and gives everyone a chance to shine and be heard, displaying the magic of Mases as a producer. The lyrics are haunting and are a huge part of why this album is so good!

Back To Eden is another amazing song from the tones of the guitar to the arrangements and the execution. If it wasn't for the magic the band brought into it, it could have easily ended up a very mediocre song. Like every song, Butler really announces his presence and helps Iommi create a nice foundation to solo over. There are moments when the song sounds so modern at the same time. You can hear some classic 70's influences.

The album's epic track, *The Hand That Rocks The Cradle*, was given a video treatment, but sadly no one saw it. This one is very heavy, expressive, and loud and harkens back to HEADLESS CROSS. The almost progressive moments make the song into a classic piece. Too bad the majority of fans didn't get to hear this one or give it a chance. This is Black Sabbath at their best!

"The Hand That Rocks The Cradle was a radio hit in Pittsburgh!" - Greg Uhrlen (Pennsylvania)

Due to a misprint on the album's sleeve, "Sin, Cardinal Sin" was just shortened to *Cardinal Sin*. It is an average song that really has that *Kashmir* da-da-da guitar going that after a while gets a bit distracting for me. Before the solo, the song really seems to just lose its place and kinda fall apart. It has a slight Iron Maiden intro/build-up that really goes to waste when it goes into a different direction.

"Tony gave me a lot of freedom, allowing me to play whatever I wanted." – Bobby Rondinelli

The last song on the disc is a very Dio-sounding song called *Evil Eye*. This song sounds like it's right out of the DEHUMANIZER session, but with a more expressive voice. There have always been rumors that Eddie Van Halen helped write and played on the track but didn't get credit for contractual reasons. According to THE VAN HALEN SAGA by Ian Christie, the guitar hero did co-write the song but didn't play on it. For me, this is a song that I could hear Dio and Osbourne singing. It just fits right in the middle.

"Having a jam with Eddie (Van Halen) and letting go, it gave everyone a boost." – Tony Iommi

The Japanese release got the very interesting bonus track, *What's The Use*. It is a good song that I could take or leave except for the pure Rainbow sound of it. Obviously, with a former Rainbow drummer and an incredibly versatile singer, Black Sabbath almost created their own version of *Death Alley Driver*, a song from STRAIGHT BETWEEN THE EYES, the 1982 release that featured Bobby Rondinelli. Listen to Iommi play the solo channeling Richie Blackmore. Very cool.

Back in a pre-digital world, if you wanted to take pictures at a concert, you needed an actual camera and not get caught with it. These historic photos are from the camera of Michael Suilleabhain during the CROSS PURPOSES tour, one of his 82 times seeing the band.

DAY, DAY AFTER NIGHT

If Black Sabbath had reunited with Ozzy as planned or was able to keep the Dio line-up moving along, tour plans and the venues played would have been so much different. Instead of the band playing the bigger halls, they were once again regulated to small theatres and clubs, especially in the U.S. The CROSS PURPOSES tour started in America at a bowling alley-turned club (a real cool club I might add) in New Britain, CT, called The Sting on February 8, 1994, and finished up 25 shows later in Florida. I didn't see the band at The Sting because I was just married, no extra money, and my wife wasn't as tolerant of my music as she is now. Opening for Black Sabbath was death metal band Morbid Angel and the legendary Motorhead. From March to June the band played in Japan and all over Europe with a show being recorded for a possible live album and video at the Hammersmith, Apollo, in London.

"Of course, there's no food on their (Motorhead) rider at all, only booze." – Tony Iommi

The set list would really be a trip in and out of the band's vast and ever-growing history. Of course, you would have the few new ones like *Psychophobia, I Witness, Immaculate Deception*, and *Cross Of Thorns* inserted into the set with the return of *Sabbath Bloody Sabbath*, a song that, as memory served, hadn't been played on any tour, EVER!

"I think he did the Dio stuff better than the Ozzy. He was more suited for that." – Geezer Butler

The band would finish the tour playing a festival in Seinajoki, Finland, on June 11, 1994, and planned to take a few months off before some big festivals in Chile including KISS and Slayer. Before rehearsals for the Monsters Of Rock shows, drummer Bobby Rondinelli came at the band asking for (or demanding) a raise. The drummer wasn't coming from any real position of power. He was told not only told no, but that his services were no longer required. Since the reunion shows with Ozzy, Iommi and Butler had been in contact with Bill Ward, and knowing the commitment was only four shows (despite playing to over 100,000 fans per show), they all agreed to have their original drummer back. Following rehearsals and a modification of the set list, ¾ of the original Black Sabbath played a 12-song set made up of almost all Ozzy material, except *Neon Knights, Heaven and Hell, Children Of The Sea, Time Machine*, and *Headless Cross*.

You can find one of the shows on YouTube, called Black Sabbath – Live In Buenos Aires, Argentina. The band put together a high-energy show with Bill Ward doing a solid job behind the kit. The tracks were all songs that Ward recorded except one, *Headless Cross*, that still fit in perfectly with the set of classic material. Also, notice a clean-shaven Tony Martin channeling his inner Ozzy with his stage presence and how he works for the crowd.

Paying Tribute

On October 4, 1994, Sony Music released the compilation, NATIVITY IN BLACK – A TRIBUTE TO BLACK SABBATH. The collection features only Ozzy-era Black Sabbath songs performed by some of the heavier bands of the day like Biohazard (*After Forever*), White Zombie (*Children Of The Grave*), Sepultura (*Symptom Of The Universe*), and Megadeth (*Paranoid*), all bands that were influenced by the Sabbath sound. There were even some great guest appearances like Bruce Dickenson with Godspeed (*Sabbath Bloody Sabbath*), Faith No More (*War Pigs*), and Ozzy Osbourne with Therapy? creating a new version of *Iron Man*. An unknown band called the Bullring Brummies recorded an excellent and quite festive version of *The Wizard*. In all fairness, the Bullring Brummies were a band featuring three Birmingham musicians you may have heard of: Rob Halford (vocals), Geezer Butler (bass), and Bill Ward (drums) who were joined by guitarists Scott Weinrich (Vitus) and Brian Tilse (Fight). The "Bullring" in their name comes from the major and well-known shopping center in Birmingham and "Brummies" is the slang term for someone from Birmingham.

Years since its release, I have really come to enjoy this album more than I did upon its release. Back then I wasn't into the death, speed, or goth rockers that were featured so heavily on the album, except Megadeth, but now I can listen to it and take away something special from each song. NATIVITY IN BLACK – A TRIBUTE TO BLACK SABBATH would receive a Gold certification in 2000 for sales over 500,000 copies and Megadeth would receive a Grammy nomination for their cover of Paranoid but would lose to Soundgarden.

Put Your Trust in Me

Unfortunately, this was probably as far down as Black Sabbath and Tony Iommi could go. Following the conclusion of the tour, Geezer Butler was gone, again returning to Ozzy Osbourne while he planned his next move. Bill Ward was also gone, deciding not to stay unless the line-up was all the original members. Once again, it was Iommi, Tony Martin, and Geoff Nicholls who had to try to pick up the pieces. But let's not condemn CROSS PURPOSES on the line-up falling apart or not even listen because it wasn't Ozzy or Ronnie. Let's judge CROSS PURPOSES on the music inside the cellophane wrappings. The album is awesome! It is that simple. Everyone put their best foot forward and provided a very enjoyable and moving listening experience. It is hard to blame the band's chart failures and downsized venues on anything other than the change in music and how we consumed it. It was next to impossible for not just Black Sabbath, but David Lee Roth, Richard Marx, Motley Crue, and The Smithereens to compete with Green Day, Soundgarden, Oasis, R.E.M., and Stone Temple Pilots for sales of music and concert tickets.

CROSS PURPOSES is full of great music delivered by Tony Martin, who had a voice as big as anyone before him. He just lacked the star power. I place this one at #13 out of 19 studio albums. Despite it being lower in the charts, it's only albums 15 to 19 that I don't really enjoy, and some of those are coming in the next chapters. This one has a solid and loyal following among the Black Sabbath faithful, who also place it at #13 out of 19. Finally, we all kind of agree on something.

"After the tour ended, Geezer went back to Ozzy. Things needed to change." – Tony Iommi

BABY IF YOU'RE FEELING GOOD!
GENE SIMMONS (KISS)

For most of the hard rock/heavy metal fans who grew up and discovered their musical identity in the 1970s, KISS was the gateway drug to a much better world. For me, Gene Simmons embodied everything cool and magical about music and taught me to follow my dreams, work hard, and believe in myself. In Boston, I was able to tell Gene how his words helped me to believe that I didn't have to be a kid who stuttered, and I could be who I wanted to be. When I told Gene this, he didn't quite know what to say and afterward gave me a big hug.

www.genesimmons.com

CROSS PURPOSES - LIVE (I.R.S.Records)
Released on April 4, 1995
Produced by Black Sabbath
Tony Martin (vocals), Tony Iommi (guitar), Geezer Butler (bass), Geoff Nicholls (keyboards) and Bobby Rondinelli (drums)
All songs written by Butler, Iommi, Osbourne and Ward except where noted

TIME MACHINE (Butler, Dio and Iommi)
CHILDREN OF THE GRAVE
I WITNESS (Butler, Iommi and Martin)
INTO THE VOID
BLACK SABBATH
PSYCHOPHOBIA (Butler, Iommi and Martin)
THE WIZARD
CROSS OF THORNS (Butler, Iommi and Martin)
SYMPTOM PF THE UNIVERSE
DRUM SOLO (Rondinelli)
HEADLESS CROSS (Iommi, Martin and Powell)
PARANOID/ HEAVEN AND HELL (Butler, Dio, Iommi and Ward)
IRON MAN
SABBATH BLOODY SABBATH

"This one was really enjoyable for a change." - Geezer Butler

WHAT ARE YOU GONNA DO?

This will be a very short chapter.

It may have been an odd time for Black Sabbath to release their second official and authorized live album, but here we were, with the very original and cleverly titled CROSS PURPOSES – LIVE! Odd that the band would release a live album as their popularity was waning, but at the same time live concerts for the home video market were becoming quite lucrative, especially for fans of particular bands who would buy anything. For the artist, they were able to get product to the stores with very little work and cost, and it was an inexpensive way to see a band, or in the case of Black Sabbath, the only time to see the band since there were a lot less tour dates thee days. Since I wasn't able to see Black Sabbath, this was the best I could do.

Produced by the band, CROSS PURPOSES – LIVE was packaged two ways. First was a CD-only that featured 14 songs recorded live at the Hammersmith Apollo in London on April 13, 1994. This comes with the usual booklet, but no pictures or liner notes, just an ad for the last three Sabbath albums. With the lack of extras (stuff you expect from a live album), you feel kinda cheated and look at this as something that was just thrown together without care or thought. I felt right away we were missing the stuff I wanted to see, such as details about the show and the players like other live albums normally do. The next purchase option was a cool CD/VHS collection that came housed in an oversized VHS case with the CD in its own jewel case. The VHS's 17 songs, featured *The Mob Rules, Anno Mundi*, and *Neon Knights*, which were not on the CD and also contained the performance video for *Feels Good To Me*. By this time, VHS tapes were becoming more affordable to consumers and more collectible, so many fans, like myself, scooped this one up at a fairly good price. I do remember the only reason I knew this was out was that the box was too big to stuff into the CD bin at Music Outlet in Enfield, CT, and I saw it, bought it, and loved it! I felt a little cheated because I thought it also came with a concert shirt because the sealed box was a bit puffy.

"Tony Martin had a fabulous voice, but we were always on top of him about his performance. Overnight he went from working venues in Birmingham to big stages everywhere." – Tony Iommi

CLOSE THE CITY

If you know going in that Tony Martin wasn't feeling 100% for most of the CROSS PURPOSES tour, this may explain a bit of the rasp in his voice. This is not to say that he sounds bad on the audio and/or video, because he sounds fantastic, but you can hear a slight strain in his voice, mostly trying to hit the lower Ozzy notes. Martin really sets the pace from the first song, *Time Machine*, a Dio track that he hits perfectly and was well received by the audience. The collection has a few surprises that, if you weren't at the show(s), you didn't know about. These include *The Wizard* and *Sabbath Bloody Sabbath*, two of the Ozzy-era songs rarely played that Martin really makes his own.

"It is a pleasure to be able to play that song (The Wizard) for you tonight. It hasn't been played for 24 long years." – Tony Martin

And how cool is it to see Geezer Butler and Tony Iommi together on stage together again? Hearing it on CD is one thing, but seeing the two of them on the same stage together and happy to be there is just really cool. Playing songs they helped create together like *Children Of The Grave, Paranoid* and *Black Sabbath* makes the songs so much more powerful. Drummer Bobby Rondinelli is a solid and underrated musician who plays much more in the style of Cozy Powell and Vinny Appice than Bill Ward, so he makes everything sound heavier and louder. Always the showman, Rondinelli gets the obligatory and energetic drum solo that leads right into the bombastic *Headless Cross*. Sadly, Geoff Nicholls gets little fanfare or screen time here, but his subtle keyboard work on the older songs as he plays under Iommi's soloing gives the music added depth. I think the only time we would see Nicholls was when he accidentally got into a shot.

"I once heard somebody describe it as the most underpromoted release of all time." – Tony Iommi

CROSS PURPOSES – LIVE would be a CD/VHS/DVD collection that would see many releases, in many different forms, and better covers.

Listening to the CD is a great way to relive some musical history but watching the VHS (which has been re-released on DVD a crap ton of times) really brings the experience to life. Being able to see and feel what the crowd in attendance adds a lot to the experience. There are some great camera angles, and cutting to different cameras isn't as distracting as many concert films can be. What you see is what you get, and what you get... is really, really good.

Never seeing the Tony Martin-led Black Sabbath live, this was my first time seeing him as the frontman. Martin has been slagged by fans, and, unfortunately, his own bandmates, for being nothing but a club singer on a large stage without the presence to rate it. That may have some merit, but this is who Tony Martin was as the vocalist for Black Sabbath. He doesn't have the edgy persona of Ozzy Osbourne, the relaxed but quite intense Ronnie James Dio delivery, or even the devil-may-care swagger of Ian Gillan, but he delivers where it counts, and that is with his voice.

WHAT IS THIS THAT STANDS BEFORE ME?

My biggest issue with the collection starts at the cover, because it's horrible. It seems like all they did was take a hard-to-see, blue-lit concert shot of each member (except Geoff Nicholls) and put them around the angel with burning wings. It is incredibly hard to distinguish any of the images, and when you look at it, not knowing what it is, you may think it's just a bunch of bluish shapes in a swirl of black with some fire. When you consider the amazing cover art of 1983's LIVE EVIL, this becomes even more of a letdown. I don't even think it's better than the artwork for LIVE AT LAST.

I remember getting mine at my local record shop, Music Outlet in Enfield, CT. The only reason I knew it was a thing back in the day was that the set came in a puffy box too big to fit in the regular CD racks and was out in the open. I also thought there was a shirt in there, but nope!

Looking at the set list, this isn't bad at all considering how much great material Black Sabbath can choose from. You go into this knowing the songs the fans really want to hear are from the Ozzy Osbourne era like *Iron Man, Children Of The Grave,* and *Paranoid*. I would have loved to see more of a focus on the Tony Martin era, like anything from THE ETERNAL IDOL and TYR. How would Martin handle *Trashed* or *No Stranger To Love*? Overall, this is a solid live release from a band really trying to survive.

Trip to M.A.R.S.
Tony MacAlpine

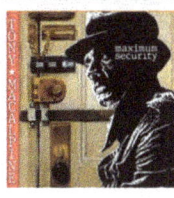

In 1984 it was big news that both Rudy Sarzo and Tommy Aldridge, now ex-Ozzy Osbourne members, would be teaming up in a new band. With so many vocalists and guitarists to be rumored coming in and out of the line-up, it would be Springfield, MA, native Tony MacAlpine who would get the job as the band's guitarist. Now called M.A.R.S. (the letters for the member's last names), it featured vocalist and fellow Springfield MA, native, Rob Rock. The band would release PROJECT: DRIVER. Currently, Tony MacAlpine is still out there, shredding and releasing new music like 2017's DEATH OF ROSES. Another bit of Black Sabbath/MacAlpine crossover is that the guitarist was the opening act for the last show on the BORN AGAIN tour, in Springfield, MA, also the last to feature vocalist Ian Gillan.

www.tonymacalpine.com

FORBIDDEN (I.R.S.Records)
Released on June 20, 1995
Produced by Ernie C
Tony Martin (vocals), Tony Iommi (guitar), Neil Murray (bass), Geoff Nicholls (keyboards) and Cozy Powell (drums)
All songs written by Martin, Iommi, Murray, Nicholls and Powell except where noted

THE ILLUSION OF POWER (additional lyrics by Ice-T)
GET A GRIP
CAN'T GET CLOSE ENOUGH
SHAKING OFF THE CHAINS
I WON'T CRY FOR YOU
GUILTY AS HELL
SICK AND TIRED
RUSTY ANGELS
FORBIDDEN
KISS OF DEATH

LOSER GETS IT ALL (Japanese Bonus Track)

"I want to say "crap," but it's actually not." – Tony Martin

you want to be my friend

In putting the touring HEADLESS CROSS and TYR album line-up back together, it was easy to secure bassist Neil Murray, but not as easy to get drummer Cozy Powell. Where Murray looked at it as just another job, Powell felt betrayed by Iommi, who he thought (with good reason) traded in their partnership and what they were building for the cash grab reunion with Ronnie James Dio. Not to mention replacing him right away with Vinny Appice following his horse accident. Once fully recovered, Powell and Murray worked with Brian May on his stunning post-Queen debut, BACK TO THE LIGHT, and toured as part of his band, opening for Guns N' Roses on their USE YOUR ILLUSION tour. On this album, if you never listened to it, Brian May channels his inner Freddie Mercury and on most tracks is complemented with the trademark pounding of Powell.

With Powell's return to Sabbath, it was time to make an album that he hoped would rival the heaviness and energy of HEADLESS CROSS. Unfortunately, that wasn't going to happen. Work started at Parr Street Studios in Liverpool, England, in 1994, before a ten-day recording session at Devonshire Studios in Los Angeles, California. The band was feeling good about the writing and rehearsing of the new music that, according to everyone involved, was classic Black Sabbath...very heavy, a bit challenging, and very loud. When the record label, I.R.S., heard the songs, they thought it was more of the same and looked to make some drastic changes. With the current flavor of the month being Limp Bizkit's fusion of metal and rap, creating something called Nu-Metal, the label was hoping an established band like Black Sabbath could cross over into this market with the right producer and direction. Naturally, the band members were all resistant but at the mercy of the record label due to their lack of sales and the dreaded contractual obligation of owing I.R.S. one more release. Iommi was beginning to tire of the constant struggles to keep Black Sabbath alive, and, possibly for the first time in his career, wanted it to be all over. He knew that, with their record deal fulfilled, there was another legal hurdle out of the way, possibly creating the chance to work with Ozzy Osbourne again under the Black Sabbath name.

Begrudgingly, Black Sabbath met with producer Ernie Cunnigham, professionally known as Ernie C., known for his work the controversial band, Body Count. Body Count had a very polarizing song, Cop Killer, that overshadowed the exciting music the band was creating, music that was heavily influenced by early Black Sabbath. Growing up in Compton, CA (with Body Count singer Ice-T), and surrounded by Rap and Hip-Hop music, Ernie C developed a serious appreciation for hard rock music and taught himself how to play guitar. A left-handed player himself, Ernie C's stage wear is all black with a large shiny cross...much like one Tony Iommi. Never feeling comfortable with his place in the band, especially now, Tony Martin heard Ice-T was going to be on the album but was never sure if it was for a song or the entire thing.

"I was told that Ice-T was gonna be doing it and they couldn't or wouldn't tell me if he was doing the whole thing or just one track. I still didn't know the answer to that when I was in the studio singing the tracks. They said they were gonna see what Ice-T wanted to do." – Tony Martin

In 1986, Aerosmith resurrected their careers by teaming up with Run-DMC for a reimagining of the band's huge 1975 hit, *Walk This Way*. The song became a massive hit and introduced both band's audiences to each other. Stylistically, it made a lot of sense, considering Run-DMC used many rock songs in their raps. The members of Body Count were huge fans of Black Sabbath and it showed in their music. For Black Sabbath, there was not much, if any, understanding of the music and the culture of the streets that Body

Count came from.

"Body Count is Black Sabbath!" – Ernie C

Communication issues began to have an impact on the sessions when Iommi and company would basically record and hand over the production and have no say in what was done, including the guitarist. If there were any problems or concerns, things weren't taken care of in a timely fashion (or at all) because both Powell and Murray had other commitments, something that irked Iommi. All the members claim the songs they recorded were not the music that was produced, again causing problems with everyone involved. Changing up Black Sabbath and making them relevant again needed a bit of street credibility, so in came Ice-T who gave a spoken word message during the song *The Illusion Of Power's* bridge.

With the album completed in old-school fashion (very fast), the band returned to England to wait for the final mixes and the album, now called FORBIDDEN, to see release.

"I think it was absolutely the wrong move!" – Tony Iommi

The entire piece for the cover created by artist Paul Sample is a great work of art, but it isn't good for this type of album.

you don't care what i'm feeling

They say never judge a book by its cover. Regaarding FORBIDDEN, you certainly can and be pretty accurate! A Black Sabbath cover featuring the Grim Reaper under a full moon with body parts strewn all over the place really can get your mind racing and heart pounding with excitement. However, the image I just described is done in a very cartoonish style with a bad choice of colors and textures. What could have been the greatest cover ever turns into a sad caricature of itself and represents exactly where Black Sabbath was at the time.

The art by Paul Sample is not bad at all. In fact, if this was a cover to a comic book or this book, I would love it because the art is awesome. Where the rendering gets lost is that Black Sabbath is a serious band and creates an image in the minds of its fans. When fans are delivered an album cover like SABBATH BLOODY SABBATH, it works, and when they're given a cover like FORBIDDEN, it doesn't. Where it gets really bad is the back cover or the inlay for the cassette, where it folds out to reveal the Reaper moving toward a smoldering serving platter featuring all sorts of stuff, including the heads of the band members. Fans of Sample's long-running cartoon strip, ORGI, could see his style and flair and appreciate

appreciate it more than those who don't know what they are even looking at.

"Most of us weren't really happy with the way it turned out." - Neil Murray

do you want to be a part of me?

Less than 15 months after the release of their last studio album and just two months after the release of a live one, Black Sabbath released their eighteenth (and most controversial) studio album, FORBIDDEN, to an unsuspecting world on June 20, 1995...and one noticed. In the music world, all I cared about in 1995 involved reunions, including the possible return of the original members of KISS following their amazing KISS UNPLUGGED special, the Beatles releasing the so-so Free As A Bird, Bruce Springsteen putting the E-Street Band back together, and Journey recording their first new album in almost a decade. There was even talk of the Sex Pistols reuniting. Hell was freezing over, reunions were big business, and Black Sabbath was just a blip on the radar.

As expected, FORBIDDEN flopped bad... really bad, and it seemed like this was expected. It didn't chart in the US at all becoming the second from the band not to do so in the US, the first being the far superior TYR. In the UK where the band always had a supportive fanbase, even during the lean years, FORBIDDEN gave the band their worst chart showing ever, only going to #71, 30 spots lower than their previous release, CROSS PURPOSES. It was bad, but the band tried to keep a brave face.

Before the album's release, Cozy Powell, in an interview with MTV UK, said there was a video being finished up for the song *Get A Grip*. I didn't even know this video existed, and, to be honest, it made me like the song a bit more. In the animation style of the album's art, it's not bad... not Black Sabbath, but not bad! But now, what is a legendary band to do when you have hit your lowest career point? Hit the road, of course, and hope for the best.

"We had a good following over in Japan, but we weren't there. We were making our way to Australia, but we never got quite that far." – Tony Martin

does it really still the fears?

Musically, the album starts off pretty intense with riff-filled fury from Tony Iommi on *The Master of Illusion*. Unfortunately, 30 or so seconds in, it all falls apart. Tony Martin is singing/speaking his lines in an odd tempo that confuses me and must have confused drummer Cozy Powell because it doesn't make sense, doesn't sound good, or makes you feel anything but uncomfortable.

"It was kind of scary in some respects because I never worked this way before." – Tony Martin

Up next, *Get A Grip* isn't a horrible song, but we hear Martin and Powell singing and playing in another odd tempo. It's not as bad as the first song, but again, not Black Sabbath. It sounds a bit like Black Sabbath doing an Aerosmith impersonation. The only cool thing going on here is the bridge that leads into a really cool and heavy solo by Iommi. Other than that…a hard pass.

Another un-Sabbath song that really has too weird a vibe to describe, *Can't Get Close Enough* is a very slow, droning song at the beginning that once it picks up gets pretty good. Heavy drums, tasty riffs, and thumping bass by Neil Murray charge this song ahead, but it still isn't what we want, even if Sabbath is trying something different. Just don't try this.

"We might have changed a few things if it wasn't for Ernie C." – Tony Iommi

It starts off like a juggernaut, but then *Shaking Off The Chains* turns into more off beats and vocals not following the melody and coming across as very forced and uninspired. There is a great Iron Maiden moment in the song, which saves it, but too little too late.

Finally, a good song, a very good song! *I Won't Cry For You* has a very slow introduction with some great vocals by Martin and inspired playing. This one is the lighters-out ballad for the album. Despite being pretty solid, it has some strange moments like the drum beats and vocal melody always sounding like they should be going somewhere else.

"Ice T was supposed to be the producer, but he said no." – Neil Murray

Guilty As Hell is a very HEADLESS CROSS thumper which is probably the only song on the entire album that has a Black Sabbath feel throughout. Unfortunately, the production flattens it out a bit and doesn't give any depth to anything. It feels like everything is just there on one flat line. Martin also doesn't sound inspired at all, but still good.

Introduced by fury from Cozy Powell (but not a Cozy Powell-type fury), *Sick & Tired* is a very good song that has a deep blues groove to it. At times, it seems like the vocals are too much for the verses, meaning a word or two too much for the music being played, almost sounding like catch up. Powell and Murray play their best Gary Moore-inspired chops within Iommi's slide guitar, but it just comes across as a bit forced, again.

Rusty Angels is a very interesting song because it almost sounds like Black Sabbath doing Dokken's *Burning Like A Flame*. Not saying this is a bad song, because it isn't, but it's hard to get the Dokken out of my head when I listen to it. With a little more work and a time machine back to 1988, this song would have been listened to and judged a little less harshly.

The title track, *Forbidden*, is a pretty solid entry, again feeling like something off of HEADLESS CROSS. This one has a lot of quality moments, but Martin seems off. The verses have Peter Gabriel moments that just don't sound right here.

The last song on an album can tell a story about where a band wants to go. Well, *Kiss Of Death* is a long, kind of boring goodbye, never really feeling like it has a place to go or, if it did, the directions to get there. More of the same as above, with great music but vocals and melodies that don't quite fit what the song is trying to do. This seems to be the story of the entire album.

"This is not a band that is afraid of experimenting with music." - Tony Martin

For Japanese fans, there is another song, *Loser Gets It All*, that is the best song I have heard from FORBIDDEN. Sad that this one gets regulated to "bonus track'"status, but it is an easy, straight-ahead rocker that has a nice groove to it. Martin really hits this one and the solo by Iommi is so good and full of character. Again, so sad that this was the bonus track.

As much as I (and most fans) rail on most of these songs, once I heard the jam tracks from the writing sessions and tracking stages, you hear that what we got on the record was NOT what was written, recorded, and intended. When I would read comments like "this album sounded better in rehearsals" or "this isn't how we wrote it," I thought it was just defensive answers to the millions of questions, but about 10 years ago I found out the truth! Enter FORBIDDEN – ROUGH MIX! These are the songs that appeared on FORBIDDEN from the writing and rehearsal session. Before Martin's vocals were added, you hear some amazing songs and ideas floating about. There is plenty of blame to go around, as to who and why the album's final mix came out as it did, but here you hear it wasn't necessarily the band's fault. The most noticeable change is in the most controversial song from the album, *The Illusion Of Power*, where musically it is very much like the Sabbath of old and features some incredible Cozy Powell double-kick drum action!

"I don't think any day is the right day to end Black Sabbath as long as the people want to hear it. I'm proud of the Sabbath stuff." – Tony Iommi

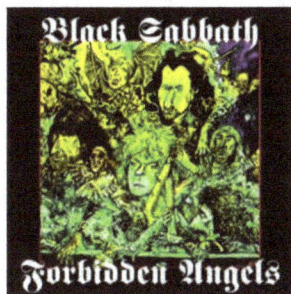 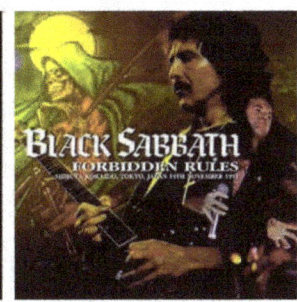 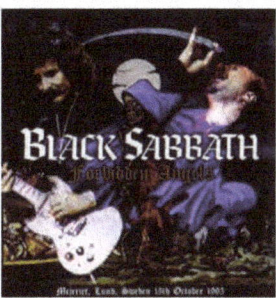

A few recordings from the ill-fated FORBIDDEN tour. Despite the reaction to the album, Black Sabbath always gave 100% on stage.

got no holes in my shoes

Black Sabbath, Motorhead, and German band Tiamat hit the United States and Canada for a series of dates that saw the band playing smaller and smaller venues than ever before like the legendary Toad's Place in New Haven, CT, on June 29, 1995. Before their trip across the pond, the band played two big festivals, Esbjerg Rock Festival in Denmark (with ELO II, Fleetwood Mac, Saxon, and a host of others). Up next was a two-day show in Sweden (again with Fleetwood Mac on the bill) where the band played incredibly, captivating the audience and keeping the new songs to a minimum...one or two, tops. Following their final show in the US on August 3, 1995, at the Universal Amphitheater in California, drummer Cozy Powell, fed up with it all, left. Before the European dates, beginning a mere two weeks later, Bobby Rondinelli was brought back in to fill the vacant drum spot. In total, Black Sabbath spent over a month in North America before spending the next three months in Europe and then made their way to South Korea, then Japan (where they added Changes to the setlist) with visits to China and Thailand. The band was scheduled for shows in Australia, the Philippines, and Vietnam, but the promoters, with many different reasons given, canceled 10 of the band's last 12 shows.

There is a bootleg (soundboard recording) floating around called BLOODY WIZARD, recorded in Chicago, Illinois, on July 7, 1995, and showcases how heavy and brilliant the band sounded live, especially Powell and Murray, who are up very high in the mix or lack of mix. New songs like *Get A Grip* and *Can't Get Close Enough* are certainly heavier than their album counterparts, but still have odd pacing and are tough to get into, but listen to *Sabbath Bloody Sabbath* and all will be forgiven.

On December 14, 1995, Black Sabbath played the final gig of the FORBIDDEN tour and the last show of the Tony Martin era. There was no fanfare... that was it... no final curtain call... just the end, a sad and unspectacular ending to an amazing story!

"The phone just stops ringing." – Tony Martin

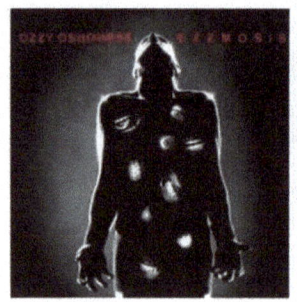  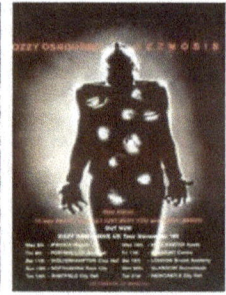

dancing by the roadside

While Black Sabbath hit a creative and financial all-time low with FORBIDDEN, Ozzy was doing what he did best, writing and recording amazing albums that the fans loved and bought by the millions! Following his retirement and subsequent return, Osbourne and Zakk Wylde worked with an all-star band on his seventh studio album, OZZMOSIS. Joining the duo were keyboardist Rick Wakeman (YES), drummer Deen Castronovo (Bad English/Hardline), and bassist, wait for it...Geezer Butler. Since this album wasn't supposed to happen due to Ozzy's medical misdiagnosis, Zakk Wylde had already begun his post-Ozzy career plans, so in came the brilliant Steve Vai (Frank Zappa/Alcatrazz/David Lee Roth/Whitesnake). Wylde had auditioned for Guns N' Roses (didn't get the gig) and then recorded his solo debut with his new band Pride & Glory, featuring two amazing players in James LoMenzo (bass) and Brian Tichy (drums).

Unfortunately for music fans, the pairing of Ozzy and Vai didn't last, with both sides admitting it just didn't work as they had hoped. Fortunately for those same music fans, Zakk Wylde would return! Only one song, My Little Man, survived from this pairing, also written with Lemmy from Motorhead. Feeling there was too much record company interference involving producers and styles, Osbourne spoke to the press, saying he may never record another album again.

OZZMOSIS would spawn several singles and radio hits, such as *Perry Mason* and *See You On The Other Side,* and would be his highest-charting album in the US (#4) and do well in the UK (#22) and Canada (#7). Sales in the US alone would be phenomenal, selling two million copies when many heavy metal/hard rock bands were distancing themselves from their former glories. On the road, Ozzy wouldn't be joined by Zakk Wylde for the first time since 1988, being replaced by Testament's Alex Skolnick, then Joe Holmes, fresh from a stint with David Lee Roth. Butler would make most of the tour, ultimately being replaced by Mike Inez. To augment the vocals, former Lynch Mob vocalist Robert Mason would come in and help to round out the sound from behind the stage.

 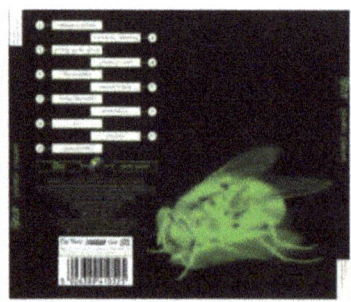 

finally...and wow, this is pretty brutal

The sticker on the wrapping said "featuring Geezer Butler, formerly of Black Sabbath," so fans knew that on October 26, 1995, Geezer Butler and his band G//Z/R (Geezer without the E's) had released their debut album PLASTIC PLANET, on TVT. If you were expecting something that sounded like Black Sabbath or at least close to the sound of his aborted Geezer Butler Band, be ready! This album, featuring vocals by Fear Factory's Burton C. Bell, is more of the modern metal, a bit too heavy, and vocally not my cup of tea. From the screamo Cookie Monster-style vocals, I was put off almost immediately...OK, right away. Musically, I love the heaviness that Butler, Pedro House (guitar), and the brilliant Deen Castronovo (drums) put together, but this was a bit more than I could handle.

The biggest push for G//Z/R was having the song *The Invisible* featured on the soundtrack for the film, MORTAL KOMBAT, in 1995. Being part of the soundtrack introduced the band to the fans of an incredibly popular franchise and showed Butler that he was in touch with the current metal scene. PLASTIC PLANET received solid reviews, especially for those who felt that Black Sabbath had lost touch with the music scene, and in 1995 who could disagree? Here, Butler let the younger musicians he was working with really push this into what it became, a bone-crushing collection.

the light is always shining

If Black Sabbath versus Ozzy 1995 were a boxing match, it would be over in literal seconds and an ambulance would be bringing a corpse to the hospital. When I.R.S. Records forced the changes to Black Sabbath's sound, they destroyed everything that made Black Sabbath great and original. Before we get upset with the band, within their rights as the employer who was paying the bills I.R.S. had the right to dictate terms and expect a sellable product, or their version of one. As expected, FORBIDDEN was just the wrong album at the worst possible time. Fans that may have been holding on now left and stopped supporting the Black Sabbath brand. For Osbourne, no matter the challenges or obstacles put in his way, the singer just seemed to always come up the better for it. Much had to do with the committed and incredibly forceful management that represented Osbourne, his wife Sharon. Despite her (at times) ruthless drive and push, she has always had her husband's best interests at heart, and it showed.

As far as keeping the music relevant, only G//Z/R's release, PLASTIC PLANET, embraced the modern metal sound of the day, which is what I don't like. But embracing changes is what do to survive. This album was bought by many non-Black Sabbath fans because they loved the music inside. In the tale of the tape, OZZMOSIS outsold FORBIDDEN by at least 2 million units and charted in the US at #4 in compared to Black Sabbath not even charting. There is a segment of the Black Sabbath fanbase that absolutely loves this album and that is cool because most of my choices aren't fan favorites. But still, the album for me ranks #18 out of 19 studio albums, not the worst, but pretty close to it. The Black Sabbath fans of the World Wide Web made their mark, calling this one the worst out of every Black Sabbath album.

"(FORBIDDEN was a) filler album that got the band out of the label deal, rid of the singer, and into the reunion. However, I wasn't privy to that information at the time." – Tony Martin

tangled in the web
robert mason (lynch mob/warrant)

In 1993, Robert Mason replaced Oni Logan in Lynch Mob. In 1990, Mason brought a street-wise style to their second album LYNCH MOB, a record that was as good, if not better, than the band's classic debut, WICKED SENSATION. Mason's vocal style is very pure, honest, and comes from the heart as I witnessed firsthand over the past few years seeing Mason with Lynch Mob and Warrant. I met Robert following an interview I did with George Lynch where he told me "that was a great interview, man." I love this guy even more! With Warrant, he has mighty big shoes to fill, but does it with grace and incredible balance, showing respect and bringing his own style.

www.warrantrocks.com

The New Testament
Black Sabbath

The Book of Sabbath
Chapter 7

Resurrection 1:7

With many broken promises and pain, the remaining giant stood alone.
Forbidden to move and grow alone, this became a time in the land
for one to become two, then two to become four!
The people in the land rejoiced like never before
as the four giants brought balance to a land
that had lost its way.
Many of the lesser would follow
and make the sounds forged in
fire and smoke come alive again.
But, when four became three,
the giants would call for The End,
and live out their days in peace for once.

REUNION (Epic Records)
Released on October 20, 1998
Produced by Thom Panunzio (live) and Bob Marlette (studio)
Ozzy Osbourne (vocals), Tony Iommi (guitar), Geezer Butler (bass) and Bill Ward (drums)
All songs written by Butler, Iommi, Osbourne and Wrd except where noted

WAR PIGS
BEHIND THE WALL OF SLEEP
N.I.B.
FAIRIES WEAR BOOTS
ELECTRIC FUNERAL
SWEET LEAF
SPIRAL ARCHITECT
INTO THE VOID
SNOWBLIND
SABBATH BLOODY SABBATH
ORCHID / LORD OF THIS WORLD
DIRTY WOMAN
BLACK SABBATH
IRON MAN
CHILDREN OF THE GRAVE
PARANOID
PSYCHO MAN (Iommi/Osbourne)
SELLING MY SOUL (Iommi/Osbourne)

TIME WILL TELL IN THEIR POWERFUL MINDS

Following the last date on the FORBIDDEN tour, Black Sabbath was all over. With their contract to I.R.S. Records nearly completed, it was time for Tony Iommi to call it a day and put a death date on the Black Sabbath tombstone. For Iommi, the struggle to keep a consistent (or any) line-up together was becoming too much trouble, especially when the industry and fanbase were not supporting his best efforts. Black Sabbath was still providing quality music (except the last album) on well-produced albums that went far beyond nostalgia. But either the fans discovered new music to digest or just wanted the nostalgia and history that the band provided. There seemed to be no place in the world for the band.

The contractual obligation greatest hits package from Black Sabbath that would free the band and more importantly, the name!

On April 29, 1996, I.R.S. Records would release THE SABBATH STONES everywhere but North America. The collection features at least one track from each of the band's last eight albums including Ian Gillan, Glenn Hughes, Ronnie James Dio, and Tony Martin on vocals. The cover had a featured list of most of the players to appear in the collection and managed to misspell Vinny Appice's first name (not the first time), calling him Vinnie. Full disclosure, I have him as Vinnie on my cell phone. In total, 16 tracks featuring 16 different members of Black Sabbath and 11 different producers, as well as Queen's Brian May. THE SABBATH STONES proved the quality and consistency of the music never waned, despite the revolving door of members. Included was the Japanese only Loser Gets It All from FORBIDDEN. As expected, THE SABBATH STONES didn't chart anywhere it was released. Now, contractually, emotionally, and legally, Black Sabbath was officially over.

"I had no idea that FORBIDDEN was Black Sabbath's last studio album." – Tony Iommi

TIME TO FACE REAL LIFE

Since his massive fall from grace and near loss of his career, Glenn Hughes considers his disaster on the Black Sabbath tour to be the beginning of his fall to rock-bottom. He couldn't get any work, and, even if he could have, he was in no condition to perform. But, by 1991, Glenn Hughes was a recovering drug addict. He had his struggles, but with his health and faith repaired, he was able to face obstacles and challenges that came his way. From 1994 to 1996, Hughes released four solo albums, all diverse and excellent yet flying far below the radar. In 1996, Hughes, Tony Iommi, and former Judas Priest drummer Dave Holland began working together on new music at DEP Studios in Birmingham, England, with no plans, no expectations, just… music. Hughes was so thankful to be able to show Iommi how far he came and hopefully make up for the SEVENTH STAR tour debacle. Musically, the trio didn't stray too far away from their combined roots (Black Sabbath, Trapeze, and Deep Purple) and kept the music hard and loud but with a lot of heart and soul. The recordings would not be released but would circulate as a highly sought-after bootleg (I highly sought and never found).

Despite his many health scares and inner demons, Ozzy Osbourne's career seemed to be on the rise. At the time, the hottest tour was the annual Lollapalooza tour, created by Jane's Addiction vocalist Perry Farrell as a farewell tour for his band, but annually grew bigger and better. Inclusion in the line-up was at the time limited to non-mainstream artists (or alternative/grunge-based acts) with the exclusion of any hard rock/heavy metal because the festival was a "peaceful" event. When Sharon Osbourne inquired about including her husband, organizers said no, but didn't stop there. They publicly insulted Ozzy, calling him a drugged-out has-been. Embarrassed and looking to show up Farrell, the Osbournes conceived their own festival, featuring all styles and genres within Heavy Metal, and settled on the ultra-cool name, Ozzfest!

"It's time, Ozzy! Hatchets buried. once and for all!" – Sharon Osbourne

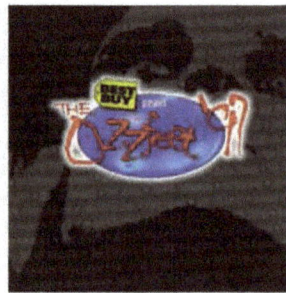

A poster promoting Ozzfest '97 with Black Sabbath and two cool CDs from Ozzfest that featured Slayer, Ozzy, and Sepultura. Thank you to Mike Demelio of WA for sharing his cool stuff and stories about trying to get to the event in a car that didn't want to go.

Following a small launch of Ozzfest in 1996 (only three shows), Sharon Osbourne reached out to Tony Iommi and Geezer Butler to see about the possibility of reuniting with Ozzy for a 22-show run in the US? Over the past few years, Iommi and Osbourne had talked and worked out many issues the two had, the biggest according to Ozzy was why he was fired from Black Sabbath in 1979. To make things work, it was now up to the guitarist and Butler to iron out their more recent issues. With the three in agreement and ready to go, it was decided that Bill Ward would not be in the band because of concerns about his playing due to years of inactivity and questions about his health. In his place would be Mike Bordin, Ozzy's current drummer from his solo band. As Ward worked himself into shape, the three-quarters reunited Black Sabbath received rave reviews for their amazing, but short (under an hour) set, following a solo set by Ozzy.

"I hadn't seen or spoken to Tony in about three years. A lot of bad things were said to each other, things we'd heard through other people." - Geezer Butler

Following the end of the Ozzfest dates, the band decided to play two shows in their native Birmingham and record the special event. What would make this a true reunion was, of course, the return of Bill Ward. With contracts in place, the band rehearsed a set of classic Sabbath music, and, on December 4th and 5th, the original members played two blistering sets that were recorded for a live album and video. For Ward, it was a personal success because of his ability to prove to his former members (and detractors) that he could perform at the highest level again, despite some serious health issues.

The summer of 1998 would see Butler, Iommi, and Osbourne tour throughout the US and Europe, proving they were still a huge concert draw decades after their heyday. Before the tour, plans were almost derailed when Bill Ward suffered a heart attack while in rehearsals. In his place would be logical choice, Vinny Appice, also featuring Geoff Nicholls performing off stage. While the band was on the road, plans were being put in place for more dates that would feature the entire original Black Sabbath line-up with Bill Ward plus Geoff Nicholls, as long as Ward was healthy and could perform. Vinny Appice would remain with the band as insurance if Ward was unable to perform either a song or an entire show. This move created some serious friction with Ronnie James Dio, who couldn't understand why his drummer would rather wait in the wings with Black Sabbath (with whom he was still quite angry) rather than be performing DIO's new music along with the hits they created together. Opening the majority of the shows on the tour was hotter-than-anything Pantera and the ultra-cool Helloween! Full disclosure, I'm not a fan of Pantera, then or now.

"If we go up there and we look like four idiots, they're going to go what the f#$%'s this?"
– Ozzy Osbourne

Sadly, on April 5, 1998, former Black Sabbath drummer Cozy Powell was killed in a car crash on his way to see his girlfriend. While on the phone she heard him say "oh s#!t!" and then a large crash. He was driving his car (a Saab 900) too fast for conditions before losing control in bad weather on the M4 outside of Bristol, England. Police reports would also list his blood-alcohol level was above the legal driving limit and he wasn't wearing a seatbelt, which caused his ejection from the vehicle. Powell's last sessions would be with Colin Blunstone (of The Zombies) for his THE LIGHT INSIDE album. Cozy's final solo album, ESPECIALLY FOR YOU, would be released the following year. From Rainbow to Michael Schenker Group, from Whitesnake to Emerson Lake & Powell and Black Sabbath, Cozy was always one of my favorite drummers, always in the Top Three with Carl Palmer and Keith Moon! His look, his sly smile, and his aggressive but controlled style were, to me, what a rock drummer should be. Cozy Powell will forever be missed.

"It was a real shock. I was stunned. All the years I knew Cozy, he was a bit of a wild character. A talented musician and good mate." – Tony Iommi

WE ARE RECORDING TONIGHT'S SHOW...

On October 20, 1998, REUNION was released almost a year after the shows were recorded to an audience that was chomping at the bit for anything new featuring the original line-up. Produced by Thom Panunzio, who had produced everyone from Bruce Springsteen to Metal Church, the album helped bring to life this amazing concert that only those in attendance were so fortunate to be able to see, hear, and feel. Featuring 16 live songs, the band tore through the expected list that included *War Pigs, Paranoid,* and *Iron Man,* but also brought out some favorites like *Fairies Wear Boots, Behind The Wall Of Sleep, Spiral Architect,* and the underrated and unexpected *Dirty Woman.* Here, Black Sabbath sounded amazing, especially Ozzy's vocals, that over the past few years have been a bit suspect. We all knew what the band was capable of individually, but here they delivered their classics as a unit with impressive precision and left everything on the stage. Give a listen to REUNION and find out. Serious hats off to Bill Ward who rolls, smashes, and hits his way through the show with perfection.

For many fans, the big attraction of this release was the inclusion of two new Black Sabbath studio songs, *Psycho Man* and *Selling My Soul,* both written by Osbourne and Iommi, and produced by Bob Marlette.

Sounding a bit more like an Ozzy solo song, *Psycho Man* is a good track that, at times, is a bit plodding and boring until after the solo by Iommi picks up the pace a bit more. *Selling My Soul* is more enjoyable due to the really cool time changes, even though the drums are not by Bill Ward, but a drum machine. Both Osbourne and Iommi would describe the writing sessions for the two new tracks as anything but easy, considering they hadn't written together since NEVER SAY DIE! Although Iommi wrote the same way, Ozzy did not.

"Everything went so well that we decided to have a go at making a new album together." – Ozzy Osbourne

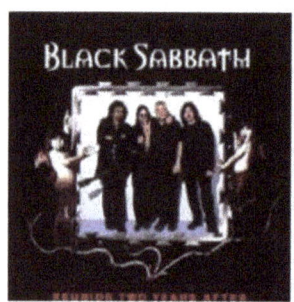

A recording from the Reunion tour, the Japanese pressing of the same album, and an awesome, one-of-a-kind fully autographed copy of REUNION belonging to Chris Giard of CT. This was a gift from a friend who waited in Boston to get it signed... the bestest friend ever!

Although the band worked at writing songs for a new album, the inspiration, desire, or chemistry wasn't exactly there to make the magic happen. Instead, we at least got a live concert album and video, two new songs, and a creepy cover with two devil-looking kids that make for an excellent listening experience. After all, this was the Black Sabbath that everyone wanted back, right? REUNION was released on Epic Records and easily went Platinum in the US and Canada and Silver in the UK. Impressive numbers indeed and proved that the world needed the original Black Sabbath together. Chart-wise, the album did amazing, going to #11 in the US, #41 in the UK, and #6 in Canada. To put the album's importance in perspective, REUNION was tied for the second highest-charting of a Black Sabbath album in the US. As much as I loved the Tony Martin era of Black Sabbath and didn't want it to end, it seemed like Black Sabbath's future was now the past.

"Among, uh... among bass fisherman our next guests are considered the preeminent heavy metal band, their new live CD double album is called REUNION... please welcome the four original members of Black Sabbath." – David Letterman

In December of 1998, Black Sabbath (with Bill Ward back behind the kit) would embark on a 22-date US tour that started with a fantastic and explosive appearance on the David Letterman show on October 29th. This tour would be the official support for REUNION and also feature Geoff Nicholls and Vinny Appice, again waiting in the wings in case of emergency. The set list included the expected tracks with the only major hiccups being shows postponed and moved around due to Osbourne suffering from throat nodules. For most of 1999, Black Sabbath would remain on the road, spending the summer as part of Ozzfest, and, from August to December, on their own headlining tour.

I CAN MAKE YOU ANYONE
RON 'BUMBLEFOOT' THAL

One of the most talented musicians, versatile players, and coolest human beings I know, Ron "Bumblefoot" Thal can do it all! When called into service with the hard-rocking Guns N' Roses in 2006, the full-on prog/rock attack of Sons Of Apollo in 2017, or providing vocals for ASIA in 2019, Bumblefoot can adapt to any musical style or situation, especially those in the Black Sabbath Family. If he isn't shredding at the Randy Rhodes Memorial, covering Paranoid with Davis Ellefson at Basstory, or performing Gates Of Babylon and Diary Of A Madman with Sons Of Apollo, Bumblefoot is bringing his talents to the world of hot sauces. Be warned, Bumblef***** the sauce will kill you!

www.bumblefoot.com

2000-2010
YOU SAY GOODBYE AND I SAY HELLO

    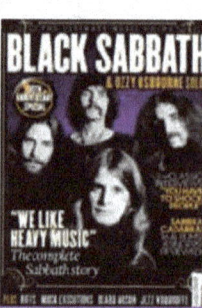

    The reunion of Tony Iommi, Ozzy Osbourne, Geezer Butler, and Bill Ward after so many years was not only magical but incredibly profitable, bringing the band back to levels not seen since the early 1980s. Black Sabbath was hot, big news, and really helping revitalize the dying Heavy Metal/Classic Rock world by reminding people who influenced bands like Nirvana, The Smashing Pumpkins, and Alice In Chains. By now, most of those bands that were given the key to the rock city a few years prior and hailed as the future of music had broken up and/or become less relevant. It was time for our music to make a strong comeback.

    Also changing in a big way was the landscape of the music industry, thanks in part to Napster and the decline of physical record sales with vinyl no longer being issued (except as collector's items) and CD sales dropping off quite a bit. By 2000, there were only five major players in the business, Warner Music Group, EMI, Sony Music, BMG, and Universal Music Group. None had the power or financial strength they had only a decade before, and were very choosy on who they put their money and energy behind. Independent labels, always so vital to the industry (especially for the Heavy Metal and Punk bands), were seeing a lot of big-name bands come their way and that was good, but without physical sales and a network of record stores to sell them, the indies were forced to be as critical as the majors regarding who they signed.

    This would have a ripple effect on the touring side of music, especially in the US. Without labels to provide seed money for tours until it became self-sufficient, many acts couldn't hit the road to promote their latest albums. If they were able to get on the road, it was only into smaller clubs and halls that may not pay as much as before, forcing bands to get by on much tighter budgets and package tours, hoping to make their money on merchandise. It was at this time you began to see artists begin to sell their music at shows. For the reformed Black Sabbath, this wasn't a problem, but for bands like DIO, they struggled to make ends meet despite releasing some amazing music and putting on the best shows imaginable. The fans just weren't there anymore and the labels they were on at the time couldn't cover the loses.

    There would also be a flood of live albums, soundboard recordings, official bootlegs, and compilations hitting the market, not just for Black Sabbath, but many bands on the other side of their commercial rainbow. The hope was that the extra releases would recoup the staggering losses of sales of physical product. Three of my favorite bands, ASIA, Marillion, and UFO, were bands that did this, mostly released by the record labels, trying to squeeze out the last bit of cash from fans for older material. By figuring that half the fanbase wasn't buying music anymore, the bands and labels counted on the other half to pick up the slack. Some of this material was good, some bad, and there was plenty of it. For example, my ASIA collection, a band that released only 13 studio albums, numbers almost 50 CDs. If they release it with the band's logo, I will buy it... and they knew it. If you want to find out more, I know a great book, ASIA – TIME AND TIME AGAIN! I forget the author's name.

This chapter will be a snapshot of the goings-on in the world of Black Sabbath and the extended family of players who worked and sometimes struggled to navigate the changing waters. Looking back at where I was in my life at this time, I was married with two young daughters and just moving into our first house, probably like many of you reading this. With the added responsibilities of life, money and time weren't as available as before. My concert attending was relegated to special shows that we could afford. This meant absolutely no club shows because of the unpredictable start times and the knowledge that a babysitter was waiting at home for us to return with cash in hand, requiring extra if we were late.

2000
AND THE WINNER IS...

FEBRUARY 23, 2000 - Black Sabbath would begin to get back at the establishment who shunned them for so long. The first step was to win a Grammy Award for Best Metal Performance for *Iron Man* (live) from REUNION. Beating out Ministry, Motorhead, Nine Inch Nails, and Rob Zombie, Black Sabbath finally received their due for their hard work, amazing songs, and rich history. Despite *Iron Man* not even being the best song on the album and a track 30 years old, no one cared. Black Sabbath and the fans won, despite most of the awards that night going to Santana. "And the Grammy goes to Black Sabbath!" Still weird to say that out loud.

 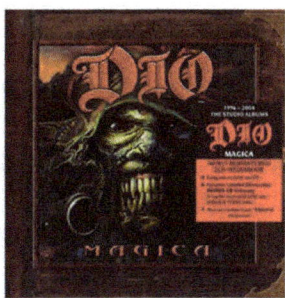 

MARCH 21, 2000 - After a lengthy break from recording, DIO returned in 2000 with one of his most critically acclaimed and ambitious albums ever, MAGICA, released on Spitfire Records. Before the album was recorded, there was a rumor circulating in Europe that a Rainbow reunion featuring Richie Blackmore and Ronnie James Dio would happen, but with Blackmore tied up with Blackmore's Night and a new DIO album being the first of a proposed trilogy, all the talk eventually went away.

"This is an album about people who are good and bad." – Ronnie James Dio

A lot had changed musically for Ronnie James Dio since 1996's ANGRY MACHINES. The biggest was the loss of guitarist Tracy G, who Dio felt was the right guitarist for the music the band was creating but was not the right choice for the fans and band management. As writing and recording began in 1999, Dio knew a change had to be made and tried to talk Tracy G into playing rhythm guitar for a new lead player. As expected, Tracy G said no and left, creating the perfect opportunity for the return of Craig Goldy. Goldy last appeared with DIO on DREAM EVIL (1987) and left under mysterious circumstances, but his return helped create the album many consider DIO's strongest since HOLY DIVER. Also returning was bassist Jimmy Bain and drummer Simon Wright, who helped this concept album become something really special. Songs like *Turn To Stone*, the epic *Eriel*, and *Losing My Insanity* had the classic feel and excitement (courtesy of Goldy's flashy leads) but retained the heaviness and serous lyrical content of Dio's last few releases. There are times when a concept album gets lost in the pompous attitude of the creator, but not MAGICA. The album wouldn't make the US album charts but would go to #13 on the Independent charts.

OCTOBER 17, 2000 - Taking almost five years to put together, Tony Iommi would finally release his solo debut, IOMMI on October 17, 2000, on Divine Records, the label formed by Sharon and Ozzy Osbourne. Considering the many previous attempts at a solo album, it was exciting to see the guitarist finally get to create the album he always wanted to do. Featuring 10 songs sung by as many vocalists, the album seemed to feature Iommi and yet not be all about him. With such diverse talents as Henry Rollins, Dave Grohl (Foo Fighters), Billy Corgan (The Smashing Pumpkins), Ian Astbury (The Cult), Phil Anselmo (Pantera), and Billy Idol, to name just a few, each song is not just a showcase for Iommi's talents but also his versatility to adapt to the different singers. IOMMI also features Black Sabbath partners Ozzy Osbourne and Bill Ward, bassist Lawrence Cottle (who played on HEADLESS CROSS), old friend Brian May, and many players from the then-current rock scene like John Tempesta (White Zombie), Peter Steele (Type-O Negative), and Ben Shepherd (Soundgarden). Produced and co-written by Bob Marlette, who produced the two studio tracks on Black Sabbath's REUNION, the album sounded fresh and modern while still maintaining the classic sound that Iommi was known for. There was a lot of writing and some recordings that never saw the light of day. Despite not being a fan of the Smashing Pumpkins at all, I felt that *Black Oblivion* was possibly the best song on the album, and that says a lot considering how great the songs are.

IOMMI would receive massive support from Sharon Osbourne (including a big launch party) and critical praise, going to #129 on the US charts when nothing good was hitting the charts. It's a solid album and a real fun listen. As much as he would have enjoyed doing one, a solo tour was out of the question due to touring commitments with Black Sabbath and just needing a break to rest his body.

2001
NEVER SAY DIE...AGAIN?

In 2001, Black Sabbath made their first real attempt at writing and recording new material for a new album. Only one song, Scary Dreams, made it beyond the writing and arguing stage. Ozzy Osbourne described the writing process with Iommi labored and forced, with Iommi having a completely different takeaway. Songs were recorded and handed over to producer Rick Rubin, but suddenly Osbourne left to finish work on his solo album that would become DOWN TO EARTH. The sessions would end when Ozzy went to finish his album, followed by another Ozzfest tour, and then would unexpectedly, and, possibly reluctantly, become a TV icon. Black Sabbath would return for Ozzfest 2001, sharing the stage with Marilyn Manson, Slipknot, Papa Roach, Linkin Park, Black Label Society, and many more bands representing every sub-genre of Heavy Metal. Ozzy Osbourne, Tony Iommi, Geezer Butler, and Bill Ward (along with Geoff Nicholls) would play 34 dates in North America and feature a shortened 10 song set list that would feature the usual suspects like *Paranoid,*

Paranoid, Iron Man, and *War Pigs*, but also include a brand-new song that Black Sabbath was working on called *Scary Dreams*.

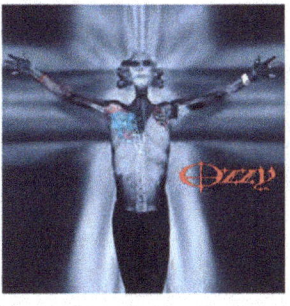
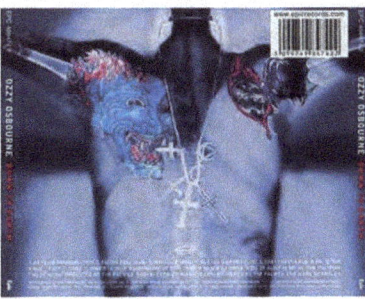
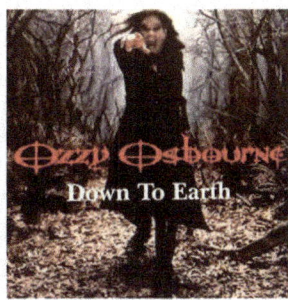

OCTOBER 16, 2001 - Ozzy Osbourne would release his eighth solo album, DOWN TO EARTH, on Epic Records. Not wanting to just make another album, continue to tour, and produce his soon-to-be-released TV show, THE OSBOURNES, the singer spent the previous year in and out of the studio with his band, featuring Zakk Wylde (guitars), Robert Trujillo (bass), and Mike Bordin (drums). It's interesting to note that the true sound and drive on this album is the new rhythm section, who give the album a Faith No More/Suicidal Tendencies groove to it, mixing things up a bit. Wylde was not involved in the songwriting at all because most of the songs were written while Joe Holmes was the guitarist. The lack of Wylde's heaviness and thunder in the writing has an effect on the overall feel and heaviness of the album. Not that it's bad at all, DOWN TO EARTH is one of Ozzy's best, but with the help of so many outside writers, it has so many different flavors. The John Lennon-sounding (and amazing) *Dreamer*, the rocking *Facing Hell*, and the sup-cool *No Easy Way Out* present The Prince Of Darkness in a more varied and controlled environment.

DOWN TO EARTH would be a huge hit for Ozzy, going to #4 in the US, #19 in the UK, and go Platinum. Of course, Ozzy would follow the release with a co-headlining tour with Rob Zombie called the Merry Mayhem Tour and then move right into the DOWN TO EARTH TOUR 2002.

2002
THE SUE ME SUE YOU BLUES

MARCH 2002 - Ozzy once commented to Sharon that they should film the interviews that he gave simply because the calamity and craziness that happens around the interviews is fun to watch. Sharon brought the idea to MTV, who jumped at the idea, and put a reality show based on the daily lives of Ozzy, Sharon, and their kids, Jack and Kelly, on the air. Their oldest daughter. Aimee, declined to participate in the project and lived in a guest house to avoid being filmed. When the show aired on March 5, 2002, it became an instant hit and the series would become MTV's most viewed series.

The reality show featuring Ozzy, Sharon, and two of their children, Jack and Kelly, was based on the day-to-day lives of the family. The show was criticized for the all-too-real look at the family, warts and all, but at the same time, many praised the show for the same reasons. For all its cartoonish portrayals, the show also showed the family dealing with Sharon's battle with cancer and Ozzy's near-death and recovery following his ATV accident. The series lasted four seasons and not only was MTV's highest viewed program but also won an Emmy in 2002 for Outstanding Reality Program. Many people (including famed TV dad Bill Cosby) publicly objected to the wild behavior, language, and lack of respect the children showed to their parents and other authority figures, failing to understand that despite being a reality show, much of the antics were staged. The years would show whether Ozzy or Cosby was the better human being.

MAY 21, 2002 - DIO would return once again with another excellent and slightly underrated album on May 21, 2002, with the aptly titled, KILLING THE DRAGON (Spitfire Records). As the music and imagery of DIO began to become more in line with what fans (especially me) wanted, the dragon in the title refers to technology and the threat it has on modern society. Writing sessions began with Craig Goldy (guitar), Jimmy Bain (bass), and drummer Simon Wright, but by the time the band settled into Total Access Recording in California, Goldy was once again out and replaced with former Bad Moon Rising/Burning Rain guitarist, Doug Aldrich, a modern player with an 80's flair and style. The band put together some excellent songs like *Better In The Dark, Before The Fall*, and the title track. Co-writing those three songs and most of the new album was Bain, who proved on this album his true value as a songwriter.

Produced by Ronnie James Dio, the album went to #199 on the US charts but #19 on the now viable US Independent charts. A comical video was made for the amazing song, *Push*, and featured Tenacious D, the rock/comedy duo of Jack Black and Kyle Glass. Ronnie James Dio also played himself in the film, TENACIOUS D IN THE PICK OF DESTINY. Another song on the album, *Throw Away Children* (co-written with Goldy), was planned to be used for a sequel to the Hear 'N Aid charity project, but for many reasons it was canceled.

"The thing about Ronnie is he is a real perfectionist." – Doug Aldrich

DIO would tour to support the album and find themselves playing smaller venues but really having a good time on the road. Following the tour, Aldrich would leave, ending up in Whitesnake, and Jimmy Bain would leave, showing up a few years later with former DIO members Vivian Campbell and Vinny Appice, along with the amazing Andrew Freeman, in the band Last In Line. Sadly, in 2016, Bain would pass away from an undiagnosed case of lung cancer while on the Def Leppard's Hysteria On The High Seas cruise.

OCTOBER 22, 2002 - As expected, with the sudden interest in Black Sabbath's history and the nostalgia for all things good, Rhino Records, along with Warner Bros., took notice. Along with Sharon Osbourne's input, SYMPTOM OF THE UNIVERSE: THE ORIGINAL BLACK SABBATH 1970 – 1978 was released on October 22, 2002. The two-disc set features 29 of the band's greatest hits, all remastered and sounding brilliant! The importance of the tracks getting remastered was to create a cohesive listening experience due to the different producers and techniques used on the original albums. For newer fans of the band, this was a perfect and inexpensive way to get the best of Black Sabbath and to hear for themselves what the hype was all about like older fans did with WE SOLD OUR SOUL FOR ROCK 'N' ROLL way back when. With such an interest collecting music again, this set is well worth the price. Also, with Black Sabbath now a featured act as part of the hugely successful Ozzfest, what better collectible for fans, old and new.

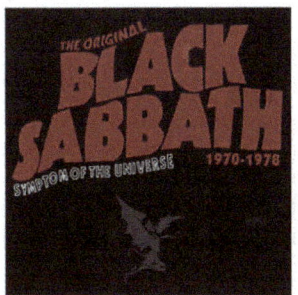

In 1998 bassist Bob Daisley and drummer Lee Kerslake sued Ozzy and Sharon Osbourne for unpaid performance royalties and album credits. In 1986, the duo successfully sued Jet Records and Don Arden for the same reasons and won that case, placing all their credits rightfully on DIARY OF A MADMAN. As Osbourne claimed in his book, I AM OZZY, the original agreement signed by the two proved there was no validity in their claims because both Daisley and Kerslake (and for that matter Randy Rhodes) received a rate for both studio work and road work and were never part of a band, but players on a solo project. This was a standard agreement. In revenge for filing the suit, Sharon Osbourne had the two albums re-recorded with Daisley and Kerslake's performance removed, re-recorded by Ozzy's current players, Trujillo and Bordin. Now, any albums sold had no performance royalties due to Daisley and Kerslake. The suit was eventually thrown out, but ill feelings between the players (and Sharon Osbourne) were sadly never resolved. The re-issues of the first two Ozzy albums were certainly a bad move that really alienated fans as well as the players involved.

2003
GOING OFF THE RAILS

What started as a casual ride across his estate In London almost ended the life of Ozzy Osbourne. On December 8, 2003, the singer was riding his ATV when he lost control, causing eight broken ribs, a broken vertebra, and a broken left collarbone. At the scene of the crash, Osbourne had to be resuscitated by his assistant, Sam Ruston, which saved his life. Ozzy had emergency surgery to repair a damaged blood vessel and would be in a coma for eight days. As expected, all tour and recording plans were canceled.

2004
DEP, BOXES, AND THE COW JUMPED OVER THE MOON

APRIL 27, 2004 - To celebrate (and capitalize) on the return of the original Black Sabbath, Rhino/Warner Bros. Records released BLACK BOX: THE COMPLETE ORIGINAL BLACK SABBATH 1970-1978 on April 27, 2004. Since the reformation of the original line-up, it seemed that the wave of Black Sabbath nostalgia was gaining strength. Everyone who had the license to produce a greatest hits collection did! The BLACK BOX was a collection for the serious fan! It contained the first eight studio albums, digitally remastered, each coming in its own case and complete with graphics from their original release. There were no bonus tracks included in order to preserve the original running order, but BLACK SABBATH would feature the songs *Evil Woman* and *Wicked World* that appeared on both the US and UK releases. The collection would contain an extensive 80-page book, complete with stories and photos of the band to would bring their early history to life. Fans were able to get an incredibly collectible set that was loaded with every song from BLACK SABBATH to NEVER SAY DIE! Also included was a bonus DVD featuring four live songs from the early days, extensive liner notes, and the lyrics to every song in the collection, checked for accuracy by Geezer Butler himself.

"We just enjoyed what we were doing. We influenced generation after generation and that's kind of an eye-opener for me because I didn't think anything we did was spectacular." – Ozzy Osbourne

JULY 2004 - With Ozzy on a break from his hit show and still recovering from his ATV accident, he would join Tony Iommi, Geezer Butler, Bill Ward, and Geoff Nicholls (off stage) for a summer run through the US, beginning on July 10, 2004. Sharing the Ozzfest stage was Lamb Of God, Lacuna Coil, Slayer, Black Label Society, and Judas Priest, who had recently reunited with vocalist Rob Halford. The shows would receive rave reviews sell a lot of tickets, with the only hiccup being a show in Camden, New Jersey, where Ozzy was unable to perform due to losing his voice. In stepped Rob Halford, once again helping his friends and fellow Brummies, just after completing a full set with Judas priest. Always the one to deliver the bad news, Bill Ward explained to the crowd what was going on and there was a bit of booing, anger, and disappointment.

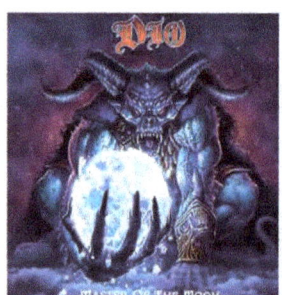  

SEPTEMBER 7, 2004 - Two years after the release of KILLING THE DRAGON, DIO would return with one of my favorites from their catalog, MASTER OF THE MOON, released through Sanctuary, SPV Steamhammer, and Victor worldwide. With an amazing cover and great music, the album features returning (again) guitarist Craig Goldy, bassist Jeff Pilson, drummer Simon Wright, and keyboardist Scott Warren. Continuing with more of what we expected and wanted from RJD, the songs contained here are big, full of story, and loaded with stimulants for the imagination. *Master Of The Moon, The Man Who Would Be King*, and the Japan-only *The Prisoner Of Paradise* create a cinematic experience and find DIO with another stellar release. Unfortunately for DIO and MASTER OF THE MOON, their label, Sanctuary Records, had some massive financial losses and began to cut staffing, and, of course, production and promotion of new music releases. Whatever got shipped at release was possibly all that was going out.

When DIO hit the road, being supported by Fireball Ministry and the John Bush-led Anthrax (in support of their stellar WE'VE COME FOR YOU ALL), Jeff Pilson wouldn't go out with the band due to touring commitments with Foreigner. In would step the ultimate utility man (and brilliant player), Rudy Sarzo. As much as I love the early DIO albums, I feel that Craig Goldie may have been the band's best guitarist, playing heavy when he needed to and not always relying on supersonic speed in a solo to make his point. In an interview I did with Goldie in 2016, I became aware of the reverence for and relationship with RJD that Goldie had. It isn't a surprise their music seems so natural.

SEPTEMBER 2, 2004 - As mentioned earlier, Tony Iommi, Glenn Hughes, and Dave Holland recorded eight songs in 1996 at the studio owned by UB40 called DEP. This was a way for Iommi to get away from the Black Sabbath bubble that had contained him for over 30 years. Following years of being bootlegged and passed among fans, it was time for the album to see a proper release. On September 28, 2004, THE 1996 DEP SESSIONS was released but with a twist. Due to the bad press and conviction of Dave Holland on charges involving a child, Iommi insisted the drums be re-recorded. In for the job was Jimmy Copley, a player with an impressive resume including Ian Gillan, Paul Rodgers, Glenn Hughes, and Jeff beck. Also added were keyboards from Don Airey and Geoff Nicholls that helped the tracks sound less like demos and more like completed tracks. As usual, Hughes sounds brilliant and once again shows my ears why he is the best voice in rock and seems to have a serious connection with Iommi. *Don't Drag The River*...wow!

The DEP Sessions and interview disc. Also, my friend and the biggest (good) music fan I know, Edward Lashua (MA) with Glenn Hughes.

This is an amazing listen that features some brilliant playing and even better vocals. There are a few times you can hear the drums being a bit off because of the fact that it is quite difficult to play drums to something already recorded and try to copy a style, not to mention the perfect timing.

2005
HALLOWED HALLS OF FAME

Honoring musicians (of any nationality) for their contributions to the music business in the United Kingdom, the UK Music Hall of Fame started in 2004 by inducting The Beatles, Elvis Presley, Bob Marley, Madonna, The Rolling Stones, Queen, Michael Jackson, Robbie Williams, Cliff Richard (with The Shadows) and U2. In 2005, the Hall welcomed in 10 new inductees including Pink Floyd, Jimi Hendrix, The Who, The Kinks, Black Sabbath, and Ozzy Osbourne. The following year's inductees (including Led Zeppelin, Rod Stewart, Prince, Brian Wilson, and Bon Jovi) would be the last for the Hall, due to lack of funding and overall non-support, The UK Hall Of Fame would cease to be an entity. For that I blame Madonna.

MAY 10, 2005 - Looking to sate his creative needs, Geezer Butler returned with OHMWORK on May 10, 2005, from his band GZR. The music from Butler's solo projects has always been much heavier and more industrial than his work with Black Sabbath. Where Iommi, Dio, and Osbourne play it closer to the Sabbath sound, GZR tends to focus on the sheer heaviness of the classic Sabbath sound. Joining Butler is longtime guitarist Pedro House, vocalist Clark Brown (who made his debut on 1995's BLACK SCIENCE), and drummer Chad (E.) Smith, who is not the player from the Red Hot Chili Peppers, hence the 'E'). Also making an appearance was vocalist/actor Lisa Rieffel on Pseudocide. Although incredibly heavy with industrial roots, OHMWORK was more accessible than past releases with songs like Misfit, Pull My String, and the rap-inspired Prisoner 103.

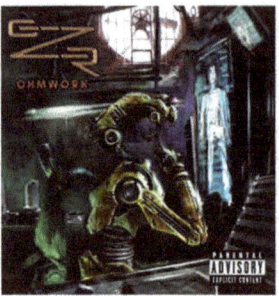 

JULY 11, 2005 - Anytime Tony Iommi and Glenn Hughes team-up in the studio, absolute magic happens. In 2004, Iommi, Hughes (bass/vocals), Kenny Aronoff (drums), and Bob Marlette (production, keyboards, and bass) teamed up to record 13 songs (10 for the album) that bring out the best of Iommi and Hughes. The result was FUSED, released on July 11, 2005, on Sanctuary Records. If you listen to FUSED and didn't know it was Iommi on guitar, you may be quite surprised. Never a one-dimensional player, Iommi really brings his A-game to this record, creating some great sounds and textures that haven't always been present in Black Sabbath recordings. *Resolution Song, Wasted Again*, and *I Go Insane* not only show off the guitarist's skills, but Hughes delivers a performance like no other, and that says a lot considering his brilliant history. Throughout his solo career, Hughes tends to play it more soulfully than the hard rock many of us want to hear, and on FUSED, the Voice Of Rock brings it!

NOVEMBER 1, 2005 - What do you do when you have done it all and possess one of the most unique voices in music history? How about a cover album? In November 2005, Ozzy Osbourne released studio album number nine, UNDER COVER, on Epic Records. Produced by Mark Hudson, a member of the 1970's trio, The Hudson Brothers, Ozzy put a unique spin on some of his favorite songs while not changing the spirit of the original tracks. Some songs seem to be a solid fit like *Mississippi Queen* (Mountain), *21st Century Schizoid Man* (King Crimson), and *All The Young Dudes* (Mott The Hoople), but others really struggle to make sense and fit Ozzy's unique voice. What is impressive is the love he put into *In My Life, Woman*, and *Working Class Hero*, songs originally sung by his hero, John Lennon.

A surprise from the album was the bonus track, *Changes*, a cover of his Black Sabbath classic sung (and re-worked a bit) with his daughter Kelly, to produce unexpected tenderness and soul. The song would be a number-one hit in the UK and go Top 20 in several countries in Europe. Featuring Jerry Cantrell (guitar), Chris Wyse (bass), and Mike Bordin (drums), UNDER COVER didn't do great saleswise, only hitting #134 in the US and #67 in the UK, but Ozzy finally got his wish (sort of), to be a Beatle.

"I owe my career to them because they gave me the desire to be in music." – Ozzy Osbourne

NOVEMBER 8, 2005 - Following several team-up releases with Dario Mollo under the name The Cage, Tony Martin released his second proper solo album, SCREAM, on MTM Records. Once again, Martin shows what a true talent he is, writing all the songs (or co-writing with Geoff Nicholls), producing, and playing most of the instruments. Where BACK WHERE I BELONG was softer, album-oriented rock, SCREAM is much heavier, and, at times, a bit more sinister. The only negative about this album is many fans didn't even know it existed, and my hand is raised.

SCREAM is one great song after another including the title track, *Faith In Madness*, and *Field Of Lies*. It's interesting to note that the album's first song, *Raising Hell*, was originally from the sessions before Ronnie James Dio's return for DEHUMANIZER, and features the original drum track played by the late great Cozy Powell. Another interesting note... the additional guitar for the album is played by Joe Harford, Tony Martin's son. This album is a must-have.

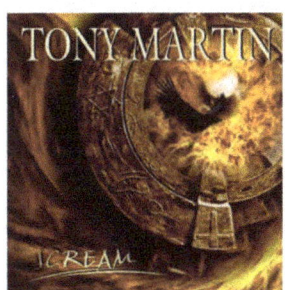 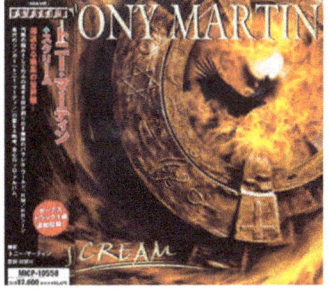

2006
HELLO CLEVELAND

The criteria to become eligible for the Rock And Roll Hall Of Fame is simple. You must have made an impact on music and it must be 25 years since your debut album was released. If the world were a place that made sense, Black Sabbath would have been inducted into the Hall in 1995 on their first year of eligibility. Instead, the Hall Of Fame said no, inducted so many less deserving performers, and ended up waiting eleven years before inducting them. The list of artists who got in before Black Sabbath is a look at how out of touch the Rock And Roll Hall Of Fame is with rock and roll, but now, inducted by Lars Ulrich and James Hetfield of Metallica, Black Sabbath was where they belonged.

2007
THE WORLD IS STILL FULL OF KINGS AND QUEENS AGAIN

With Black Sabbath on a brief hiatus as Ozzy Osbourne and his family filmed, baskeing in the success and glory of the TV series, THE OSBOURNES, Tony Iommi and Geezer Butler were just waiting in the wings. As more compilations were planned and released, there was a proposed collection that would feature every Black Sabbath album released on Vertigo/Warner Bros. Records, from BLACK SABBATH to THE ETERNAL IDOL. The idea was modified, with Rhino records suggesteing another compilation like GREATEST HITS 1970 – 1979, but this time focusing on the next most profitable era, the Ronnie James Dio years. What would make this compilation so special was the inclusion of three newly recorded tracks, featuring Iommi, Butler, Dio, and Appice. But first…

APRIL 3, 2007 - Following the DEHUMANIZER debacle, the bad blood between Ronnie James Dio and Tony Iommi would begin to pass as they began communicating with each other, something they had never done before. Iommi and Dio exchanged ideas virtually and Dio flew to England to work with Iommi to mold them into songs. Butler and Ward came in to record the three new songs, but difficulties with Ward forced the band to find another drummer. Claiming musical differences for the split, in stepped Vinny Appice for a third time replacing Ward. With the world enjoying one Black Sabbath reunion, how about another one? The record label was excited about two new songs but because the process went so fast with the band, they were able to record a third.

BLACK SABBATH – THE DIO YEARS was released on April 3, 2007, and was a solid remastered collection of amazing songs including *Neon Knights, Children Of The Sea* (live version), T*he Mob Rules*, and 10 more celebrating the three studio and one live album of the Dio era. The three new songs written by Dio and Iommi were *The Devil Cried, Shadow In The Wind*, and *Ear In The Wall*. For many fans, this was something they thought would never happen again, considering the way Dio's time in the band ended. In many interviews following the DEHUMANIZER break-up, Dio was honest about his feelings toward Iommi and Butler, and it sounded like a third time would never happen. The success of the album and the pure enjoyment of the collaboration prompted the band to do the unthinkable…tour. It was decided that the band couldn't go out as Black Sabbath, to avoid confusion with the now Ozzy-led band, so they decided to name themselves after the first Dio-led, Heaven & Hell. The album would do very well on the US Charts, going to #54 and #151 in the UK, charting higher than the GREATEST HITS 1970 – 1979 the year before.

A Canadian promoter put together a series of dates in Canada (with Megadeth and Down in support) that were quickly followed up with a full World Tour. In all, Heaven & Hell played almost 100 dates together, and, more importantly, the members all got along. With the band not being called Black Sabbath, there wasn't any one person in charge or legacy to work around, so there were no pressures or expectations, especially on the set list. At the Classic Rock & Roll of Honors awards, the tour was awarded Comeback

Of The Year. With the issues in the past seemingly behind them, what were the members of Heaven & Hell to do once their tour was over?

AUGUST 28, 2007 - With an incredibly successful and profitable tour as Heaven & Hell, the band decided to release a live album to commemorate the tour! On August 28, 2007, Heaven & Hell released, technically, their debut album on Rhino Records. LIVE FROM RADIO CITY MUSIC HALL is a double CD (and some sets contained a DVD) that featured Heaven & Hell live at the famed Radio City Music Hall on March 30, 2007. With the pressure off to only perform music from the Dio era (HEAVEN AND HELL, MOB RULES and DEHUMANIZER), the band was able to stay away from the Black Sabbath legacy and work from within their own sub-history with the band, something I'm sure made RJD very happy. Considering the wealth of material, the band must have known the set list would contain no filler on this tour.

Listed as producers were all the individual player's managers, but in reality, it was the band who put this together. Joined by Scott Warren on keyboards, Heaven & Hell tear through 15 songs, including the must-haves like *Children Of The Sea, The Mob Rules, Heaven And Hell*, and, of course, *Neon Knights*. My only issue with the album and the performances is the fact that *E5150* is followed by the more mellow I than the heavy *Neon Knights* instead of where it should be, in front of *The Mob Rules*. A small nitpick I know, but a big takeaway from this album (and any Ronnie James Dio performance) is the way he speaks to the crowd instead of yelling at them. By every account, RJD was the perfect gentleman. He didn't have airs and looked at himself as just a fan that happened to be on stage.

LIVE FROM RADIO CITY MUSIC HALL was an unexpected release from a completely unexpected reunion, and so worth the price. Also, get or at least watch the concert DVD to see four masters controling a stage and commanding an audience.

2008
THE RULES OF HELL

MAY 22, 2007 - Ozzy Osbourne would release solo album number ten on Epic Records called BLACK RAIN. It featured Zakk Wylde (guitar), Mike Bordin (drums), and new bassist Rob Nicholson (who replaced Jason Newsted, who replaced Robert Trujillo who joined Metallica). It was produced by Ozzy with Kevin Churko, whose past credits included Britney Spears, Shania Twain, Michael Bolton, and Celine Dion, certainly not rockers, but obviously, chart-toppers. Churko didn't mellow Ozzy's style or smooth out any rough edges, but what he did bring was a lot of varied sounds and textures like the almost-danceable *I Don't Wanna Stop*, the mellow *Lay Your World On Me*, and the typical, expected Ozzy rockers like *Black Rain*. But the best song on the album has to be the very Beatles-inspired *Here You Are*...just beautiful.

Recorded at the Music Machine in Beverly Hills, CA, BLACK RAIN was released in different versions with different covers, with the logo on a brown background or the painting of Ozzy standing in black rain. US editions came with a code to redeem for tickets to a pair of Ozzfest shows, now jokingly referred to as Freefest! Since this was now the age of digital downloads and online music services, there were three bonus tracks recorded for different platforms, *Nightmare* (amazing song), *I Can't Save You* (another awesome track), and *Love To Hate* (not bad).

Although reviews weren't good, BLACK RAIN went to #3 in the US, Ozzy's highest chart ever in the states, #3 in the UK, and #5 in Canada. In other media, *I Don't Wanna Stop* was used in video games, by the WWE, and on the WFAN morning drive radio show on WFAN, starring Boomer and Gio, a show I'm a HUGE fan of! Of course, Ozzy would spend time on the road in support of the album, sharing the Ozzfest stage with Iron Maiden. That changed when comments on stage by vocalist Bruce Dickinson about reality TV shows caused a national media frenzy. Obviously, this upset the Osbournes, who were more than happy to see Iron Maiden exit with a handful of shows left on the tour.

APRIL 28, 2009 - Following their unexpected and very successful tour, Ronnie James Dio, Tony Iommi, Geezer Butler, and Vinny Appice had time in their schedules and the desire to work together again. In 2008, they jumped back into the studio to record a full album under the Heaven & Hell banner. Not feeling the constraints of the Black Sabbath name and legacy or being resentful because someone was taking over their baby, Dio and Iommi were able to rekindle the solid relationship they had while recording HEAVEN AND HELL. The band decided to produce the album themselves (well, Iommi, Butler, and Dio) and also planned on recording the album live, meaning everyone together in the studio with a minimum of overdubs. There would be some production and engineering by Mike Exeter, Iommi's right-hand man/tech, but all the decisions were made by the band. This process would also keep everyone together and working at the same time, something that created issues the last time the four recorded together, as well as the LIVE EVIL production mess. This also kept everyone involved in the arrangements, thus making everyone happy and feeling they were all contributing.

On April 28, 2009, THE DEVIL YOU KNOW was released on Rhino Records (Roadrunner in Europe). It is very much a follow-up to DEHUMANIZER, and, for the most part, DIO's MASTER OF MOON. The music is as heavy as ever, the subject matter is a bit dark, and the music is exactly where the band wanted to be. One listen to songs like *Bible Black, Fear*, and *Breaking Into Heaven* finds Dio's voice a bit lower in register and more guttural but every bit as intense as expected. Many fans (including myself) looked at this album as what they hoped DEHUMANIZER would be. There were three additional tracks recorded for Japan and two live ones as an iTunes bonus.

THE DEVIL YOU KNOW, with its amazing cover (changed for Wal-Mart buyers) would impressively hit the charts, going to #8 in the US, #21 in the UK, and #24 in Canada. The album would also receive an award for Best Album at the Metal Hammer Golden Gods Awards. As expected, Heaven & Hell would hit the road to support with 98 dates worldwide. The band would finish the tour in Atlantic City, New Jersey, on August 29, 2009.

Heaven & Hell as seen through the camera of Rob Smith (MA). The last picture with a smiling Ronnie James Dio blew me away because of the pure enjoyment of performing and being with his fans. He didn't know Rob had a camera on him, so the smile is all-natural.

MAY 2009 - Behind the scenes and out of the public eye, Tony Iommi and Ozzy Osbourne had gone back and forth as to the ownership of the Black Sabbath name. On May 26, 2009, the talking between bandmates/friends ended and Ozzy decided this needed to be settled in the courts. Ozzy was seeking 50% ownership of the trademark in the hope that the suit would eventually lead to equal ownership among the four original members.

"It is with great regret that I had to resort to legal action against my long-term partner, Tony Iommi, but after three years of trying to resolve this issue amicably, I feel I have no other recourse. As of the mid-1990s, after constant and numerous changes in band members, the brand of Black Sabbath was literally in the toilet and Tony Iommi (touring under the name Black Sabbath) was reduced to performing in clubs. Since 1997, when Geezer, Bill, and myself rejoined the band, Black Sabbath has returned to its former glory as we headlined sold-out arenas and amphitheaters playing to upwards of 50,000 people at each show around the world. We worked collectively to restore credibility and bring dignity back to the name

Black Sabbath, which led to the band being inducted into the UK and US Rock & Roll Hall of Fames in 2005 and 2006, respectively. Throughout the last 12 years, it was my management representatives who oversaw the marketing and quality control of the Black Sabbath brand through OZZFEST, touring, merchandising, and album reissues. The name Black Sabbath now has a worldwide prestige and merchandising value that it would not have had by continuing on the road it was on before the 1997 reunion tour.

Tony, I am so sorry it's had to get to this point by me having to take this action against you. I don't have the right to speak for Geezer and Bill, but I feel that morally and ethically the trademark should be owned by the four of us equally. I hope that by me taking this first step that it will ultimately end up that way. We've all worked too hard and long in our careers to allow you to sell merchandise that features all our faces, old Black Sabbath album covers, and band logos, and then you tell us that you own the copyright. We're all in our 60s now. The Black Sabbath legacy should live on long after we have all gone. Please do the right thing." -Ozzy

Iommi's only public rebuttal was that for 41 years, he was the only constant in Black Sabbath, the one who appeared on every album under the name and kept the banner waving when no one else wanted to. He finished by commenting that when members left the band, they relinquished their rights to the name and its use.

JULY 22, 2008 - To promote (or as a cynic would say, capitalize) on the success of Heaven & Hell and their upcoming Metal Masters Tour with Judas Priest, Motorhead, and Testament, Rhino Records released a much-expanded version of THE DIO YEARS collection with THE RULES OF HELL, a 5-disc set featuring remastered versions of all the Dio era Sabbath. Released on July 22, 2008, this collection is an easy way to get history in a box, or at least one box. Each CD contains extensive liner notes that help tell the rise and fall... and fall of this era in Black Sabbath history. Easily the remastered version of LIVE EVIL is the gem of this collection, bringing back to life an album that suffered from a very muted original production. If you bought the collection at Best Buy you received a bonus 5-song concert disc, LIVE AT HAMMERSMITH ODEON. Other retailers offered a download of the three new songs from THE DIO YEARS.

2010
SOMEONE TURNED THE SUN AROUND

MAY 2010 - In 2009, Heaven & Hell planned on getting back together to record a follow-up to their monster hit, THE DEVIL YOU KNOW, and tour heavily in 2010. European dates with Iron Maiden were being worked out, but plans were forced to be changed when in November vocalist Ronnie James Dio was diagnosed with stomach cancer. While the band was on their last tour, the band all knew that Dio was in pain and that something was wrong. Despite all the physical issues, Dio performed to his usual high standards, and, following the tour, went to see his doctors where he was properly diagnosed. Although the prognosis was good at first for recovery, the cancer soon spread to his liver, and, despite his best efforts to fight, the dragon would eventually defeat him. On May 4th, Heaven & Hell announced the cancelation of all summer shows to give time for Ronnie James Dio to recover from his treatments. But, 12 days later, the vocalist would leave this world forever on May 16, 2010, at the age of 67.

Words cannot describe the impact that Ronnie James Dio had, not only on music but in so many people's lives. His songwriting, storytelling, and, most of all, the ability to imbue you with hope even when things looked their bleakest, continues to have a profound effect on so many people. When I first heard his voice on Gates Of Babylon from Rainbow along with the fluid leads of Richie Blackmore, the heavy percussion of Cozy Powell, the holding-it-all-down bass work of Bob Daisley, and the swirling keyboards of David Stone, it showed me how a vocalist and lyricist can tell such a deep story... and not just sing a song.

On May 30, more than 1,200 fans gathered inside Forest Lawn Memorial Park's Hall Of Liberty in Los Angeles, CA, for a day of healing and celebration in memory of Ronnie James Dio. Hosted by metal DJ and friend of Dio, Eddie Trunk, the service featured band members past and present, as well as friends and family, of the fallen singer. Geoff Tate, John Payne, Glenn Hughes, Joey Belladonna, Scott Warren, and Paul Shortino were among the many who performed spoke, performed, shared memories, and told stories.

An amazing view of Ronnie James Dio with the people who loved him by Heath Zeller, and that he, in turn, loved back. Paying his respects to a friend, Jim Hoefelt, at the tomb of Ronnie James Dio and embracing the singer (embraced back) a few years before his passing.

  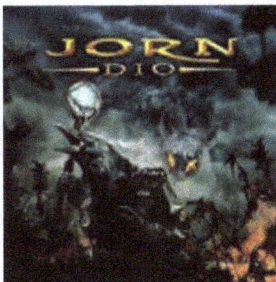 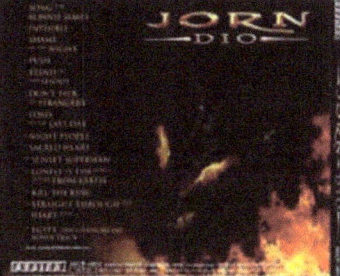

A few tributes to the memory of RJD. Heaven & Hell at High Voltage (the tribute show) and the cool tribute album by the great Jorn!

On June 4, 2010, it was announced via the media that the lawsuit between Ozzy Osbourne and Tony Iommi was settled regarding ownership of the name Black Sabbath. The true issue behind the suit filed by Osbourne was about merchandising the name Black Sabbath, not necessarily who was in the band, although that played a part. As Sharon Osbourne would explain, Iommi and Osbourne would each own 50% of the band name, making it impossible for the band to exist without those two in total agreement. This is much like the agreement UFO made in 1995 to get Michael Schenker back into the band, making the only UFO that can legally exist is if Schenker was involved. This forced vocalist Phil Moog and bassist Pete Way to record any new music under the name Moog/Way for a few years. Following some financial and career problems, Schenker did right by the band and their fans, giving the name back to Phil Moog. Want to read more about it? Try UFO – YOUR FAVORITE BAND'S FAVORITE BAND. It's a pretty good book (this is a shameless plug).

On July 24, Tony Iommi, Geezer Butler, and Vinny Appice performed for one last time as Heaven & Hell at the High Voltage Festival in London. Initially, the band canceled their appearance following the death of Ronnie James Dio, but promoters convinced the band to make the set a tribute to Dio, giving fans a chance to celebrate the legacy and say goodbye in their own way. Joining Iommi, Butler, and Appice would be two heavy hitters, Glenn Hughes and Jorn Lande. Hughes was a longtime friend of Dio and Lande is an amazing vocalist who sounds so much like Dio. Together, the band performed their festival set list of 11 songs that was a fitting send-off for a band born from a legacy. For many, like me, this was my first introduction to the amazing voice and talent of the Norwegian-born Lande. Not only does he have a big voice much like RJD's, but he has his soul, as well. Listen to his band Jorn (especially THE TRAVELER) and hear the uncanny similarities. On July 2, 2010, Jorn released an amazing album called DIO on Frontiers Records, a 14-song love letter to his hero and inspiration. Consisting of songs from DIO, Black Sabbath, and Rainbow, and the beautiful Song For Ronnie James, Jorn received a bit of undue criticism for cashing in on Dio's memory, but I think it is a fitting tribute by someone talented enough to cover his music and who loved him.

JUNE 2010 - Originally to be called SOUL SUCKA, Ozzy Osbourne released his 11th studio album, SCREAM, on June 11, 2010, on Epic records. Again co-produced with Kevin Churko, the album was a bit of a departure from the usually expected sounds created by Ozzy. With bassist Rob Nicholson and drums played by co-producer Churko (although credit is given to tour drummer Tommy Clufetos), the album was the first in years not to feature Zakk Wylde, who was focusing on his amazing band, Black Label Society. In his place was Konstantinos Karamitroudis, better known as Gus G, a Greek burner of a player from the band Firewind. Gus G's sound was a lot thinner than Wylde's, but the music recorded seemed to ask for this style. Also featured is keyboardist Adam Wakeman, who has been Ozzy's tour player since 2004, and is the son of his friend, YES's Rick Wakeman.

  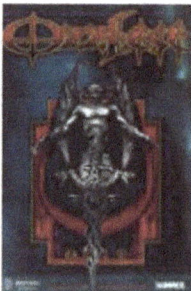

Despite a few really good songs, the best being *Life Won't Wait*, SCREAM failed to match the longevity and sales of previous releases, still going to #4 in the US, #12 in the UK, and #4 in Canada, but the album would slip off the charts as fast as it got there. Ozzy and the band would do a short European tour before a shortened Ozzfest tour in the US and then a full world tour, bringing Ozzy and the band to Europe, the Middle East, and Japan before a return visit to North America, followed by South America, and a return to Europe, consisting of 93 shows. At most of the shows, Ozzy was supported by Halford and Slash.

Also in 2010, Ozzy recorded a single and shot a video covering John Lennon's *How?*, released in support of an Amnesty International event during what would have been John Lennon's 70th birthday. The amazing and touching video shows Ozzy walking around New York City with a bouquet of purple flowers and leaving them on the Imagine memorial in Central Park. I'm in tears now watching it and thinking about my emotional visit to that same spot earlier last year.

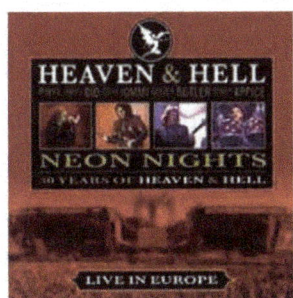  

On November 16, 2010, NEON KNIGHTS 30 YEARS OF HEAVEN & HELL LIVE IN EUROPE (called LIVE AT WACKEN in Europe) was released worldwide to a fanbase still trying to recover from the loss of Ronnie James Dio. The 11-song collection was recorded on July 30, 2009, at the Wacken Open Air Festival in Germany. Listening to this collection or watching the DVD and knowing now what we didn't know then about the physical issues Ronnie James Dio was enduring makes this an even more impressive collection of performances. Just hear how Dio leads the massive audience through Heaven And Hell and what a gentleman he was on the stage, always respectful of his audiences.

Of course, when you hear these songs it breaks your heart knowing the singer was in pain and how hard it must have been to sing these songs while trying to keep a brave face. As for Tony Iommi, Geezer Butler, and Vinny Appice...brilliant! Featuring the best of the Dio era of Black Sabbath, like Neon Knights and Children Of The Sea, mixed in with a few from THE DEVIL YOU KNOW, this is a nice way to connect with the voice, and the man, we are all still missing.

2011
REUNITED AND IT FEELS SO GOOD...FOR NOW

On November 11, 2011, Black Sabbath hosted a party at the Whiskey a Go-Go in Hollywood, CA, hosted by former Black Flag singer-turned-popular-public-speaker Henry Rollins. Here, the original members of Black Sabbath announced they would be officially reuniting with a full tour and, finally, a brand-new studio album, produced by Rick Rubin. The plans would feature an appearance at the 2012 Download Festival and see the band touring Europe in May and June of 2012 with North American dates to be announced following the party. Following a Q & A hosted by Rollins, Iommi, Osbourne, Butler, and Ward stood together as a solid, one-for-all unified front. Unfortunately, this wouldn't last long, with managers and band members behind the scenes scrambling for the best deal possible for themselves and their clients. Unfortunately for one of the original four, they wouldn't be able to reach a deal and would find themselves left behind.

2012
KILLING YOURSELF TO LIVE (F*** CANCER)

While Black Sabbath worked on their new album in the United States, Tony Iommi went to the doctor to have a painful lump looked at near his groin that he feared was Prostate Cancer. Fearful not to act, it was Ozzy Osbourne who spoke to him about getting it checked, remembering Sharon Osbourne's success fighting cancer due to early detection. Iommi had surgery to remove the mass and everything went as hoped, but when the biopsy on the lump came back, they found cancer. At age 64, a few years younger than his friend Ronnie James Dio was when he was diagnosed, the guitarist was in the early stages of lymphoma. Determined to beat this, Iommi began treatments right away, but he and the band knew it would weaken him and force Black Sabbath to move the recording sessions for the new album back to the UK. It also put the band's tour plans for

2012 in serious jeopardy. Forced to change his eating habits and time management, Iommi would keep to a regimented schedule to recover from his chemotherapy treatments.

As Black Sabbath continued to work on new music and with their guitarist's condition, Bill Ward took to social media and announced that, after months of negotiations, he would not participate in the Black Sabbath reunion unless he received a signable contract. A few days later the band called him on his threat (also on social media) commenting that they were saddened that Ward decided publicly to not participate in the band's touring plans in 2013 or the recording of a new album.

Did Ward play the odds and lose? Did he overestimate his own worth? When we think of a band, we think that all the members split the pie equally, are all part of the creative process, live in the same house, and just enjoy each other's company all the time. Obviously, this isn't the case and only happened with the Beatles (HELP) and The Monkees (their entire TV series). Both sides said they hoped things could be worked out, but by May Ward's images were removed from the band's official website, blacksabbath.com, and that was the final nail in the coffin. Geezer Butler expressed sadness about the situation with Ward and at the same time said the band was rehearsing with Tommy Clufetos, Ozzy's solo drummer. In June, Ozzy told the press that Black Sabbath had written about 15 songs so far for the new album with a later interview speaking about one of the new songs, *God Is Dead?*.

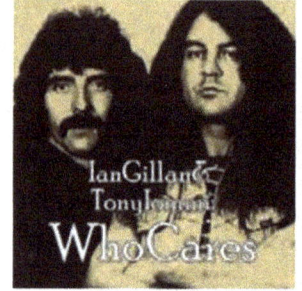

With awards being bestowed on Black Sabbath at a record pace, it was time for Tony Iommi to get acknowledgment for his humanitarian work that he, Ian Gillan, and Geoff Downes (ASIA/YES/The Buggles) had done for Armenia following the destruction of a devastating earthquake in 1988. While touring the country, they discovered a music school in Gyumri, Armenia, that was basically a shack with a few old instruments. Inspired to help rebuild this school and create a vibrant music program, Iommi, Gillan, keyboardist Jon Lord (Deep Purple), drummer Nicko McBrain (Iron Maiden), bassist Jason Newsted (Metallica), and guitarist Mikko Lindstrom (HIM) teamed up as WhoCares and released the single Out Of My Mind b/w Holy Water. The single raised significant funds, but on July 13, 2012, a full album, IAN GILLAN & TONY IOMMI: WHOCARES, raised even more funds. The double-disc collection featured the two new songs plus over an hour of reworked classic tracks, rarities, and surprises from the histories of Black Sabbath, Deep Purple, and the solo works of Iommi and Gillan. This album is one of the most underrated releases from either of the two with some incredible songs like an unplugged version of *When A Blind Man Cries* (Gillan with Steve Morse) or *Smoke On The Water* featuring Gillan and Ronnie James Dio. Former Deep Purple keyboardist Jon Lord would sadly pass away on June 16, 2020, three days after the album's release, making this his final recording.

With Tony Iommi being weakened from his cancer treatments, Black Sabbath would only manage to play three shows in 2012 with Ozzy's drummer Tommy Clufetos behind the kit, but they were three big shows. On May 19th, it was at the O2 Arena in London, June 10th at the Download Festival in Leicestershire, and an odd one, a satisfying set at Lollapalooza in Chicago on August 30th, a decade after the organizers called Ozzy a has-been, thus creating Ozzfest.

Since a Black Sabbath tour has already been booked in Europe (just not announced), Ozzy and Geezer Butler agreed to honor those dates, but not as Black Sabbath, since Iommi wasn't able to travel. The band would be called Ozzy & Friends and feature Zakk Wylde, Tommy Clufetos, and Adam Wakeman from Ozzy's solo band, as well as guests like Slash, Gus G, and Rob Nicholson. The set would be quite solid, featuring classic Ozzy material like *Suicide Solution, The Ultimate Sin*, and *Shot in The Dark*, as well as Black Sabbath must-play numbers like *Rat Salad, Iron Man*, and *Into The Void*. More than anything, this series shows helped pacify the promoters who had Heaven & Hell shows canceled in 2010 and the Black Sabbath gigs missed in 2012. Playing over a dozen shows from May to July, it was now time to get serious and finish their new album.

ANOTHER MAN FROM M.A.R.S.
ROB ROCK (IMPELLITTERI)

Springfield, MA native Rob Rock was a big part of the local rock scene (that I was a bit too young for) as the vocalist for Vice. In 1986, he joined former Ozzy bassist Rudy Sarzo, drummer Tommy Aldridge, and fellow Springfield musician, guitarist Tony MacAlpine, in the supergroup, M.A.R.S., for their album, PROJECT DRIVER. Following their lone release the band split, with Rock joining Chris Impellitteri.

www.impellitteri.net

13 (Vertigo Records)
Released on June 10, 2013
Produced by Rick Rubin
Ozzy Osbourne (vocals), Tony Iommi (guitar) and Geezer Butler (bass)
Additional musicuan Brad Wilk (drums)
All songs written by Butler, Iommi and Osbourne

END OF THE BEGINNING
GOD IS DEAD
LONER
ZEITGEIST
AGE OF REASON
LIVE FOREVER
DAMAGED SOUL
DEAR FATHER

METHADEMIC (Saturn/Best Buy/Spotify/Deluxe Edition bonus track)
PEACE OF MIND (Saturn/Best Buy/Spotify/Deluxe Edition bonus track)
PARIAH (Saturn/Best Buy/Spotify/Deluxe Edition bonus track)
NAIVETE IN BLACK (Japanese/Best Buy/Spotify/Deluxe Edition bonus track)

"It's now or never. We get along great. Everything's really good." – Tony Iommi

THE BOMBER'S MOON WILL SHOW US LIGHT

As 2013 began, an interview with bassist Geezer Butler revealed not only the progress of the new album, but the title of the forthcoming Black Sabbath as 13. In true Butler fashion, he followed up the statement by saying it also may not be called 13. The band began to release a short series of documentaries on YouTube showing them hard at work in the studio (of course minus Bill Ward) and had the band explaining how excited they were to be working with a life-long fan in producer Rick Rubin. From creating Def Jam Records as a high school senior to his retooling of The Beastie Boys, signing of Public Enemy, and guiding Run-DMC, Rubin had seen a lot of success as a creator and producer, including 20 Grammy nominations, winning 8 of them, and, most recently, 21 from Adele. Unable to keep the news under wraps any longer, Black Sabbath soon announced the drummer for the new album would be Bill Wilk from Rage Against The Machine and Audioslave, two bands that Rubin produced and had great success with.

"I've been a fan of Black Sabbath my whole life." – Rick Rubin

Before Wilk was announced as the player on the new album several drummers were considered, including the obvious choice of Vinny Appice. But, in 2011, Appice had just formed Kill Devil Hill with bassist Rex Brown (Pantera), guitarist Mark Zavon, and vocalist Dewey Bragg, and at the moment was touring to support their solid self-titled debut album. Asked and interested but due to commitments couldn't do it was the amazing Carl Palmer. A fellow Brummie, Palmer would have added such a flair and technicality to the new album, considering (in my opinion) he is one of the top 5 drummers to ever live. But his band, ASIA, was recording their 13th album, GRAVITAS, so this never could go beyond the "what if" stage. Rubin was excited to work with Wilk again, considering he was quite familiar with his style and knew he would be a perfect fit for Black Sabbath. Both Rubin and Iommi praised Wilk, knowing the fact that it isn't easy to drum in Black Sabbath considering that the music isn't just heavy, but that there are a lot of blues and jazz elements to incorporate into the sound.

With Iommi feeling better, Black Sabbath was finally able to finish recording by January 2013 and hand over everything to Rubin. Their desire was for him to work his magic, the same magic that helped sell a lot of albums for The Beastie Boys, Slayer, Tom Petty, and The Cult years before. What would Rick Rubin bring to the table as far as the overall sound? Would he let Black Sabbath be...Black Sabbath?

"After about a week and a half I realized they poop and pee just like me." – Brad Wilk

LOSING CONTROL OR ARE YOU WINNING?

Obviously, the cover for this big album had to be spectacular, catch the eye, and represent the music that Black Sabbath was making now. With the title 13, there were many things the band could have done to illustrate this evil/unlucky number, but I think they did a great job making it classy, spooky, and typical Black Sabbath. Created by Nick Dart and Neil Bowen of Zip Design, the cover art for the album 13 was revealed to the world on April 4, 2013. Before getting the Black Sabbath cover, Zip Design did work for ome very non-Black Sabbath artists and many compilations, so they seemed like an odd choice but, eventually, the right one.

"The magic is back." – Geezer Butler

Keeping it quite basic but very striking we get the large number 13 made in wicker and burning in a dark field with a foreboding sky behind the fire's orange glow. The image would be brought to life by sculptor Spencer Jenkins and photographed by Jonathan Knowles, who all did a fantastic job creating the perfect shot.

I can remember being a bit confused as to why the album was called 13 since there were eight songs, this was their 19th studio album, and the 9th featuring Ozzy Osbourne as the vocalist. No matter what I did, the numbers just didn't add up to 13 until I realized it was going to be released in 2013...plus 13 has a spooky and supernatural connotation...so there you go.

"We recorded the album, basically live." – Tony Iommi

REACHED OUT FROM INSIDE

With the hype, most people expected 13 to do well, but not as good as it actually did. Released on June 10, 2013, the album was an immediate hit with old fans and new, going to #1 in the US, UK, and Canada. The album would also go to #1 in Holland, Germany, New Zealand, Norway, Sweden, and Switzerland, and go Top 10 everywhere else in the world, except France (#15). The first single, *God Is Dead?*, was released a month before the album's release and received substantial airplay on Rock Radio, with the video viewed by millions on YouTube. To really get people talking, the band even made an appearance on the season finale of CSI: VEGAS in the episode "Skin In The Game." They were shot performing The End Of The Beginning in a bar to a lot of young hotties (I'm sure guys wished that was the typical Black Sabbath audience) and looked great. If the goal was to get non-CSI people to watch the show, they got their wish. That episode was my first and last.

Ozzy was even given a speaking part (playing himself) and did an excellent job being funny, charming, and Ozzy. 13 received mostly positive reviews but there was a lot of criticism regarding the production. Many people felt it ruined the vibe of the music by compressing the sound too much and making it sound just like everything else out there. I thought the production was a modern take on the sound Rodger Bain created on their debut album and didn't have a problem with it. I was upset at the lack of good or memorable songs to notice the production.

Despite my personal feelings about the album, Black Sabbath would receive more awards and accolades for 13 and the song *Is God Dead?* would win a Grammy Award for Best Metal Performance. The album would win a (Metal Hammer) Golden God Award, a (Classic Rock) Roll of Honor Award, and Revolver Golden Gods Award for Best Album. Not bad, not bad at all.

"It's been a fantastic year for us. You couldn't wish for anything better." -Tony Iommi

NOW MY BODY IS MY SHRINE

Black Sabbath began the 13 tour in New Zealand on April 20, 2013, with drummer Tommy Clufetos and keyboardist Adam Wakeman. There they would play two shows before a five-show run in Australia with New Zealand rockers Shihad and one in Japan (an Ozzfest date). After a few months off, the band would hit the road in the US with Andrew WK (playing DJ) just as the album was beginning to generate a massive buzz. The first leg of the North American tour would finish in September and a month later kick off again in South America and Mexico with Megadeth before another month off. After that, they would hit Europe with a final show in Birmingham on December 22. Black Sabbath would take a much deserved few months off, with Iommi still getting his cancer treatments, and return to North America for 12 dates, then back to Europe, finishing up 2013 July 4th in London. Reviews were positive for the band, despite Iommi still not feeling himself but getting stronger. Butler, Iommi, and Ozzy on average would play a 16-song set and include two or three new songs into the line-up, *Is God Dead?*, *End Of The Beginning*, and *Age Of Reason*.

By the way, you should really give Shihad a serious spin. As I did the research for this chapter, I gave them a listen, and wow... great stuff if you like 70's punk with a modern sound. These guys have it, plus some great videos.

HOLY PHONY EMPATHY

13 started off with promise. *End Of The Beginning* is the way you would hope this album would start. Like their debut album all those years ago, we hear Tony Iommi playing sparse but incredibly meaningful riffs, Ozzy Osbourne speaking his vocals over the thunderous bass of Geezer Butler, and Bill Ward-inspired fills provided by Brad Wilk. The song is epic and has a lot of great moments to love.

"It wasn't that he wanted a blues album. He wanted the blues feel from us." - Ozzy Osbourne

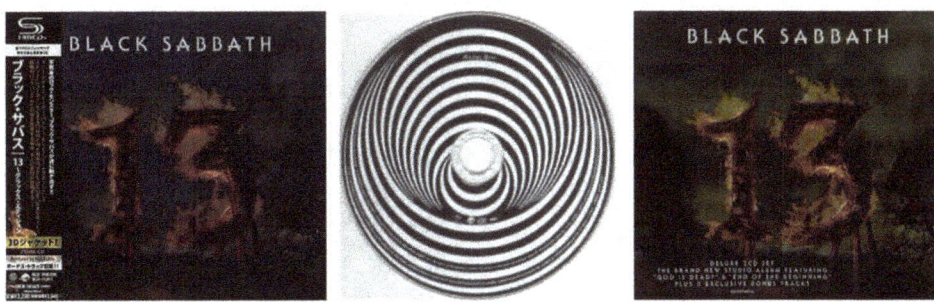

The Japanese release of 13, the super-cool throwback Vertigo label as the CD face, and a special 2-CD set of 13 containing bonus tracks.

The first single *Is God Dead?* sadly, for me, brings the album down a couple of notches due to its monotone delivery and almost nine minutes of going nowhere. Lyrically, it is a great song and there are certain parts musically that really create an amazing experience, but not enough to make it resonate. The tones Iommi uses in the guitar solo are ultra-cool, but...not enough for almost nine minutes.

Loner doesn't make the situation any better. Ozzy's vocals seem very uninspired as the band seems to be playing a different song altogether. The only part of note is the two Iommi solos with Butler and Wilk just exploding behind him. Again, just too boring.

"I didn't want it to be a follow-up to NEVER SAY DIE!" – Ozzy Osbourne

Finishing off the side one (if we are counting sides) is *Zeitgeist* and....another one that just doesn't do anything for me, but I know so many fans that love it. Trying to do their best modern take on *Planet Caravan*, the song has a distorted Ozzy singing over acoustic guitar and bongos and dancing bass lines. Again...it doesn't really go anywhere. It just is.

Age Of Reason kicks off what would be side two, and, sad to say, so much more of the same. A riff, uninspired vocals, fluid bass, and drums that seem to be the only thing on this track with life. For seven minutes the only release we get is some cool interplay between Iommi and Butler, but then it just returns to the same drudgery. As the song winds down, there are some cool choral vocals within the solo, but that's it!

"We're trying to get back to the way they worked when they were Black Sabbath." – Rick Rubin

By now, to save the album, every song has to be the best thing ever. Although *Live Forever* starts out as boring as the rest of the songs, it picks up into something a bit better than the rest, with Ozzy singing along with the melody. The music between the verses with Wilk riding the symbols under the guitar is a real treat, but it isn't enough to make me think, "wow, that song was awesome."

With everything so far just not being what I hoped for or wanted, *Damaged Soul* was really the final nail in the coffin for me. Its only redeeming quality are the jamming moments. The rest is absolutely nothing. Lyrically, it sounds like a battle between good and evil, God vs Satan, and well....to be honest, no one wins here.

The last song on the album we waited so long for, *Dear Father*, is another one that really makes the point that this album's songs aren't very good. This is so sad. Even the raining, bell-ringing ending wasn't enough to save it.

Black Sabbath released bonus material for the different formats it was released in. Up first was the rocky and chugging *Methademic!* Musically the song has a lot of cool factors, including the driving beat by Wilk playing with the guitar and bass to create a nice moment. Ozzy's voice isn't much here, but it certainly fits the song and the mood of the recording. The chorus is right out of solo Ozzy 1980s and that gives it bonus points.

"Whatever Sabbath does, people usually misunderstand it anyway." – Geezer Butler.

The only thing wrong with *Peace Of Mind* is that it should have been on the album, not regulated to bonus track status. It is a mid-tempo rocker that finds Ozzy in his best creative place. Leading into the time change, the band is playing some interesting and very impressive things that make this song come to life.

Starting off very slow and moody, *Pariah* could possibly be the best song from the sessions. The chugging riffs and the thumping bass really bring back the classic Black Sabbath feel, and Ozzy's vocals are much livelier here, not the dark, morose voice we had on the rest of the tracks. This should have been the second track and the first single released.

Heavy and loud, *Naivete In Black* gives you a *Never Say Die!* vibe to it. The song has no intro or warning, it just starts, goes and that's it...and that's all you need. The song, to my ears, captures another Sabbath moment of fanatic riffing and a distorted, almost thrashy, solo. Whoever decided to make this one a bonus track and not part of the album, you blew it!

I DON'T WANT TO LIVE FOREVER

As you can probably gather from the last few pages, 13 is not an album I was very fond of at all. The positives...the band sounds awesome! Tony Iommi pulls out some great riffs and solos, Geezer Butler really dances his way around the songs (when he isn't lost in the mix) and Brad Wilk plays so well, dare I say...you don't miss the playing of Bill Ward, but you do miss the spirit he brought to the band. The negatives...Ozzy Osbourne's vocals are incredibly monotone. I understand he doesn't have the voice he used to due to no fault of his own. It's just life and the lifespan of a singer. But the songs after a while all begin to just sound the same like the album is just made up of one loonnngggg song. There isn't much to separate the tracks, not a lot of variety, and, to me, is why the album suffers so much.

Another big wall that gets in my way is that the songs, dare I say it, aren't that great. I know my expectations may have played a major part in my initial reaction, wanting the Black Sabbath of old, but I think what we got was a rehash of the debut album, almost song for song. As a die-hard fan, I asked myself these same questions for years. What did I want and what did I expect? Well, I'm not quite sure, because after DEHUMANIZER I tried to always keep my expectations to a very low bar. But if there was something I wanted from this album, it was a bit more life to it, something I could go back to and say, YES....this I love! When the bonus tracks make up a better album than the album, this is a problem.

The good news/bad news on this is that I'm not alone in this assessment. I rank this my least favorite release of the 19 studio albums, a 19 out of 19. The ever-growing Black Sabbath Facebook family, when asked to rank all the albums, they put 13 slightly higher, #17...just above The ETERNAL IDOL and FORBIDDEN.

A JAG ACT OF 'DETH
CHRIS BRODERICK

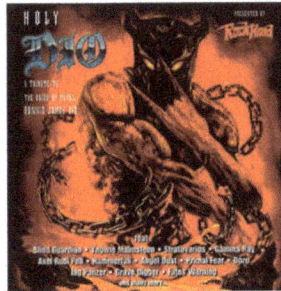

Guitarist Chris Broderick is known for his speed and heaviness, being a member of Megadeth from 2006 to 2014 and his current, very heavy band, Act Of Defiance! As a member of Jag Panzer in 2000, Broderick was able to show off his inner Tony Iommi when the band contributed an incredible version of Children Of The Sea to the album HOLY DIVER – TRIBUTE TO RONNIE JAMES DIO.

www.chrisbroderick.com

THE END
(2016-2017)

The title above the stage says it all...THE END!
Captured by Chris Hebert at Mohegan Sun in Uncasville, CT...
this really felt like the end.

Following a few years away from everything, Ozzy Osbourne, Geezer Butler, and a still recovering Tony Iommi would make an announcement that would create a whirling cornucopia of emotions for fans. The trio would announce a world tour that would be the final page in the Black Sabbath story. Called THE END, this final tour cycle would bring this very long and prolific journey to an end. Incorporating the logo from MASTER OF REALITY, THE END was going to be one final world assault that would start on January 20, 2016, in Omaha, Nebraska, and end over 80 shows later in the band's home of Birmingham, England, on February 4, 2017, bringing their incredible story full circle. The band had hoped to have a new and final album put together and released before the tour, but Butler and Ozzy expressed their desire not to have to do another record, considering the time it took for the last one to complete. If there was going to be another album, a final release, it would be a live album from the tour.

"If we were to do an album, it would take three or four years to complete." – Ozzy Osbourne

THE END EP that was released for the tour. The last picture is a touching tribute that Black Sabbath did on December 4, 2016, in Sao Paulo, Brazil. The flag represents the logo and colors of Associação Chapecoense de Futebol, the soccer club that was involved in a plane crash on November 28, 2016, where all but three members of the team perished. The picture was sent by Paulo Franzmann

Instead of a full album, Black Sabbath would look to put together an eight-song EP consisting of four leftover songs from the 13 sessions and 4 live cuts recorded on the last tour. Despite it being an EP and not quite a full album, the running time was only three minutes shorter than 13. Sadly, for those who struggled with the last album, three of the songs, *Season Of The Dead, Take Me Home,* and *Isolated Man* tends to sound just like everything else from the album (riff-driven, monotone, and crashing cymbals) with only *Cry All Night* having any spark of coolness, mostly from Iommi's Tom Morello guitar moments. The CD called THE END would be sold exclusively at the shows on the tour and would be limited to the quantity produced. As expected, the CD was bought by fans at the venues, creating a big demand. The simplistic cover art was created by the company OBEY, whose style is inspired by the awesome Rowdy Roddy piper film, THEY LIVE, a movie about aliens that have infiltrated all segments of society and are in prominent roles in the media, law enforcement, and politics. Life imitating art?

Memories of THE END, courtesy of Mike Stull. Some incredible images of the band playing their hearts out followed by a final bow.

"When you're on stage, seeing the audience, and there's people out there crying, it was all sorts of emotions. It was really great to see all these people from all over the world, but it was also emotional, because it's the last time you're going to be seeing these people." – Tony Iommi

On February 4, 2017, Black Sabbath played their final show in their hometown of Birmingham, England, at the Genting Arena, also known as the NEC (National Exhibition Center). The band, with drummer Tom Clufetos and keyboardist Adam Wakeman, would fly through an emotional 16-ong set that started with Black Sabbath and would end, of course, with Paranoid. It is hard to imagine what was going through the heads of the band members as they played these songs for the last time. It was reported that Ozzy had prepared a speech to finish the night as the balloons and confetti fell, but all he could muster was an emotional "Thank You," and that was enough.

On November 17, 2017, Black Sabbath, via Eagle Vision, would release a live album/DVD/Blue Ray called THE END: LIVE IN BIRMINGHAM, recorded at their last concert in Birmingham. Released in so many formats (CD, Blue Ray, or DVD with or without CD or triple vinyl, yes, vinyl), this concert is the perfect ending to the story that is Black Sabbath. When you listen to or watch this show, the amazing thing is how tight and together the band is and how everything you see and hear was how the fans in attendance heard it and saw it that night. Remember, you only get one chance at your final concert. Featuring 17 amazing songs, everything is clear, emotional, and full of joy, no matter the subject matter. From the opening track, *Black Sabbath*, to the final two, *Children Of The Grave* and *Paranoid*, Black Sabbath show everyone who were the true masters of heavy metal!

"I was physically there, but I remember thinking, 'F@#$%^& hell." – Ozzy Osbourne

But the most special gift any Black Sabbath fan could get was a bonus disc called The Angelic Sessions. Here and for one last time, Ozzy Osbourne, Tony Iommi and Geezer Butler (with drummer Tommy Clufetos) go back to the studio and film/record themselves performing 5 songs: *The Wizard, Wicked World, Sweet Leaf,*

Tomorrow's Dream, and an emotionally packed *Changes*. This was recorded days after the final show, and, like the interviews with The Band at the end of THE LAST WALTZ, it really brings home that this was the end. If you don't understand my reference to THE LAST WALTZ, finish this book super quick (you're almost done, anyway) and watch one of the greatest and most amazing concert films ever. Unfortunately for The Band, only one member wanted it to all be over. Everyone in Black Sabbath knew it was time.

Geezer Butler, Ozzy Osbourne, and Tony Iommi on stage and Black Sabbath off-stage with Tod Clark in San Antonio, Texas.

"We didn't rehearse anything for the sessions," Butler says. **"We were all sort of coming down from the whole Birmingham thing, and we wanted to get out as quickly as possible. I think we work best that way. The first four albums were done straight off the cuff."** – Geezer Butler

THE FINAL WORD ON...EVERYTHING!

Wow, here I am at THE END. This book was started in the pre-COVID 19 world of 2019. I'm thinking now about the plan, origins, twists, and turns this book took from the basic idea of chronicling the story of Black Sabbath, Deep Purple, Led Zeppelin, and Uriah Heep to over a hundred pages in deciding to just focus on the entire world and extended family of Black Sabbath. What I have rediscovered about Black Sabbath is how amazing and timeless the music truly is, and how their story, their tragedies, and their triumphs are so interwoven with my own life. For the past 50-plus years that I have been alive I have watched their story unfold right before my eyes and felt a part of their story. I loved researching the albums, reestablishing a relationship with a particular song or an event in their/our history, and saying hi to some great memories. There were times I dove back into a particular record and thought "I thought I liked this album more" or "how did I miss that incredible piece of awesomeness?" With my musical awakening happening around 1980, I missed most of the golden era of Black Sabbath the first time around. I've spent so many years and so much time playing architect and historian, listening to and soaking in every riff, and feeling all the emotions of the band in their heyday.

The album/CD and the Blue Ray captured forever the last concert of Black Sabbath. If this is it, the band ended the story properly.

Writing a book (on any subject) is an emotional exercise, as it is to create music, so I hope these past 200-plus pages brought a smile to your face, a rush of endorphins to the music-loving part of your brain, and a greater appreciation for the incredible wealth of music and hard work that Black Sabbath poured into every groove. In 1977, KISS put their blood into the red ink that printed the KISS comic, Marvel Comics Super Special #1. An awesome marketing strategy to say the least, but Black Sabbath poured their blood into everything they did...even the bad albums and songs.

The Black Sabbath story may be over, but the legacy and the legend will never end!

God Bless and thank you so much for spending some time with me...

NOT ALWAYS THE LAST IN LINE
ANDREW FREEMAN

In 2012, former DIO members Vivian Campbell, Jimmy Bain, and Vinny Appice looked to create a project where they could not only celebrate the music they made in the past with DIO but also rekindle their musical partnership. Along with vocalist Andrew Freeman, Last In Line was born. The band toured, performing DIO music, but in 2015 released HEAVY CROWN, an incredible album of great rock 'n' roll that has a lot of originality, NOT a DIO soundalike. When I met and interviewed Andrew on the band's tour to support the album, II, I found an incredible vocalist who understands the comparisons but welcomes the opportunity to impress, and he does.

www.andrewfreemanmusic.com

ENCORE
FOR WHOM THE (JIMI) BELL TOLLS!!!

Connecticut in the 1980s was an incredible place to be. Financially it was one of the richest per capita states in the union, there was professional hockey (The Hartford Whalers), but more importantly for this story...there was an incredibly vibrant music scene. Being almost halfway between Boston and New York, we were blessed to have an endless supply of rock clubs, bars, and small theatres to support bands playing original music to packed houses every night. One of those groups working the Tri-State market was Joined Forces, Connecticut's most popular band. Featuring guitarist Jimi Bell, Joined Forces would play every weekend, either headlining their own shows at the legendary The Agora Ballroom in West Hartford, CT, or opening for Lynch Mob at Toad's Place in New Haven, CT, my only time ever seeing Joined Forces live. Unfortunately, Hartford County wasn't a place where a band could make it big, but Jimi Bell would take advantage of every opportunity provided him. Bell would catch the ear of Kramer guitars, who would endorse him, joining Eddie Van Halen, Richie Sambora, and Vivian Campbell as reps for the company. Bell would join such an elite company even though he wasn't signed to a record deal and was working mostly on the East Coast.

In 1986, following dates with Joan Jett and The Blackhearts, Joined Forces were picked to play the fictional club band, The Hunzz, in the Joan Jett/Michael J. Fox feature film, LIGHT OF DAY, that would be released the following year. Playing constantly to large crowds, Joined Forces were looking to make the jump to the big time until Bell would receive a phone call that would change his life forever.

"I got a call and was told you are going to go out and audition for Ozzy. I asked "When, next week?" and was told, "No, now! Sharon Osbourne has already booked your ticket."

With a plane ticket waiting for him at Bradley International, Bell took a cross-country flight to California for an unexpected audition that over 500 hopefuls had already been through...and failed to get the gig. Not knowing a lot of Ozzy songs well, Bell learned as much as he could on his long flight, getting himself ready emotionally for the next few days. It wasn't known to Jimi at the time, that Ozzy had (almost) already decided on a clean-cut young guitarist from New Jersey, Jeffery Wielandt, who would soon change his name to the much more rock 'n' roll Zakk Wylde.

Jimi got to his hotel, received an envelope of cash for expenses, and was almost immediately brought to a small studio where bassist Phil Soussan, drummer Randy Castillo and Sharon Osbourne were working out (and weeding out) prospective and hopeful players who would make the next cut. Sharon was very interested in seeing if the guy she saw on a tape sent by Kramer guitars was as good as the guy who was ready to audition. As he played with Soussan and Castillo for Sharon, Bell was put through his paces and got the approval of all three. He was now ready to play for/with Ozzy Osbourne. Later that night, as Bell tried to relax in his hotel room, a knock came at the door by a blonde stranger bearing gifts.

"Zakk came to my room with two Coca Colas and wanted to see what I played like. He brought in a Rockman amp and two pairs of headphones, so we were both playing through it and hearing each other. I heard later that Zakk was blown away by my playing."

On the day of the audition, Jimi spent time in the audience with Sharon Osbourne watching another player hit the stage before him. This guitarist, a Swedish player (no, not that one) hit the stage and decided to go off script and play the solo to *Flying High Again* his way, not THE way. This infuriated Ozzy, standing behind the guitarist, to the point of standing behind him and using stabbing gestures and choking motions to show his displeasure for what he was hearing. When the guitarist turned to Ozzy, his mannerisms did an about-face and morphed into smiles and thumbs up. Now it was Jimi's turn to show what he was made of. Taking the stage with confidence and nerves, the left-hander knew to follow the songs close to the way Randy Rhodes played them originally, but add a bit of his own flair, just not play them in the key of Yngwie!

"I have my own style of playing. You take little bits and pieces of everything and make it your own. The first song I did was "I Don't Know," and Ozzy was at the microphone and it just sounded great. When it came time for the solo section, Ozzy got down in front of the amp and just listened to me play."

Following the audition and some positive conversation where Bell was told it was between him and Zakk, he went out to dinner with Ozzy, Sharon, and their entourage that ended up with the forever memory of Ozzy's hands in Jimi's salad, eating it by the handful. Following dinner, the group descended on Ozzy's bungalow where Bell got to see another side of Ozzy. As MTV played an old performance video of Black Sabbath doing *Paranoid*, Ozzy picked up his young daughter, Aimee, brought her to the TV, and boasted proudly, "Look Aimee, it's your daddy!"

Later that night, Bell joined Phil Soussan and Randy Castillo out on the town, ending up at one of the L.A. music scene's most legendary spots, The Troubadour, in West Hollywood, CA. Despite the lack of sleep, Bell was running on pure emotions and enjoying the life of a young rock star in L.A., meeting people and feeling like a part of the scene. The next morning, Bell woke up and was told he was going home. A car was waiting and a plane ticket at the airport had his name on it. History shows that the guitar job went to Zakk Wylde, who would become Ozzy's right-hand man on and off for the next 20-plus years. Jimi knew in his heart he wasn't the choice but was never told officially he didn't get the gig and only found out like most of us when a formal announcement was finally made to the press.

For many hopefuls that never got that far, thousands would have loved to be runner-up or the second choice, but for Bell, he took it really hard. He came back to Connecticut with an experience of a lifetime, but no more band. Once Bell got on the plane to audition, Joined Forces broke up. Now without a band and understandably feeling low about everything that happened over a few days, Bell let this get the best of him and began to partake in the party lifestyle more than normal.

"Coming in second was very difficult for me. I almost wished I wasn't at that point."

A few months passed and again Bell received another phone call, this time from Geezer Butler. Looking to (re)start his own band, former Black Sabbath bassist Geezer Butler was on the hunt for a hot, flashy young guitarist who could not only play but write songs. Following his departure from Black Sabbath after the BORN AGAIN tour, Butler created the first version of the Geezer Butler Band that didn't go further than a few shows and a live bootleg CD. Butler and Bell hit it off immediately and the duo began to write songs with the plan to go to and record them for the band's debut album. Being told they had signed with MCA Records, the band now featuring Carl Sentence (vocals), Gary Ferguson (drums), and Jezz Woodroffe (keyboards) began to record music like *Heat In The Steet, Computer God*, and *Master Of Insanity*. Butler wanted the music to be heavy but exciting, melodic music that was nothing like Black Sabbath, and he wanted Jimi Bell.

"Can you write a song like a Black Sabbath song?" – Geezer Butler

Unfortunately, the staffer who signed the band to MCA was fired, and, as is the normal procedure in the music business, everything he had anything to do with was now canceled. This meant the end of the Geezer Butler Band, and, with a call from Gloria Butler explaining the situation, another major blow came to Jimi Bell. This was much harder to deal with than Ozzy considering the time, emotions, and hard work that went in. Bell returned to the States with nothing to show for the time with Butler but a bunch of songs and a funny story about carrying a young Aimee Osbourne down a dark spiral staircase at Warwick Castle in Birmingham, England.

"For some reason, Gloria Butler was babysitting Aimee and Kelly Osbourne and one of them got in trouble for spilling red paint, so we went to the castle. It was Geezer, his sons Biff and James, myself, and Aimee. We were coming down the lookout tower at night with no light inside and I was holding Aimee, leaning against the wall trying to feel my way down the circular staircase and not fall. I'm thinking if I ever fall with Ozzy's daughter, he's gonna bite my head off."

The music industry is not known to be a very nurturing or loyal place, and Bell found that out twice, again shattering his dreams and making him question himself. Undaunted, Bell was raised to never give up and keep trying, and that is what he did. In 1988, bassist Billy Sheehan had just left David Lee Roth's band and was looking to put together his own band. With the help of Mike Varney (from Shrapnel Records), Sheehan reached out to Bell after seeing a tape of him playing and told him about a new project he was working on. Sheehan prefaced that his plan was to feature Paul Gilbert, the amazing player from Racer X who had recently left the band. Sheehan asked Bell if he would be interested if Gilbert didn't work out, and, of course, Bell said yes. Gilbert would join Sheehan, vocalist Eric Martin, and drummer Pat Torpey to form Mr. Big.

With the club scenes not what used to be, and also without a band, Bell focused on his talents as a guitar teacher. In 1992, Bell heard, like many of us, that Geezer Butler, Ronnie James Dio, and Vinny Appice would be returning to Black Sabbath with Tony Iommi for a new album that would eventually become DEHUMANIZER. He also heard that his song, *Master Of Insanity*, would be going on the new album. Knowing one of his songs would be sung by Ronnie James Dio was so special and an honor for Bell, but once again the business side of the music business pulled the rug out when Bell was told that he couldn't receive any songwriting credit. However, following the upcoming tour, he would receive payment for the song. It was explained to Bell that there was no way a song could or would appear on a Black Sabbath album written by a guitarist other than Tony Iommi. That was just the way it was going to be.

"I was gracious, thanking Gloria Butler for the opportunity. Honestly, it started to get to me that Black Sabbath was playing the song live, proving Master Of Insanity wasn't a throwaway track."

Following the tour, Bell endured another setback when he didn't receive any money for the use of the song. In an interesting and weird twist of fate, Jimi Bell ended up on the phone with Ronnie James Dio, who spoke to Jimi about how he felt about the situation and how he fought to get the guitarist paid to no avail.

"The recording on the DEHUMANIZER album is exactly like the demo, except for the solo."

In 1997, DIO was appearing in Hartford, CT, at the Webster Theatre where Jimi Bell was at a special dinner for fans of the band. The plan for the evening was for Dio and the band to meet and break bread with several lucky fans. There as a guest, Bell finally got a chance to meet face to face the legendary voice and found him to be incredibly kind, very personable, and incredibly genuine. A surprise for the guitarist was Dio's ability to recall every detail of their phone call.

"Jimi Bell! Master Of Insanity!" – Ronnie James Dio

Bell and Dio stood by a pinball machine for almost 45 minutes talking about the song and the lack of credit or payment, with the singer being incredibly empathetic and supportive of Bell's feelings. Dio knew that Bell wrote the song and would ask those in charge, "why don't you just pay the guy?" Getting the credit and pay for writing the song would have been the right things to happen, but to have Ronnie James Dio acknowledge his work and share in his frustrations meant the world to Bell.

"How many people can honestly say they wrote a song that Ronnie James Dio sang? That is something that I will cherish forever."

Some amazing images of Jimi Bell in action with Beyond Purple and House of Lords, courtesy of Lea Caffery of Morning Star Reflections.

As Jimi Bell and I sit in my dining room talking about events that happened a lifetime ago, I asked him if he did get the Ozzy gig, where does he think he would be now? His answer is completely humble and in character for Bell, saying he might not be alive today if he got the job in 1987, but he is quick to point out that God just had other plans. Currently, Jimi Bell, a member of Black Sabbath history, is the guitarist for House Of Lords, a position he has held since 2005, releasing 8 albums including the spectacular SAINT OF THE LOST SOULS in 2017. In 2019, Bell was asked to replace Steve Lynch in Autograph, which he, the band, and his many fans were incredibly excited about. When not on the national stages, Jimi keeps busy with Beyond Purple, a band that covers not only Deep Purple but Rainbow, Whitesnake, and Dio. He also is a member of local legends, Maxx Explosion, a pure rock band that mixes great originals and some well-placed covers. Jimi has also been presented a Lifetime Achievement Award from All That Shreds Magazine in 2018 and is now a member (in good standing) of the New England Music Hall Of Fame.

www.jimibell.com
www.autographband.com
www.houseoflordsband.com

So much has changed since I started this project on September 28, 2019. First, the book itself went from a focus and study on the Original Big Four (Deep Purple, Led Zeppelin, Uriah Heep, and of course Black Sabbath), to just a book about Black Sabbath. Second, my family and I sold our home of 20 years in Springfield, MA, and moved to a beautiful lake house in Palmer, MA. This house has given me the most incredible office and recording studio to write and record and made the creative process that much more, well, creative. Third, reality had gone from us doing what we wanted to quarantine, masks, social distancing, and fear. As I write this on October 24, 2020 (listening to the Moody Blues and wearing my official Black Sabbath-Black Lives Matter shirt), we are still wearing masks and almost waiting for the next wave of God knows what! But we will survive this... we are fighters.

Socially, politically, and racially we have all been challenged, for the better, I hope. Many have chosen to make a stand when they probably shouldn't and let things go that truly deserve a fight. We have seen people compromise values to further a cause that really doesn't deserve to be furthered. I have lost friends over the stands I made, I have argued with family and alienated those I don't agree with, because the art of conversation has seemingly been lost forever. This makes me sad.

Despite all this, I have made so many new friends through you, the Black Sabbath Family, no.... my Black Sabbath Family! I have discovered that no matter where you grew up or how you were raised, we are all the same. We grew up being told Black Sabbath would destroy our souls and lead us down a path of destruction. We would never amount to anything, no one would love us because we wore a Black Sabbath shirt, saw the band live, or bought a Black Sabbath album. You were a dumb burnout who will never get a good job and become a productive member of society. If you were a person of faith like I am... forget the above issues...you were going to Hell! This was something I was told in church youth groups throughout my teens that used to really affect me, but now Jesus and I have an understanding. I put him first in my life, I do his work on Earth, I love my neighbors, and let his spirit shine in me. If I do all that, he'll let the Black Sabbath thing slide.

So, this brings us to the end and the big question...is Black Sabbath truly over? As much as I love the band and how much they have meant to me for over 40 years, I hope the answer is yes. Black Sabbath took their final bow and that is how I want to remember it, not a goodbye followed by something else. Earlier this year Ozzy Osbourne released an amazing album called ORDINARY MAN, an album I didn't like at first because it wasn't BLIZZARD OF OZZ or DIARY OF A MADMAN. It was a man reflecting on his life and coming to an understanding of where he is as a 71-year-old, and I respect that so much. It's Ozzy's real John Lennon moment.

As is a tradition with my book writing, when I get to the final page, I pop on the Pet Shop Boys 1987 hit, What Have I Done To Deserve This? Why this song? I have no idea.... but I do love it! I am relieved that the writing is all over and I can get back three to four hours a day, resume writing weekly album reviews, focus on my podcasts, and spend more time my family. But I will miss all of you and I will miss the music that has consumed me for the past 13 months. Sure, I will still listen to Black Sabbath and the extended family, just not as critically and with an ear to every little detail. Now I go back to being just a fan.

And now... THE END! ...this time for real. Honest.

www.ingramcontent.com/pod-product-compliance
Lightning Source LLC
Chambersburg PA
CBHW051119110526
44589CB00026B/2976